Keep in Touch

Other Word books by Al Bryant

Daily Meditations with F. B. Meyer
LoveSongs: Daily Meditations for Married Couples
Near the Sun: A Sourcebook of Daily Meditations from
   Charles Haddon Spurgeon

366 Day Starters for Young Adults

Al Bryant

WORD BOOKS
PUBLISHER
WACO, TEXAS

KEEP IN TOUCH

Library of Congress catalog card number: 80–53257

ISBN 0-8499-0277-0

To

Ann

who
lights
up
my
life

Foreword

It's been my joy to write and compile a number of devotional books in the last twenty-five years or so—and one must learn some things in the process of working with words, his own or others. As I've read the writings of Christian authors past and present, I've been enriched in my own soul by the majestic thoughts that have entered into and filtered through my mind. Even if no one had ever read these compilations, I would have been strengthened spiritually and encouraged in my own walk with the Lord by what I've read.

I've learned that, by and large, older Christians are seeking solace and uplift in their devotional reading. Younger people, on the other hand, are looking for a challenge, a banner to serve under, a flag to follow. That is the criterion I have used in selecting these excerpts from the thoughts of writers ancient and modern, and it is the emphasis of my own contribution to these pages. These meditations are not "preachy," however. Rather, they confront us where we are and demand our best in response.

I have titled this book *Keep in Touch*—for that is what we must do. We must make it a daily practice to be constantly in touch with our heavenly Father and Guide. Life is a journey, and one needs a map if he is to find his way most effectively. The Bible is the road map for life, and the meditations in *Keep in Touch* are Scripture-based and Christ-centered. The theme of God's guidance runs throughout, and it is my prayer that you will discover lasting truth herein as you peruse these pages.

You will discover that this book is exhaustively indexed to enhance its usefulness beyond just as a daily devotional text. We hope that you will find these thoughts to be discussion starters and "probers" as well as thought-provoking daily meditations. In order to "go with the flow" of these daily thoughts, we have grouped them as follows:

January—Growing in God
February—Living in Christ
March—Depending upon God
April—Trusting in God
May—Giving Your Life to God
June—Living for God
July—Guidance from God
August—Learning from God
September—Looking at Life Through God's Eyes
October—Living in the Spirit
November—Living Thankfully
December—The Understanding Life

I want to thank Robin Hardy for the "labor of love" she bestowed on this book. She went far beyond her duty as an editor in arranging and styling the meditations in *Keep in Touch*. I'm also grateful to the many people of God, some living here on earth and some already in eternity, for their contributions to this compilation. In some cases these are footnoted as to source, but in others we have merely given the name of the author of a pithy thought we have quoted.

As *Keep in Touch* becomes a part of you, I pray it will make a meaningful contribution to your life.

AL BRYANT

Waco, Texas

January

Growing in God

They sow the wind and reap the whirlwind.

Hosea 8:7, NIV

1

THIS BOOK IS DEDICATED to my teenage daughter, Ann. She has a horse—and she and I have learned many things from that so-called "dumb" animal, lessons which I'll be sharing with you periodically in this book. But the biggest and most basic lesson we've learned is this: when you're taming a horse, you get out of her exactly what you put in, provided she hasn't been spoiled or mistreated by a previous owner.

In our case, the horse was a three-year-old who had little or no contact before with humankind, good or otherwise. She was natural and unspoiled. In fact, her previous owner said that she hadn't shown much interest in humans at all. She rather studiously avoided them—until she and Ann were mutually attracted to each other. She had never been ridden before and was barely trained to accept the halter—but in less than a month Ann was riding her bareback. A short time later we tried the saddle, and ultimately the bridle—all of which she accepted graciously and with little or no resistance. Through it all her spirit was gentle and tranquil, and today she is one of the most trustworthy and loving horses I've seen. Why? Because all she has known is love and genuine caring. She and Ann are the best of friends and inseparable companions.

The horse reflects the treatment she has known. If she had been treated harshly, she would have turned out an angry, intractable mount—or one whose spirit was so broken as to make her a nonentity. As I watched the gradual transformation from wild to tame, I was reminded of how true this is in the spiritual realm as well. Feed into life resentment and bitterness, and you'll reap the same. But invest love and compassion, and your spirit will become Christlike and caring. As says our verse for the day, sow the wind and reap the whirlwind, but sow love and love shall remain!

9

January

2
Ye have not passed this way heretofore.

Joshua 3:4

IT IS GOOD for a man to come to a future which he does not know, for then he will be completely dependent upon his Guide. It is good for you if God brings you to the borders of some promised land. Do not hesitate at any experience because it is unknown, untried. Do not draw back from any way because you never have passed that way before. The truth, the task, the joy, the suffering, on whose border you are standing, oh, my friend—go into it without fear; only go into it with God, the God who has always been with you.

Let the past give up to you all assurance of Him which it contains. Set that assurance before you. Follow that, and the new life to which it leads you shall open its best richness to you.

Only we know that with a world which needs so much, and with a God who knows its needs and who loves it and pities it so tenderly, there must be in the long year ahead some approach of its life to His life, some coming of the Lord!

PHILLIPS BROOKS

3
. . . speaking the truth in love, may [we] grow up into him in all things, which is the head, even Christ.

Ephesians 4:15

MANY PEOPLE GROW into Christian maturity very rapidly: others much more slowly, almost imperceptibly. I once saw a picture on television of flowers growing, budding, and opening. This was done by slow-motion photography over a long period of time. If you had watched the same process with your naked eye in your garden it would have taken days. In the same way, we watch our lives from day to day and often get discouraged at the slow growth. But if you wait for a year or two and then look back over your life you will see how much you have grown. You've become kinder, more gracious, more loving. You love the Scriptures more. You love to pray more. You are a more faithful witness. You will never reach that point of full maturity in Christ until you see him face to face in heaven.

BILLY GRAHAM

Quoted from *How to Be Born Again* (Waco, Tx: Word Books, 1977).

Be strong in the grace that is in Christ Jesus.

2 Timothy 2:1

4

WHERE IS THE STRENGTH with which we are to be empowered? It is in Christ Jesus. It is in no sense in ourselves. Power is not given to us as something to be used independently of him. It is *divine* power, both as to its exercise and its source. Then, again, we are not called upon here to strengthen ourselves, but rather to allow ourselves to be strengthened. The verb is in the passive voice: *"Be strengthened in the grace that is in Christ Jesus."* It is the office of the Holy Spirit of God thus to strengthen us. He does this by bringing us into the center and source of all power. It pleased the Father that all fullness of grace should dwell in Jesus Christ. It is to him the Spirit leads us. It is of the things of Christ that the Spirit takes and reveals to us. It is his might that he communicates unto us. But as we said, not apart from him, but in union and communion with him: "strengthened with all might, according to his glorious power" (Col. 1:11). When we are thus strengthened, we have no consciousness of strength in ourselves. It is then that we know our own weakness—but we have the power of Christ.

EVAN H. HOPKINS

Despised though you are, fear not, O Israel; for I will help you. I am the Lord, your Redeemer; I am the Holy One of Israel. You shall be a new and sharp-toothed threshing instrument to tear all enemies apart, making chaff of mountains. You shall toss them in the air; the wind shall blow them all away; whirlwinds shall scatter them. And the joy of the Lord shall fill you full; you shall glory in the God of Israel.

Isaiah 41:14–16, LB

5

I NEVER CEASE to be amazed at the total contrast between the way the *world* would lift and sustain its servants to the level of its highest, and the way the Lord lifts and sustains his. The world motivates her warriors to victory by an appeal to personal excellence. That's what the sales manager does when he gives his salesmen a pep talk. That's the aim of the high-priced football coach who seeks to motivate every member of his team to come out of the huddle fighting. But God doesn't make good soldiers for Jesus Christ by inflating *human* confidence. He doesn't destroy the confidence, but he gives that confidence solid foundations.

January

Its Builder and Substance is God. The King James Version calls Israel "thou worm Jacob"—but when Jacob accepts his new classification, he "shalt rejoice in the Lord." The *worm* turns—and becomes a "sharp-toothed threshing instrument" to tear its enemies apart. God can change us, too!

6

And he shall be like a tree planted by the rivers of water, that bringeth forth his fruit in his season; his leaf also shall not wither; and whatsoever he doeth shall prosper.

Psalm 1:3

PROPER PLANTING is important in growing in grace. No farmer plants where he does not expect to grow a good crop. He is looking for a harvest. In this passage we are given the guidelines for good planting. The spiritual farmer is promised prosperity if he follows the formula. Joseph is probably the outstanding example in Scripture of spiritual (and material) prosperity, although Job certainly comes to mind in this connection as well. Of Joseph, the Bible says, "And his master saw that the Lord was with him, and that the Lord made all that he did to prosper in his hand" (Gen. 39:3). Stephen, in his defense before the Jewish officials, reminded his hearers, "And the patriarchs, jealous of Joseph, sold him into Egypt; but God was with him, and rescued him out of all his afflictions, and gave him favor and wisdom before Pharaoh, king of Egypt, who made him governor over Egypt and over all his household" (Acts 7:9–10, RSV). Jeremiah echoes Psalm 1 when he writes, "Blessed is the man who trusts in the Lord. . . . He is like a tree planted by water, that sends out its roots by the stream, and does not fear when heat comes, for its leaves remain green, and is not anxious in the year of drought, for it does not cease to bear fruit" (Jer. 17:7–8, RSV). Looking for a prosperous life? Be sure you are planted right!

7

And he is the head of the body, the church: who is the beginning, the firstborn from the dead; that in all things he might have the preeminence.

Colossians 1:18

WHAT DOES IT MEAN to make Christ preeminent in one's life? The dictionary defines the word *preeminence* as putting someone or something "above and before others." Is that where I put Jesus Christ in my life? Another interesting translation of this verse that sheds additional light on the meaning of putting Christ in the place of preeminence is from the *Living Bible:* ". . . so that he is first in everything." If Christ *is* first in everything, all other aspects of my life will fall into place perfectly. If I join the psalmist, I will follow God's formula for "firstness": "[God says] Also I will make him my firstborn, higher than the kings of the earth" (Ps. 89:27). In the same context with our verse for the day, Paul describes Jesus: "Who is the image of the invisible God, the firstborn of every creature" (Col. 1:15). In Ephesians 1:22–23, Paul gives us this perspective on Christ's preeminence: "And [God] hath put all things under his feet, and gave him to be the head over all things to the church, which is his body, the fulness of him that filleth all in all." St. Augustine put it succinctly: "Christ is not valued at all unless He is valued above all."

For I will satisfy the weary soul, and every languishing soul I will replenish.

Jeremiah 31:25, RSV

8

DURING THE TRIAL of eleven communists in New York, Judge Harold Medina struggled hard to keep his composure, trying to refrain from saying anything that might cause a mistrial. Under badgering he came close to breaking down. He took frequent recesses to recoup his forces. After one of these he reported: "I asked God to take charge of things, and that his will be done. All I know is, that as I lay on that couch in the heat of the darkened room, some new kind of strength seemed to flow into my veins. After fifteen minutes I was refreshed and went back to carry on the business of my court."

The most beautiful offer in the world is from the lips of Jesus: "Come unto me, all ye that labour and are heavy laden, and I will give you rest. Take my yoke upon you, and learn of me; for I am meek and lowly in heart, and ye shall find rest unto your souls. For my yoke is easy, and my burden is light" (Matt. 11:28–30). Notice the kind of rest he offers—not inactivity, not release from all pressures. He knows we need the right kind of pressure and tension. So he invites us to take on a new pressure: his yoke. Strange way to find freedom? Not at all. His yoke is adapted to our true nature as sons and daughters of God, so it is easy and light, and

13

it makes all other pressures easier to bear. He simply meant, "Team up with me. Together we can handle any pressure and use it creatively."

T. CECIL MYERS

Quoted from *You Can Be More Than You Are* (Waco, TX: Word Books, 1976), pp. 52–53.

9   *But [that we,] speaking the truth in love, may grow up into him in all things, which is the head, even Christ.*

Ephesians 4:15

OFTEN, when we have completed a certain phase or period in our lives, such as a graduation, we feel that we've "arrived" at another level—and that "this is it." But Paul would say, as he told the Ephesians here, don't be content with where you are right now, but "grow up into him in all things." Our growth should take place in several different directions: upward, outward, and inward. We should strive to grow Godward, the *up*ward development of spiritual sensitivity. We should seek to grow outward in our relationships to others, developing a sense of servant-hood. And we should long to grow in the inner man, feeling the surge of the Spirit-filled life as it lifts us closer to the stature and fullness of Christ. It seems as if Paul is almost praying here as he concludes this brief résumé of the gifts of the Spirit which he began in verse 7 with the words, "But unto every one of us is given grace according to the measure of the gift of Christ." May this be our prayer as well!

10   *And the Word was made flesh, and dwelt among us, (and we beheld his glory, the glory as of the only begotten of the Father,) full of grace and truth.*

John 1:14

THE CHRISTIAN RELIGION began when "The Word was made flesh." God became real. All that could be said in words, the Law and the Prophets had said. But what would be made real in *life* was not made real until Jesus came. He did not only *say* the truth, He *was* the truth. He was the Incarnation of God. With all reverence, let it be said that we must become lesser incarnations of Him. We must be Christophers,

"Christ-bearers." Our lives, our words, our inspired acts, our deeds of honesty and integrity and unselfishness must be bridges across which He walks again into our world.

SAM SHOEMAKER

11

For the Lord God, the Holy One of Israel, says: Only in returning to me and waiting for me will you be saved; in quietness and confidence is your strength. . . . And if you leave God's paths and go astray, you will hear a Voice behind you say, "No, this is the way; walk here."
Isaiah 30:15, 21, LB

QUIETNESS AND CONFIDENCE are unbeatable weapons in the warfare of life, provided that confidence is in the right One—God himself! The King James Version has "In returning and rest"—rest and waiting are merely trellis virtues, worthless and weak unless they have something to climb on. We are to *rest* on God! We are to *trust* in God. Look at the text carefully. It does not say that quietness and confidence *are* our strength. It says our strength is *in* them—it reaches us through them. The *Lord* is my strength and salvation. The Israelites in Isaiah's time were asking, "What shall we do?" God answered, "Your strength is to sit still! Your protection is my Spirit!" He is telling us the same thing today!

12

Endure hardness as a good soldier of Jesus Christ.
2 Timothy 2:3

"A GOOD SOLDIER," it has been said, "both abstains and sustains." This is to endure hardness. He has not only to fight in aggressive conflict, he has to withstand in defensive warfare. His power is seen far more in what he can *bear* than in what he can *do*. How true all this is spiritually! To be a good soldier of Jesus Christ we must know the discipline of laying aside every encumbrance, every weight, every entanglement. We must learn by actual experience how to "refuse," as well as how to accept. We lose as much oftentimes by yielding to the allurements of the world as by failing to claim the provisions of grace. The "hardness" that is essential to a "good soldier" can be brought about only by the discipline of trial, and fidelity to this law of the kingdom, that we "please him who hath chosen [us] to be a soldier"' (v. 4). Character is formed by conduct, and conduct is the outcome of a living faith in a personal Savior. Thus it becomes our responsibility to "fight the good fight of faith" (1 Tim. 6:12).

EVAN H. HOPKINS

---

13   *My brethren, be strong in the Lord, and in the power of his might.*

Ephesians 6:10

THE CONTEXT TEACHES us that these words have reference to Christian conflict; to Christian conflict in relation to our great adversary, Satan, and "spiritual wickedness in high places." The words point to that step which is preliminary to successful warfare. Before the foe can be encountered the *right position* must be taken. We must be entrenched in the strength of the Lord. We must be enclosed "in the power of his might," or, as one has paraphrased it, "in the energy of him, the strong." It is in vain we engage in the conflict if that preliminary condition has not been fulfilled. In earthly warfare the soldier does not provide his own means of defense or weapons of assault. So in Christian conflict our whole equipment is divinely provided for us. He gives us a position that is impregnable—strength in the Lord; an armor that is impenetrable; and a weapon that is infallible—"the sword of the Spirit." We have by faith to take that position and continually to abide in it. We have by faith to put on that armor and wear it constantly.

EVAN H. HOPKINS

---

14   *Take heed unto thyself, and unto the doctrine; continue in them: for in doing this thou shalt both save thyself, and them that hear thee.*

1 Timothy 4:16

TWO THINGS are of primary importance—the doctrine we believe and the life we live. The apostle Paul here recognizes both aspects. It is not sufficient merely to make sure our views are scriptural and our doctrine sound. We must also be "sound in faith, in charity, in patience" (Titus 2:2), and in practice.

To take heed to ourselves does not mean to put ourselves first. It means, rather, that we should be living in a spirit of prayer and watchfulness. It means that health of the soul is as essential to the spiritual life as health of body is to the physical life. It is possible to get "below par" physically. At that point we are most susceptible to disease. Our resistance is low, or even nonexistent. How true this is spiritually as well. There is such a thing as a low spiritual condition. Holding sound doctrine will not compensate for living, active faith on the Lord's word and prompt obedience to the Lord's will. Where health of soul is poor, every spiritual faculty is affected.

And the very God of peace sanctify you wholly; and I pray God your **15**
whole spirit and soul and body be preserved blameless unto the coming
of our Lord Jesus Christ.

1 Thessalonians 5:23

WE HUMAN BEINGS are complex organisms. In this passage, Paul recognizes our complexity and plurality, and lays out for us in brief scope the three basic components of our person. The *spirit* is that part of us which alone can hold communion with God. In Jewish thought, the *soul* was the seat of a person's rational faculties. The third segment of our selves Paul mentions is the *body*—the organ of our senses. The One who preserves or keeps all this is God. Before he keeps us in holiness, he takes us into his possession. In other words, before he *keeps* us in holiness, he *brings* us into it. To sanctify is to make holy by consecrating to holy use. We "sanctify" ourselves when we each present ourselves to God as "a workman that needeth not to be ashamed, rightly dividing the word of truth" (2 Tim. 2:15). He sanctifies us when he takes us to himself—when he fills us with himself. Then comes the keeping. The way the *Living Bible* translates today's verse is meaningful to me: "May the God of peace himself make you entirely pure and devoted to God; and may your spirit and soul and body be kept strong and blameless until that day when our Lord Jesus Christ comes back again."

Put on therefore, as the elect of God, holy and beloved, bowels [hearts] **16**
of mercies, kindness, humbleness of mind, meekness, longsuffering.

Colossians 3:12

WE ADMIT that our scientific advance has outstripped our social and moral advance. Material civilization has advanced while human nature has stood still. Dictators have tried to whip human nature into line with totalitarian principles, but human nature eventually resists. Christianity sets about to change human nature and often meets with resistance, too. We all want our own way. The other fellow wants his way. There is stalemate—or war. We like to think, and we hope that others will think, only of our virtues. But neither we nor they can escape for long thinking of our sins and defects. We are not big enough to meet the moral demands of this day and age. Our day calls for a greatness of character, for an unselfishness of spirit of which we are incapable by ourselves. We must change quickly and greatly, or we may lose our precious freedom. We have misused our freedom in order to get our own way, our own spoils, and have left others to fend for themselves. The way to advance is to face these facts honestly—we all need a change of heart. Only to humble men can God speak. Only through humble men can God work.

SAM SHOEMAKER

17   *Because God is always at work in you to make you willing and able to obey his own purpose.*

Philippians 2:13, TEV

THE FORMULA for cooperating with God is this: To love God is to let God love you; to let God love you is to be completely open to what he wants to do in every part of your thinking, feeling, and attitude.

That's what I believe Paul is talking about in today's Scripture. In it he says some magnificent things about God and some motivating things about us. God is always at work in us. He chose us, loved us, and gave us the gift of faith to respond. He persists in us and will not let us rest at any stage of growth. Paul said it clearly, "For by grace you have been saved through faith; and this is not your own doing, it is the gift of God—not because of works, lest any man should boast. For we are his workmanship, created in Christ Jesus for good works, which God prepared beforehand, that we should walk in them" (Eph. 2:8–10, RSV). God knows what he is doing with us. Even the desire to want what he wants is a gift. We can trust him at every point, in the difficulties and the delights of life, because he will weave them into his ultimate plan to make us like his Son and prepare us to live with him forever. So we can relax and enjoy the journey! God will not leave us unfinished or incomplete. Therefore, we can enter into each new day with the confidence that he will make us willing to be willing to do his will.

LLOYD OGILVIE

Quoted from *Let God Love You* (Waco, TX: Word Books, 1974), p. 78.

For to me to live is Christ. . . .

18

Philippians 1:21

THE CHRISTIAN LIFE is lived on one of three levels. The first and lowest is that which is characterized as dissatisfied, discontented, and incomplete. On this level the Christian senses that there is something better, that he isn't really experiencing the fullness possible in the Christian life. Christians on this level are dully dissatisfied with where they are, but they don't know what to do about it. And then there are those who are "halfway up"—sometimes they face forward and feel uplifted, and sometimes they face backward and are defeated and discouraged. The third level is that described by Paul in Colossians 3:3, "For you have died, and your life is hid with Christ in God" (RSV). These Christians are those with a strange tranquility and contentment in the midst of a chaotic world—for nothing can disturb the contentment of the Christian who has said, "For to me to live is Christ"!

I am the true Bread from heaven; and anyone who eats this Bread shall live forever, and not die as your fathers did—though they ate bread from heaven.

19

John 6:58, LB

PHILLIPS BROOKS, perceptive preacher of the nineteenth century, said, "Feed on Christ, and then go and live your life, and it is Christ in you that lives your life, that helps the poor, that tells the truth, that fights the battle, and that wins the crown." The apostle Paul is saying the same thing in Galatians 2:20, "I have been crucified with Christ; it is no longer I who live, but Christ who lives in me; and the life I now live in the flesh I live by faith in the Son of God, who loved me and gave himself for me" (RSV). I used to have trouble with this passage from Paul, but old Phillips Brooks helped me get a handle on it and see how it

January

dovetailed with our Lord's teaching in the Gospel of John. It is my prayer that my life might indeed so reflect my Lord that others will see him instead of me. What a way to live!

---

20 *For those whom he foreknew he also predestined to be conformed to the image of his Son, in order that he might be the first-born among many brethren.*

Romans 8:29, RSV

UNDER THE RIGHT CONDITIONS it is as natural for character to become beautiful as for a flower; and if on God's earth there is not some machinery for effecting it, the supreme gift to the world has been forgotten. This is simply what man was made for. As Browning says: "Man was made to grow, not stop." Or in the deeper words of an older Book: "Whom he did foreknow, he also did predestinate to be conformed to the image of his Son. . . ."

---

21 *Out of the abundance of the heart the mouth speaketh.*

Matthew 12:34

WHAT IS THE HEART? It is that central region of our being where three things are focused: the thoughts, the desires, and the will. Everyone is constantly thinking and desiring and willing; and the nature and current of his thoughts, the character and aim of his desires, as well as the attitude and direction of his will, determine the state of his heart, his inward core. The heart is neither the evil nature or the new nature. The man who by God's grace is regenerated has received a new nature and cannot become unregenerate though he may degenerate. But his heart may change from day to day. Today the beatitude may belong to him: "Blessed are the pure in heart"; tomorrow he may lapse into sin and lose that blessing. Now it is our privilege and our duty to be cleansed in thought and in desire, to be brought into a condition of loyalty in will and purpose, and to be kept in this state of inward conformity to Christ, moment by moment. "Faithful is he that calleth you, who also will do it" (1 Thess. 5:24). And the heart which the Lord cleanses he also fills.

EVAN H. HOPKINS

What doth the Lord require of thee, but to do justly, and to love **22**
mercy, and to walk humbly with thy God?

Micah 6:8

WHAT A BLUEPRINT for a meaningful life these words from the Book of Micah suggest. They come to us in the context of the "Lord's case against Israel" as expressed by the prophet. Every dimension of life is taken into account here: duty to God, others, and self. I am "to do justly" to others, "to walk humbly" with my God, and "to love mercy," which speaks of the inner harmony I am to have because of my right relationship to God and others. I like the way Isaiah amplifies the truth of Micah's admonition: "Thus says the Lord: 'Keep justice, and do righteousness, for soon my salvation will come.' . . . I dwell in the high and holy place, and also with him who is of a contrite and humble spirit, to revive the spirit of the humble, and to revive the heart of the contrite" (56:1; 57:15, RSV). Micah really ministers to my need in this insightful verse for today.

The Lord replied, "I myself will go with you and give you success [rest, **23**
RSV]."

Exodus 33:14, LB

WE CAN DARE ANYTHING and go any place if God goes with us. His presence doesn't just go *with* us; it *surrounds* and *overshadows* us, before, behind, above, and below. In light of this truth, why are we afraid? Why do we hesitate to follow God completely? Why don't we obey all his commands and fulfill his will as he reveals it to us?

We need to recognize that this promise of God to his people, Israel, applies to the Christian today as well. Our God is alive, present in the world with us. How do I know? He has heard and answered my prayers. He has given me guidance when I asked for it. Therefore will I follow him without fear, for I will not be walking alone—my Companion is the Lord himself!

Living this kind of a guided, God-directed life implies submission on my part—a willingness to subject myself and my will to him, a willingness to walk according to his plan and purpose for my life rather than inserting my will ahead of his, substituting my way for his way. How do I know when I am in his will? Our text supplies one aspect of the answer: a restful spirit. If I am doing his will, I have a positive feeling of peace and purpose about the way I am taking. There is a solid sense of "rightness" about my path that is inescapable.

Another unerring source of spiritual direction is available to his child through his Word. Isaiah says, "He shall enter into peace: they shall rest . . ." (57:2). This promise is specifically to the righteous, the godly person, the one who puts God first in his life, who seeks his way. God has promised to walk that way with you, child of his. Walk it with confidence and a restful spirit!

24

Take thought for what is noble in the sight of all.

Romans 12:17, RSV

A CROSS CHRISTIAN, an anxious Christian, a discouraged, gloomy, exacting Christian, a doubting, complaining Christian, a selfish, cruel, hard-hearted Christian, a self-indulgent Christian, a Christian with a sharp tongue or bitter spirit—all these may be earnest in their work, and may have honorable places in the church; but they are not Christlike Christians, and they know nothing of the realities of which the Bible treats, no matter how loud their professions may be. The life hid with Christ in God is a hidden life as to its source, but it must not be hidden as to its practical results. People must see that we walk as Christ walked, if we say that we are abiding in Him. We must prove that we possess that which we profess. We must, in short, be real followers of Christ, and not theoretical ones only. And this means that we must really turn our backs on everything that is not pleasing to God, "as the servants of Christ, doing the will of God from the heart."

HANNAH WHITALL SMITH

25

Thou God seest me.

Genesis 16:13

THERE ARE CERTAIN THINGS that we do in the absence of certain holy friends that we would not for a moment do in their presence; but God is always present whether we know it or not, and if we walk in the consciousness of his presence, our lives and hearts will speedily be cleansed. As Paul says, "Walk in the Spirit, and ye shall not fulfil the lust of the flesh" (Gal. 5:16).

We become like those with whom we habitually associate. How like their parents children become! How many mothers and fathers have been startled by seeing their own imperfections and follies mirrored in their children, and husband and wife grow strangely like one another. Thus, also, the one who associates with God becomes like God.

R.A. TORREY

And Jacob awaked out of his sleep, and he said, Surely the Lord is in this place; and I knew it not.

26

Genesis 28:16

SOMETIMES WE THINK if we could change our circumstances we would become more spiritual, or happier. We imagine that it is the place that makes the difference. But we are always on holy ground if we are habitually living in the presence of God. God is always with his people, but they don't always realize it! It is for us by faith to recognize his presence: "Surely the Lord is in this place." When we say he is present with us by faith, we must not make the mistake of thinking that our very thought of him as present makes him so. No, he is there whether we realize or think it or not. "I am with you alway" is a perpetual fact that precedes our faith—not something that grows out of our faith. To apprehend or realize that fact is not to make it true, but to grasp that which was true before we grasped or understood it. It is then that fact passes into experience. For Christ is to us practically what he is to our faith.

The Spirit of God hath made me, and the breath of the Almighty hath given me life.

27

Job 33:4

THE PROBLEMS of the Christian life finally are simplified to this: man has but to preserve the right attitude. To abide in Christ, to be in position—that is all. Much work may be done on board a ship crossing the Atlantic. Yet none of it is spent on making the ship go. The sailor but harnesses his vessel to the wind. He puts his sail and rudder in position, and lo! the miracle is wrought. So everywhere God creates, man utilizes. All the work of the world is merely a taking advantage of

January

energies already there. God gives the wind and the water and the heat; man but puts himself in the way of the wind, fixes his waterwheel in the way of the river, puts his piston in the way of the steam; and so, holding himself in position before God's Spirit, he feels all the energies of Omnipotence coursing through and within his soul.

HENRY DRUMMOND

28

Have I not commanded you? Be strong and of good courage; be not frightened, neither be dismayed; for the Lord your God is with you wherever you go.

Joshua 1:9, RSV

HERE'S A COMMAND that will appeal to the youthful heart—for youth seeks a challenge. But God is not demanding the strength of mere human heroism here. He is not calling for animal courage and a conquering spirit. The strength commanded here comes through faith. It is not the strength that rests on faith, but that on which faith rests. God reminds Joshua of the earlier exhortations of Moses recorded in Deuteronomy 31:7, 8, and 23, and drives home the clincher: "for the Lord your God is with you wherever you go." It is not our prayer that makes this true, but it *is* prayer that opens our eyes to see this truth. God declares the fact, faith accepts it, and at once all fear disappears. Someone has said that to Joshua it meant "strength in the hands and firmness in the knees." Jeremiah had the same message from God: "Be not afraid . . . for I am with thee to deliver thee, saith the Lord" (1:8), and Isaiah echoes it: "Strengthen ye the weak hands, and confirm [make firm] the feeble knees" (35:3; see Heb. 12:12, 13). All that remains for Joshua—and for us—is to take possession of our inheritance: "Every place that the sole of your foot shall tread upon, that have I given unto you, as I said unto Moses" (Josh. 1:3). Take possession of your inheritance—it's yours for the taking!

29

. . . as your days, so shall your strength be.

Deuteronomy 33:25, RSV

PROBABLY NO PHYSICAL CHARACTERISTIC is more admired and desired than sheer strength, at least among young men. High school and college athletes are among the "in" crowd in any school. Indeed, physical strength seems to lie at the heart of much of what the world calls "success." Yet I don't think that is exactly what Moses had in mind here, as he reported the words of the Lord. The *Living Bible* gives this as, "And may your strength match the length of your days." The New International Version says, "your strength will equal your days." The concept here is more of an inner, spiritual strength to cope with life's struggles rather than mere physical power. Indeed, the one man of tremendous physical strength who stands out in the Bible is Samson— and he didn't fare too well in those other areas of life that really count. The promise, "so shall your strength be," is sure, however. As the need arises, the inner fiber, the outward strength, *will* be supplied. I'll go with that guarantee!

That I may know [Christ], and the power of his resurrection, and the **30**
fellowship of his sufferings, being made conformable unto his death.
Philippians 3:10

DO WE NOT FEEL the change that had come between Paul crying submissively, "Lord, what wilt thou have me to do?" looking to an outside Christ for commandment, and the same Paul crying, "Not I, but Christ liveth in me" (Gal. 2:20)—rejoicing in the inspiration of an inward Savior? This was the perfect victory for which Paul was always longing so desperately. It did not come perfectly to him in this world. It cannot to any of us. Dependent as it is upon the knowledge of Christ by the soul, it cannot be perfect till the soul's knowledge shall be perfect in heaven. The great privilege of the Christian is deepening, personal intimacy with him who is the Christian's life, the Lord Jesus Christ. All comes to that at last. Christianity begins with many motives. It all fastens itself at last upon one motive, which does not exclude, but is large enough to comprehend, all that is good in all the rest, "That I may know him."

PHILLIPS BROOKS

Awake, awake; put on thy strength, O Zion. . . . **31**
Isaiah 52:1

THESE COMPELLING WORDS are found in the heart of that part of Isaiah which speaks of comfort and assurance for the wayward nation of Israel

January

(this section begins with chapter 40 and goes on through the remainder of the book). Isaiah is speaking of the restoration of Israel following the national captivity which had lasted for an entire generation. F. B. Meyer puts these words into perspective for us: "Put on strength. We do not have to buy it, or generate it by prayers and resolutions, but we are simply to put it on. He waits to strengthen us with all power, according to his riches in glory. Do not simply pray to be kept and helped, but put on the whole armor of God." "The Lord is the strength of my life; of whom shall I be afraid?" asked David in Psalm 27:1. God indeed is the Source of our strength, both inner and outer. He supplies it, but we must put it on!

February

Living in Christ

And what is the exceeding greatness of his power to us-ward who believe, according to the working of his mighty power, which he wrought in Christ, when he raised him from the dead, and set him at his own right hand in the heavenly places.

Ephesians 1:19–20

1

I AM PERFECTLY SURE that spiritual help and power are as available to us as water or electricity. They are about us all the time, waiting to be appropriated. The air is filled with them. I am not talking vague "metaphysics" now. I believe that the help and power which we need was once and for all defined, localized, and channeled to the world in the person of Jesus Christ. When the Holy Spirit came, in fulfillment of Christ's promise, all that Christ was and did became universally accessible. Too many are more concerned with the formulas than with the results. Many in our churches say the right words, but do not appropriate or release the power.

Yet if God is behind all things, and has manifested Himself supremely in Christ His Son and in the Holy Spirit, then spiritual power is not only the most important kind of power but also the most pervasive. Some people seem to be touched by this power, some do not, some of us know it intermittently. I do not believe that this is primarily due to constitutional virtues or defects, but simply to the fact that some people seek persistently in the right way, while others do not.

SAM SHOEMAKER

Submit yourselves therefore to God. Resist the devil, and he will flee from you.

James 4:7

2

HERE'S ANOTHER KEY to victorious Christian living. The Christian life is a paradox. Where else do you win by surrendering or submitting?

February

Ours is not a *personal* struggle against evil—it's an appropriation of the means of defense God has already set up, a system outside of ourselves. Christ is our Fortress, the Armor in which we are enclosed. Resisting the devil involves wearing that armor and living in that fortress. To come out of the fortress and to discard the armor before we struggle with Satan is to invite failure and defeat. It is useless to plead for strength to resist in ourselves when Jesus Christ offers us his power for overcoming that evil oppressor. Follow God's formula—and find victory in the living God.

---

3 *If any man serve me, let him follow me; and where I am, there shall also my servant be.*

John 12:26

THE REALLY SIMPLE LIFE is the life of following Jesus. The most perplexing question will soon become as clear as day if you determine with all your heart to follow him. Satan will always be ready to whisper to you, "Such and such a good man does it"; but all you need to answer is: "It doesn't matter what this or that man may do, or not do. The only question to me is, 'What would Jesus do?'"

The more closely we follow Jesus, the more our faith in him will grow. Those who follow most closely in his footsteps have most faith. When Peter began to follow Christ afar off, his faith failed rapidly. The more denial of self, of true cross-bearing and humility there is in our lives, the more our faith will grow.

R. A. TORREY

---

4 *Show me thy ways, O Lord; teach me thy paths. Lead me in thy truth, and teach me. . . .*

Psalm 25:4–5

I CAN REALLY EMPATHIZE with David as he cries out here to God in a desperate prayer for guidance and protection. Throughout the Psalms we repeatedly see David crying out to God, and it is indicative of the relationship he had with his heavenly Father. We aren't told what his particular predicament was in this instance but since he was a man of war, of action, it probably concerned his very life, for time and time again David trod upon the very edges of eternity in his struggle to avoid death at the hands of the demented King Saul. David's difficulties drove him to a life of prayer and close fellowship with God. F. B. Meyer says on this subject of walking with God: "God does not always show us the whole plan for our lives at a burst, but unfolds our life to us bit by bit." This is the way it is with most of us—and that's why David's life is such an encouragement to me. He never "arrived." He was always on the way.

And the child [John the Baptist] grew, and waxed strong in spirit, and was in the deserts till the day of his showing unto Israel.

5

Luke 1:80

THERE ARE TWO KINDS of incompleteness—the incompleteness which is simply that which is growing to completeness: a child is a perfect human being in the sense of all his adjustments being right, but he is not a perfected human being in the sense of full growth and maturity; therefore the effort of a child to do a thing and not succeed is not in the same category as failure through willfulness. It is the limitation of his growing powers that prevents his succeeding. But alongside that is an incompleteness which comes from the presence of an opposing force, something which makes me say "I won't." A man with an impulse toward God and all that is right has also an impulse toward that which is against God, he is divided in two; it is not a question of imperfect growth but of downright opposition which not only makes for incompleteness, but makes an hiatus that cannot be bridged. No power outside God can alter that "I won't" into "I will." "I won't" is not imperfect "I will," and it will never develop into "I will."

There was no incompleteness in that sense in our Lord; he grew and "increased in wisdom and stature" (Luke 2:52), and when we are born again it means that "Christ is formed in us," then we have to "grow up in all things into Him." But that will to oppose must be dealt with before I can do that; I can't develop as Jesus did unless He takes out of me that which never was in Him. If He can do that, then I can begin to understand how He is my Example; but He is not my Example unless the Redemption has been made of practical effect in me.

OSWALD CHAMBERS

29

February

6

I keep asking that the God of our Lord Jesus Christ . . . may give you the Spirit of wisdom and revelation, so that you may know him better. I pray also that the eyes of your heart may be enlightened in order that you may know the hope to which he has called you, the riches of his glorious inheritance in the saints, and his incomparably great power for us who believe.

Ephesians 1:17–19, NIV

THERE IS SUCH A VAST message in these verses that one cannot even begin to summarize it in a few short sentences, but let me hit a highlight or two. One striking fact emerges: the power of Christ's Resurrection is available to me *right now*. That enormous power which raised Jesus from the dead will enlighten the eyes of my heart and reveal "the riches of his glorious inheritance in the saints." That power rules "not only in the present age but also in the one to come" (v. 21, NIV). We Christians enjoy "advances in grace" because his Resurrection power is available to us every step of our dusty way, right now! Here's heavenly power to propel this earthly frame. Am I putting it to use, or letting it lie dormant while I try to make it on my own?

7

Fear not; for I am with thee. . . .

Isaiah 43:5

GOD HAS A STRONG reserve with which to discharge this engagement; for He is able to do all things. Believer, till you can drain dry the ocean of omnipotence, till you can break into pieces the towering mountains of almighty strength, you never need to fear. Think not that the strength of man shall ever be able to overcome the power of God. While the earth's huge pillars stand, you have enough reason to abide firm in your faith. The same God who directs the earth in its orbit, who feeds the burning furnace of the sun and trims the lamps of heaven, has promised to supply you with daily strength. In Isaiah 41:10 He says, "Fear thou not; for I am with thee: be not dismayed; for I am thy God: I will strengthen thee; yea I will help thee; yea, I will uphold thee with the right hand of my righteousness." While He is able to uphold the universe, do not dream that He will prove unable to fulfill His own promises. Remember what He did in the days of old, in the former generations. Remember how He spoke and it was done; how He commanded, and it stood fast. Shall He that created the world grow weary?

He hangs the world upon nothing; shall He who does this be unable to support His children? Shall He be unfaithful to His Word for want of power? Who is it that restrains the tempest? Does He not ride upon the wings of the wind, and make the clouds His chariots, and hold the ocean in the hollow of His hand? How can He fail you? When He has put such a faithful promise as this on record, will you for a moment indulge the thought that He has outpromised Himself and gone beyond His power to fulfill? Ah, no! You can no longer doubt.

CHARLES H. SPURGEON

Whoever does the will of God is my brother, and sister, and mother.
Mark 3:35, RSV

8

TENNYSON WAS RIGHT, "Our wills are ours, we know not how; our wills are ours, to make them Thine." When we make our wills his will, we know the beloved communion for which we were born. But also, we come to know a new relationship with others who are also seeking his will. A great Church is born when with one voice we cry, "In our life together, thy will be done!" The family of faith results. . . .

There is no Christian growth without the surrender of the will. That's the battlefield for our souls. Augustine said in his prayers to God, "When I vacillated about my decision to serve the Lord my God, it was I who willed and I who willed not, and nobody else. I was fighting against myself. All you asked was that I cease to want what I willed and want what you willed."

That's the liberating secret! The family of God is the fellowship of people who are open to the will of God and therefore open to each other. His will is that we love him and each other. We cannot love each other while resisting his will nor can we resist loving each other if we do his will.

LLOYD OGILVIE

Quoted from *Life Without Limits* (Waco, TX: Word Books, 1975), pp. 76–77.

There is a friend that sticketh closer than a brother.
Proverbs 18:24

9

THERE IS A CONCEPT of Christ which we do not consider as often as we should. In fact, we're probably guilty of not thinking of it at all! And that's his position as our Friend. Charles H. Spurgeon, with his customary insight, put it into perspective for us: "Do not be content with an interview now and then, but seek always to be in his company, for only in his presence do you have either comfort or safety. Jesus should not be just a friend we call upon now and then but one with whom we walk every day. You have a difficult road before you; see that you do not try to go without your Guide. In every condition you will need Jesus. Keep close to your best Friend, and he will refresh and cheer you." What better Guide could you and I know than this One who is not only our Friend, but our Elder Brother?

10

For if any one is a hearer of the word and not a doer, he is like a man who observes his natural face in a mirror; for he observes himself and goes away and at once forgets what he was like. . . . But we all, with open face beholding as in a glass the glory of the Lord, are changed into the same image from glory to glory, even as by the Spirit of the Lord.

James 1:23–24, RSV; 2 Corinthians 3:18

WHAT KIND OF AN IMAGE do I reflect in my day-to-day life? Do I look into the mirror of God's Word and see myself, and then go away and forget what I saw? Or do I look into the mirror and see "the glory of the Lord"—and then go out and reflect that glory? In *The Changed Life* Henry Drummond wrote: "In looking at a mirror one does not see the mirror or think of it, but only what it reflects. For a mirror never calls attention to itself except where there are flaws in it." Unlike the mirror he describes, the mirror of the Word reflects the flaws it sees in me—and I have a choice: yield my flaws to the divine surgery and emerge with the flaws changed to crowns; or turn my back on the mirror and forget what I've seen, bent on my own path without regard to God's plan for me.

11

Furthermore, we have had fathers of our flesh which corrected us, and we gave them reverence: shall we not much rather be in subjection unto the Father of spirits, and live?

Hebrews 12:9

IMAGINE A BLIMP tied up at an airport. Untied, the blimp just blows back and forth, without any control. It needs firm mooring lines to hold it firmly in place so it'll still be flying high the next morning. Lacking them, it may fly high for a while, but it will also lose control and crash.

Faith in Christ is like that. You can directly, emotionally, experience God's goodness to you, but that alone is like the blimp without moorings. That's why people who never get into the Word of God often drift from drugs to the occult to Christianity to Eastern religions. They're flying high, but without controls they crash.

God doesn't have a skin. He doesn't give us something tangible we can physically hold onto. But he does give us, through the Bible and through Jesus, some moorings. They're things that don't change—truths we can grab onto and hold no matter how we're feeling. One is this truth—God is our Father. It'll help hold you steady while you soar.

JAY KESLER

Quoted from Jay Kesler and Tim Stafford, *I Never Promised You a Disneyland* (Waco, TX: Word Books, 1975).

As he who called you is holy, be holy yourselves in all your conduct. **12**
1 Peter 1:15, RSV

GOD IS BOTH our model and the power by which we rise toward that model. He is holy, and he has called us unto himself. We, too, therefore must be holy. By our regeneration and conversion we are set apart unto God. That setting apart unto him makes us holy as to our calling. But we must be holy now "in all [our] conduct." The influence of his holiness must be seen in our outward conduct and course of life. We are holy only in so far as we are brought into contact with the center of all holiness. God has called us, not merely out of darkness, but into the light—unto himself. It is only because of this that we can be holy. Whatever he takes possession of becomes holy. When he took possession of the bush, and dwelt in it, that bush became a holy bush (Exod. 3). God himself made it holy. So, when he calls us to himself and takes possession of us, we become a holy temple unto God. He transfigures the outer life by renewing the mind, and this by filling our whole being with himself, who is the Holy One.

EVAN H. HOPKINS

Who is the image of the invisible God, the firstborn of every creature: **13**
. . . For it pleased the Father that in him should all fulness dwell.
Colossians 1:15, 19

A GREAT MANY PEOPLE overexercise themselves in asking questions about who and what God is. They would do better to seek to discover what He is like by studying what He does, by watching the places where He has been, by tracing Him, as it were, through His footsteps. Nobody

February

knows exactly what electricity is, but we know a good deal about what electricity does. We know most about God's nature through Christ, but this often does not become personal to us until we go into partnership with God, and enjoy the effects of His power in our own experience. Many will never believe much in God until they come in contact with others who believe in Him vitally and in such a way that their belief tremendously affects their lives. Many years ago a highly privileged young man named William Borden went out from Yale University to serve God and his fellow men in Egypt. While still young, he fell ill and died. On his gravestone in Cairo are the words, "Apart from Christ there is no explanation of such a life." There are many in the world of whom something like this must be said. Some are great, some are obscure, but round them is an aura, an atmosphere, which marks them as not just of this world.

SAM SHOEMAKER

14

For who hath known the mind of the Lord, that he may instruct him? But we have the mind of Christ.

1 Corinthians 2:16

WHAT DOES IT MEAN to "have the mind of Christ"? Among the cluster of the "fruit of the Spirit" in Galatians 5:22 is "faith." We misunderstand if we assume that this faith comes from within ourselves. It comes as a gift when the Spirit rules within our lives. We don't produce it by our own efforts by imitating Christ's example. Rather, it comes as we honor the Holy Spirit, as we yield our lives to his control. He is the One who produces in us "this mind . . . which was also in Christ Jesus" (Phil. 2:5). The true imitation of Christ consists in the renunciation of ourselves, even as he ignored himself, and living by faith in the Son of God, even as he lived by the Father. To "have the mind of Christ" is to be completely controlled by him, which results in bearing fruit for him. There is no way a branch can be fruitful if it is severed from the tree, the source of its strength.

15

The Lord your God proveth you, to know whether ye love the Lord your God with all your heart and with all your soul.

Deuteronomy 13:3

NEVER LIMIT GOD by remembering what you have done in the past. When you come into relation with the Reality of Redemption God creates something in you that was never there before; it is the active working of the life of God in you. Consequently you can do now what you could not do before. Character is always revealed in crises. There are lives that seem selfish and self-centered until a crisis occurs, and they manifest the most disinterested concern and self-effacement. On the other hand, there are lives that appear unselfish and noble, and when the crisis comes they are revealed as mean and despicable. In the early stages of our Christian experience we are inclined to hunt in an overplus of delight for the commandments of our Lord in order to obey them out of our love for Him, but when that conscious obedience is assimilated and we begin to mature in our life with God, we obey His command-ments unconsciously, until in the maturest stage of all we are simply children of God through whom God does His will, for the most part unconsciously to us.

OSWALD CHAMBERS

But the wisdom that comes from heaven is first of all pure; then peace loving, considerate, submissive, full of mercy and good fruit, impar-tial and sincere.

James 3:17, NIV

16

I'D LIKE TO THINK that this striking description of the Christ-filled life could be applied to me. I don't think James misses one of the attributes that would enhance the life of a "beautiful believer." Notice, however, that these Christian characteristics come "from above" and grow out of a "pure" or transparent life. All of these are traits of the Spirit. James is not writing about physical appearance, but about spiritual beauty. He's describing the Christian spirit rather than the Christian body. These words apply to man or woman, child or adult, without depending on age or gender. J. R. Miller writes: "The things that hurt and sear our lives are resentment, unforgiveness, bitter feeling, desire for revenge. Men may beat us until our bones are broken, but if love fails not in our hearts meanwhile, we have come through the experience unharmed, with no marks of injury upon us. One writing of a friend terribly hurt in a hit-and-run accident said that the woman would probably be scarred for life, and then went on to speak of the wonderful patience of her suffering, and that the peace of God had not failed in her heart for a moment. The world may hurt our bodies, but if we suffer as Christ suffered, there will be no trace of scarring or wounding in our inner life."

February

17

That which we have seen and heard we proclaim also to you, so that you may have fellowship with us; and our fellowship is with the Father and with his Son Jesus Christ.

1 John 1:3, RSV

CLOSENESS WITH CHRIST is the inspiration and intimation of our living. A personal relationship with Christ helps us to see both our distortion of his intention and what we are to become. It was not easy to be a Christian in ancient Ephesus, nor is it now in your city and mine. The same distracting philosophies which disturbed the Christians then, trouble us now. We are tempted to make Christ an idea or theory which has little to do with our difficult weeks or days or hours. We share with the Christians to whom John wrote the seeming disadvantage of not having seen Christ in the flesh. But we can know him with the same intimacy John knew after Pentecost.

If you had a choice of being ushered back through history to be part of the band of disciples to walk and talk with Jesus in the flesh, would you want that more than knowing his presence and power in intimate friendship for your life today? I choose the latter. More than an example of life, we have the Enabler of Life who can reproduce himself in us. That's what I need for today. What about you?

LLOYD OGILVIE

Quoted from *When God First Thought of You* (Waco, TX: Word Books, 1978), p. 17.

18

Because the foolishness of God is wiser than men; and the weakness of God is stronger than men.

1 Corinthians 1:25

GOD GRANT THAT His Spirit may bring every one of us to the place where the secret is learned and enjoyed that His strength is made perfect in our weakness. The realization that my strength is always a hindrance to God's supply of life is a great eye-opener. A man who has genius is apt to rely on his genius rather than on God. A man who has money is apt to rely on money instead of God. So many of us trust in what we have in the way of possessions instead of entirely in God. All these sources of strength are sources of double weakness. But when we realize that our true life is "hid with Christ in God," that we are "complete in him," in whom "dwelleth all the fulness of the Godhead bodily," then His strength is radiantly manifested in our mortal flesh. God grant that every "spasmodic" saint may turn into a real sanctified saint, whose light and life and love shine more and more unto the perfect day.

OSWALD CHAMBERS

These things I have spoken unto you, that in me ye might have peace. In the world ye shall have tribulation: but be of good cheer, I have overcome the world. **19**

John 16:33

THESE WORDS of encouragement come at the end of our Savior's farewell message to his disciples, just before his betrayal. As Henry Drummond says, "Nothing ever for a moment broke the serenity of Christ's life on earth. Misfortune could not reach him; he had no fortune. Food, raiment, money—fountainheads of half the world's weariness—he simply did not care about; they played no part in his life; he took 'no thought' for them. It was impossible to affect him by lowering his reputation. He had already made himself of no reputation. He was dumb before insult. When he was reviled he reviled not again. In fact, there was nothing that the world could do to him that could ruffle the surface of his spirit." We, his followers today, have this same source of serenity in the face of whatever the world sends our way.

But the Lord is faithful, who shall stablish you, and keep you from evil. **20**

2 Thessalonians 3:3

FOR YEARS you may have lived a sheltered, protected life. "Lead me not into temptation"—so you have prayed every morning, and every day has brought the answer to your prayer. But some day all that breaks and goes to pieces. A great temptation comes, and is not restrained. Then you cry out for the old mercy, and it is not given—and then, behold what comes! A new mercy! You go into that temptation. Your old security perishes, but by-and-by out of its death comes a new strength. Not to be saved from dying, but to die and live again in a new security, a strong and trusty character, educated by trial, purified by fire—that is what comes as the result of the testing. Not a victory *for* you, preserving you from danger, but a victory *in* you, strengthening you by danger—that is

February

the experience from which you go forth, strong with a strength which nothing can subdue.

PHILLIPS BROOKS

---

21   *If ye be reproached for the name of Christ, happy are ye.*

1 Peter 4:14

THIS WORD, *Christian*, came to the Early Church by a process. The multitude, curiously looking on from day to day at their worship, their testimony and teaching, their life and character, could see one feature predominating all else. One name was always on their lips; one Presence they were always invoking; one word they were always repeating— *Christ*. So they came to call His disciples *Christ ones*; for that is just what Christian means, a *Christ one*.

But, is our testimony, our worship, our life today such that it would lead the world, if it knew nothing of our religion, to call us *Christians*? Would there be so much of the name, the testimony, and the Spirit of Christ in our faces, our songs, our work, and our daily lives, that the disciples should again be called *Christians*, because they were Christ ones?

"What the world wants today is not more Christians, but more Christ ones." It is not the imitation of Christ, but it is identification with Christ that constitutes vital Christianity. It is not the human trying to copy the divine, but it is the divine coming into the human and lifting it to His level, and making it second nature to be like God. "Christ liveth in me." "Your life is hid with Christ in God." Christianity is not primarily a new way of living, of believing, of worshiping, but Christianity is coming into a new relationship to a Person. It is meeting Jesus and going on with Him.

A. B. SIMPSON

---

22   *But the path of the just is as the shining light, that shineth more and more unto the perfect day.*

Proverbs 4:18

THERE IS A WONDERFUL freedom in this life of simply following Jesus. This path is straight and plain. But the path of one who tries to shape his conduct by observing the conduct of others, is full of twists and turns and pitfalls. Keep looking at Jesus. Follow trustingly where he leads.

Are you walking as Jesus walked? Are you living your life day by day, in utter disregard of your own interests, your own reputation, your own authority, your own comfort, your own honor, doing the things that will bring blessing to others, no matter what loss and dishonor the doing of them may bring to you? Then you are abiding in him: "He that saith he abideth in him ought himself also so to walk, even as he walked" (1 John 2:6).

R. A. TORREY

23

The thief cometh not, but for to steal, and to kill, and to destroy: I am come that they might have life, and that they might have it more abundantly.

John 10:10

WHAT A TREMENDOUS promise is wrapped up in these words from the lips of Jesus. Life is our first and primary need. In its deepest sense it involves a vital and continuing connection with him of whom it is written, "In him was life; and the life was the light of men" (John 1:4). In a sense, Christ's fullness is the complement of our emptiness. In Romans 5:12 Paul says, "Wherefore, as by one man sin entered into the world, and death by sin; and so death passed upon all men, for that all have sinned." In reply to that emptiness, Jesus says, "I am come that they might have life . . . more abundantly." Once we were without life, and then suddenly it is ours in Christ. But he doesn't leave us at that point. As is his nature, he goes far beyond our basic and primary need, and gives us an abundance where we once had nothing at all! This is the One with whom you can live your life. How much better with him rather than the "thief"!

24

Ye are complete in him.

Colossians 2:10

THE NATURE of the Christian life is Christ's life taking hold upon all the inner life of a man, changing, dominating, pulsating. It is seen therefore, and I do not think we can be too careful in emphasizing this, that Christian life is neither human imitation of Christ, nor correct intellectual positions concerning Christ. Neither is it a cult, or a system of thought. I may attempt to imitate Christ sincerely through long years, and yet never be a Christian. I may hold absolutely correct intellectual views concerning Christ as a person, and His power, and yet never be a Christian. It is possible for me to admire Him, and attempt with all the power of my life to imitate Him, and yet never realize Him. It is quite possible for a person to believe most sincerely in His Deity, and in the fact of His atoning work, and moreover, in the necessity for regeneration, and yet never be submitted to His Lordship, never to have personal share in the work of His atonement, never to be born again.

Nothing short of the coming into the life of the individual of Christ Himself constitutes a Christian. If Jesus Christ is external to your life there will be times when the world will not see Him and hear Him, and will not know you belong to Him. But if Christ be in you, living, reigning there absolutely, and you are obeying Him, there never will be a moment when the truth will not be evident. You cannot hide Christ if once He comes within. If the light is there, it simply must shine.

G. CAMPBELL MORGAN

25 *Thou art my lamp, O Lord; and the Lord will lighten my darkness. . . . As for God, his way is perfect; the word of the Lord is tried: he is a buckler to all them that trust in him. . . . God is my strength and power: and he maketh my way perfect.*

2 Samuel 22:29, 31, 33

"HE MAKETH MY WAY perfect!" What a promise for anyone about to set out on a journey! But notice the significant words with which our text for the day begins: "Thou art my lamp, O Lord: and the Lord will lighten my darkness." It is Jesus Christ who is both the Author and Finisher of our faith. He is both the crown and the glory of our human perfection. This means far more than that he puts the *finishing touch* on the quality of our human nature. He himself *is* the finishing touch. The Lord of glory places the final climactic and indispensable beauty upon mankind, even as the finished tabernacle stood in gloom until the glory of God fell upon it. Of what value is a gem, even though fashioned by the most gifted artisan, if there is no light to show off the beauty of the cut stone? Of what service is the mightiest dam unless the waters are allowed to flow through it? How vital it is that we yield ourselves to his control so that he can truly lighten our darkness and direct us on our way.

Then spake Jesus again unto them, saying, I am the light of the world: he that followeth me shall not walk in darkness, but shall have the light of life.

John 8:12

26

WE ARE TO IMITATE Jesus in our lives. He is the pattern we are to live by. But we need to make sure we're dealing with the real pattern, not some feeling we've built up. . . . My dad tells a story about raising a barn for a man whose barn had burned. All the people in the neighborhood came together and assigned certain guys to cut the rafters. All these guys had to do was follow a pattern.

But instead of using the original pattern for each rafter that was to be cut, they would mark one, cut it, and then use it to mark the next one, and so on. Each time they marked a rafter, however, they were gaining just one pencil width in length. Each marking would only add ⅓₂ of an inch or so at each end. It doesn't amount to much, except they kept compounding it until they were one-half inch off on the sixteenth rafter. By the thirty-second rafter they were one inch off its pattern. Eventually they realized their error, and had to recut all the rafters.

Some of us are in that position when it comes to following Jesus—we're copying something somebody told us or some feeling we remember, and we're missing the mark. This is why the Bible goes to such pains to tell us what Jesus was really like. He is the pattern we're supposed to live by. The person who wants to follow Christ has to keep going back to that original pattern.

JAY KESLER

Quoted from Jay Kesler and Tim Stafford, *I Never Promised You a Disneyland* (Waco, TX: Word Books, 1975).

Quit you like men, be strong.

1 Corinthians 16:13

27

GENTLENESS AND GOOD TEMPER are not all. One may have these qualities and yet be lacking in the completeness of well-rounded character. There must be strength as well as beauty. Love is the fulfilling of the law; all the commandments being summed up in one, "Thou shalt love." But *love* is a large word. It is like one of those composite pictures into which many pictures are blended. All the elements of duty to God and to our fellows are wrapped up in the divine conception of loving. It will not do, therefore, for us to take merely the things that belong to the gentle side, and think of these as the whole of Christian character. Christ was infinitely gentle. The warmth of his heart made a tropical summer all about him. But back of the gentleness was also infinite strength. We must be like him, not only in gentle warmth, but also in truth and all righteousness. We must be to others, not only tenderness, but also strength to lean upon, and stability in which they may find refuge.

J. R. MILLER

---

28   *"The virgin will be with child and will give birth to a son, and they will call him Immanuel"—which means, "God with us."*
Matthew 1:23, NIV

IN HIS BOOK *The Kingdom Is Yours*, Louis Evans, Sr., tells the story of a student who sold aluminumware to earn his way through school. He was scared to death of his job and one day rang the front doorbell of a home with real fear and trembling. When the largest woman he had ever seen answered the door, he stuttered: "Ma-Ma-Madam, you don't want any aluminum, do you?" Her angry "Of course not!" left him beaten for the day. That night he related his tale of woe to the veteran salesman with whom he was working and moaned that he couldn't take it any longer. His friend assured him he knew what his problem was and suggested that the two work together the next day, on opposite sides of the street. "Just before you ring a doorbell," he explained, "look over at me and I'll salute you and you'll know I'm with you."

The next day the student went to another door, still scared to death. Then, remembering the words of his friend, he looked across the street. Sure enough, his friend saw him and waved—he was not alone. With renewed confidence he rang the bell and faced the smallest woman he'd ever seen. Confidently he spoke: "Madam, I know you'd like to look at some aluminumware, wouldn't you?" "Certainly," she replied—and he had a great day! Later that day the old salesman said, "You know, son, the only thing you needed was the power of a presence—to know that you were not alone." You and I need that assurance too! Isn't it great to know that Jesus is *God with us?*

Now among those who went up to worship at the feast were some Greeks. So these came to Philip, . . . and said to him, "Sir, we wish to see Jesus."

John 12:20–21, RSV

29

WHEN I WAS PRIVILEGED to share the exciting days of the birth and growth of the Winnetka Presbyterian Church some years ago, I was amazed at the hunger for Jesus Christ in that affluent, sophisticated suburb of Chicago. The more we preached Christ, studied his life and message, claimed the contemporary power of his presence, and modeled the new life made possible by his indwelling Spirit, the more people flocked to the church. The hunger for Jesus Christ was vividly communicated to me on the day we finished the new building to house the life of the emerging congregation. The night before we all had worked to finish up the preparations of the building for dedication. The next day when I mounted into the beautifully carved, new pulpit, I looked down at the Bible to read my text. There boldly staring up at me was a plaque placed over the open Scriptures. It quoted the words of the Greeks who came seeking Jesus. "Sir, we wish to see Jesus!" That not only expressed the deepest need of the congregation but its fondest hope. I later learned that the man who had slipped into the sanctuary late at night to put the startling and undeniable challenge before me was a highly educated, polished and cultured Christian who recently had found new life in Christ. He knew his greatest need was shared by the whole congregation.

LLOYD OGILVIE

Quoted from *Life Without Limits* (Waco, TX: Word Books, 1975), p. 20.

March

Depending upon God

1   *And we know that in all things God works for the good of those who love him, who have been called according to his purpose.*

Romans 8:28, NIV

SOME YEARS AGO my life hit what I thought must have been its lowest ebb. I was so low I had to reach *up* to scratch the bottom of the barrel! At the time I couldn't understand why this was happening to me—and I certainly didn't think anything good could come out of it. Strangely enough, it was at this time that my creative juices began to flow again. I began to dream new dreams—and, in effect, my family and I started a whole new life. Out of inner agitation came exciting new ideas and projects, this very book among them. Truly, as George Edward Woodberry says, "Agitation is that part of our intellectual life where vitality results; there ideas are born, breed and bring forth." This is true in the spiritual realm as well as in the intellectual, I discovered. The great Frederick Douglass, ex-slave, abolitionist, and orator said, "Those who profess to favor freedom, and yet depreciate agitation, are men who want rain without thunder and lightning. They want the ocean without the roar of its many waters." Both these men were speaking on the purely intellectual level—but the truth of what they were saying is even more striking in the spiritual sphere, as I think Paul was pointing out here in Romans 8.

Do not be anxious about anything, but in everything, by prayer and petition, with thanksgiving, present your requests to God.

Philippians 4:6, NIV

2

I WAS SHOCKED to hear that suicide is one of the prime causes of death among teenagers and young people today. Norman Mailer once said, "The natural role of twentieth-century man is anxiety." Ours is indeed a generation beset by stress—anxiety about what tomorrow might bring, worry about meeting the debts of the day. And yet Paul is saying here, "Don't worry about anything; instead, pray about everything; tell God your needs and don't forget to thank him for his answers" (LB). "Give it to God"—that should be our motto regarding the cares of the day. Of all people, Christians should be the most serene as they go through life, not because they are untouched by its troubles, but because they refuse to be anxious in their anticipation of what tomorrow might bring. Jesus told us, "Don't be anxious about tomorrow. God will take care of your tomorrow too. Live one day at a time" (Matt. 6:34, LB). Elbert Hubbard rephrased that thought well: "If pleasures are greatest in anticipation, just remember that this is also true of trouble." The ancient philosopher Seneca said, "Nothing is so wretched or foolish as to anticipate misfortunes. What madness is it to be expecting evil before it comes."

Whoso trusteth in the Lord, happy is he.

Proverbs 16:20

3

WE NEVER KNOW the meaning of trust until we learn the nature of trial. It is in the trial that we have to put into practice the theory of believing in God. Trust is to become the habit of the soul. But often the young disciple is greatly perplexed about faith, because, instead of being occupied with the object of faith, he is thinking of the act of believing. But faith never comes in this way. It has no existence apart from him who is the object of it: "Whoso trusteth *in the Lord.*" Let our thoughts be occupied with God's revealed character, with what he is to us and what he has done for us, and we shall, without *trying* to believe, begin to put our trust in him. It is with what God is that we have to be occupied. The mind then finds its resting-place. It stays itself on God. A peace then is known that could never be found in the world. We see then how true are the words, "Happy is he." Trial therefore is the school of trust. It

March

is there we learn the lesson of implicitly confiding in God, and of waiting patiently on him.

EVAN H. HOPKINS

4

Blessed is the man that endureth temptation: for when he is tried, he shall receive the crown of life, which the Lord hath promised to them that love him.

James 1:12

ONE REASON I like James is that he was so practical. He faced the fact that Christians meet temptation, and he gave his readers practical suggestions for overcoming the temptations that came into their lives (read James 1:2–4, 12–16; 4:7). Withstanding temptation can build your spiritual muscles and strengthen you immensely. As some unknown author has said: "Temptations that find us dwelling in God are to our faith like winds that more firmly root the tree." The other side of the coin is examined in an old saying quoted in *The Link:* "Temptations are like tramps. Treat them kindly and they return bringing others with them." We can do one of two things with the temptations that come our way: endure (stand up and fight against them in the strength God gives us) or yield (sit down and let them wash over us because we try to resist in our own strength). May God give us grace to withstand, and having done all, to stand!

5

The Spirit immediately drove him out into the wilderness. And he was in the wilderness forty days . . . and the angels ministered to him.

Mark 1:12–13, RSV

AS JESUS WAS TEMPTED in order to live, so are we. The source of our hope and help is the same. As Jesus was ministered to by angels, so are we. Paul discovered this and reminded the Corinthians: "No temptation has overtaken you that is not common to man. God is faithful, and he will not let you be tempted beyond your strength, but with the temptation will also provide the way of escape, that you may be able to endure it" (1 Cor. 10:13, RSV).

God is with us in our temptation. He sends his angels to sustain us through it. The word *angel* means "messenger" and is used in the Bible for spiritual and human agents who carry out God's will. Here in the temptation, "the angels" implies emissaries from God, particularized manifestations of his Spirit for the battle with evil. The result was inward peace and strength which came in the prolonged struggle for a clear understanding of the Father's will for Jesus' ministry. The same is true for us. Special messengers of his Spirit, along with people he deploys to help us, will be given in our times of temptation.

LLOYD OGILVIE

Quoted from *Life Without Limits* (Waco, TX: Word Books, 1975), p. 31.

For we have not an high priest which cannot be touched with the feeling of our infirmities; but was in all points tempted like as we are, yet without sin.

Hebrews 4:15

6

I MUST CONFESS that I have struggled with the full meaning of this verse. How could my divine Savior possibly be tempted like I am? I have no trouble with the last part of the verse, "yet without sin," but the meaning of the first part eluded me for many years. But then I happened to read this verse in the New English Bible: "For ours is not a high priest unable to sympathize with our weaknesses, but one who, because of his likeness to us, has been tested every way, only without sin." And J. B. Phillips translates it: ". . . he himself has shared fully in all our experience of temptation, except that he never sinned." The passage goes on: "Let us *therefore* boldly approach the throne of our gracious God" (v. 16, NEB). Jesus understands everything we are called upon to go through. He never loses his "cool." This is beyond you, but if you allow him to have full control of your life, he can make it possible for you to live this way too!

Watch ye and pray, lest ye enter into temptation. The spirit truly is ready, but the flesh is weak.

Mark 14:38

7

SPIRITUAL CONFLICT is at work in the heart of every believer. It is true that the Christian possesses a new nature, but the old sin nature is still

March

there. It is now up to us, day by day, to yield to the new nature which Christ dominates.

There is the story of a housewife who found a mouse in her kitchen and took a broom to it. The mouse didn't waste its time contemplating either the housewife or the broom, but got busy looking for a hole. And so it is with us when we are caught by temptation. We don't spend time contemplating the temptation but we get busy looking for a way out. The Scripture says, "God . . . will not allow you to be tempted beyond what you are able; but with the temptation will provide the way of escape also" (1 Cor. 10:13, NASB)

BILLY GRAHAM

Quoted from *How to Be Born Again* (Waco, TX: Word Books, 1977).

8   *Cast thy burden upon the Lord, and he shall sustain thee.*

Psalm 55:22

THERE ARE SOME mistaken notions current concerning the ways in which God would help us. People think that whenever they have a little trouble, a bit of hard path to go over, a load to carry, a sorrow to endure, all they have to do is to call upon God, and he will at once take away their sorrow, or free them from the trouble. But this is not the way God helps us. His purpose of love concerning us is, not to make all things easy for us, but to make something of us.

When we pray God to save us from our care, to take the struggles out of our life, to make the paths mossy, to lift off every load, he will not do it. It would be most unloving of him to do so. We must carry the burden ourselves; all God promises is to sustain us as we carry it. He wants us to learn life's lessons, and to do this we must be left to work out the problems for ourselves. There are rich blessings which can be received only in sorrow. It would be short-sighted love indeed that would heed our cries, and spare us from sorrow, and thus deprive us of the wonderful blessings which can be gained only in sorrow. God is too good to us to answer our prayers, which would save us from pain, cost, and sacrifice today, at the price of larger, better, truer life in the end. He would not rob us of the blessing that is in the burden, which we can get only by carrying it.

J. R. MILLER

My counsel is: Don't worry about things—food, drink, and clothes. **9**
For you already have life and a body—and they are far more
important than what to eat and wear.

Matthew 6:25, LB

THEODORE L. CUYLER, a perceptive and practical devotional writer of a
past generation, once said, "God never built a Christian strong enough
to carry today's duties and tomorrow's anxieties piled on top of them."
That's why the Scriptures so frequently counsel the Christian to give his
concerns and anxieties to his heavenly Father. Strangely enough, the
average Christian is just as subject to the stress caused by anxiety, if not
more so, as the average man on the street. In some instances, this stress
is caused by physical problems. Even so, an anxious Christian is a
contradiction in terms—yet the breed is quite common! Both Jesus and
Paul frequently addressed the problem. And in the Old Testament the
psalmist David wrote: "Cast thy burden upon the Lord, and he shall
sustain thee: he shall never suffer the righteous to be moved" (55:22).
The apostle Peter reminded us to always be "casting all your care upon
him; for he careth for you" (1 Pet. 5:7). While he was not a Christian
(albeit a theist), Ben Franklin had this to say on the subject: "Do not
anticipate trouble, or worry about what may never happen. Keep in the
sunlight." If he had added, "the sunlight of God's love and care," I
couldn't have agreed with him more!

Why take ye thought for raiment? Consider the lilies of the field, how **10**
they grow; they toil not, neither do they spin: And yet I say unto you,
That even Solomon in all his glory was not arrayed like one of these.

Matthew 6:28–29

CHRIST'S WORDS are not a general appeal to consider nature. Men are
not to consider lilies simply to admire their beauty, to dream over the
delicate strength and grace of stem and leaf. The point they were to
consider was *how they grew*—how without anxiety or care the flower
woke into loveliness, how without weaving these leaves were woven,
how without toiling these complex tissues spun themselves, and how
without any effort or friction the whole slowly came ready-made from
the loom of God in its more than Solomon-like glory. "So," He says,
making the application beyond dispute, "you careworn, anxious men
must grow. You, too, need take no thought for your life, what ye shall
eat, or what ye shall drink, or what ye shall put on. For if God so clothe

March

the grass of the field, which today is and tomorrow is cast in to the oven, shall he not much more clothe you, O ye of little faith?"

HENRY DRUMMOND

11

I have told you these things, so that in me you may have peace. In this world you will have trouble. But take heart! I have overcome the world.

John 16:33, NIV

THERE IS A MISCONCEPTION abroad in the world, and it is that Christianity is the key to an easy life. But Jesus never promised that, as our verse for the day makes very clear. Rather, he promised a life of hardship, with himself at the heart of it. As James L. Christensen has so bluntly put it: "The purpose of Christianity is not to avoid difficulty, but to produce a character adequate to meet it when it comes. It does not make life easy; rather it tries to make us great enough for life." Paul must have had this truth in mind when he wrote: "Nay, in all these things we are more than conquerors through him that loved us" (Rom. 8:37). He then went on to triumphantly shout: "For I am persuaded, that neither death, nor life, nor angels, nor principalities, nor powers, nor things present, nor things to come, nor height, nor depth, nor any other creature, shall be able to separate us from the love of God, which is in Christ Jesus our Lord" (vv. 38–39).

12

Many are the afflictions of the righteous; but the Lord delivers him out of them all. He keeps all his bones; not one of them is broken.

Psalm 34:19–20, RSV

I PARTICULARLY LIKE the way this passage reads in the *Living Bible:* "The good man does not escape all troubles—he has them too. But the Lord helps him in each and every one. God even protects him from accidents." No sane man goes out to seek trouble or injury. Our natural desire and instinct is to avoid trouble or pain at all costs. David, who wrote this psalm while feigning madness to escape a king's evil designs against him, had nonetheless discovered that trouble can be blessing in disguise. God can turn trouble to our advantage if we will let him. Many men of God have written on this subject, but two of the most pithy statements are these: "Troubles are often the tools by which God fashions us for better things" (Henry Ward Beecher). E. Stanley Jones cast it in an even different light: "The Christian under trouble doesn't break up—he breaks out." Seen in this light troubles can be stepping stones to greater understanding and spiritual growth. With such growth at stake, isn't a little trouble worth the discomfort and difficulty?

And the name of the second called he Ephraim: For God hath caused me to be fruitful in the land of my affliction.

Genesis 41:52

13

JOSEPH WAS FRUITFUL in spite of affliction or "suffering" as the NIV has it. When I think of Joseph's positive influence in the negative Egyptian environment in which he was enslaved, I can't help but be reminded of a modern Joseph I know—or perhaps I should say "Josephine"—for I'm alluding to Joni Eareckson, some of whose devotional thoughts you will encounter elsewhere in this book. Joni certainly has borne fruit in an unfriendly environment—complete paralysis from the neck down. In spite of her physical helplessness, she has had a tremendous spiritual ministry—through her books, the filmed story of her life, and her personal appearances on the Billy Graham crusades and other platforms. But, like Joseph's father Jacob, at one time Joni said of her circumstances, "All these things are against me" (Gen. 42:36). She even wanted to end her own life. But then she allowed God to speak to her and through her—and now she is one of his most eloquent representatives. How do you handle "affliction"?

But the God of all grace, who hath called us unto his eternal glory by Christ Jesus, after that ye have suffered a while, make you perfect, stablish, strengthen, settle you.

1 Peter 5:10

14

MARTIN LUTHER, the great Reformer and brilliant theologian, has given me a handle on this whole subject of suffering that I'd like to share with you: "Our suffering is not worthy of the name of suffering. When I consider my crosses, tribulations, and temptations, I shame myself almost to death, thinking what are they in comparison to the sufferings of my blessed Saviour Christ Jesus." I can echo that sentiment. Personally, I've not experienced much in the way of suffering, but I know many who have. Suffering can be mental or physical, and it does not bypass the Christian. In fact, many Christians have grown infinitely in the crucible of suffering. As I look at Peter's words here (and he knew what it meant to suffer for Christ!), it is my prayer that if suffering (of whatever kind) should come my way, I will allow it to "perfect, stablish, strengthen, and settle" me.

15

For whom he did foreknow, he also did predestinate to be conformed to the image of his Son.

Romans 8:29

THIS VERSE opens up a whole area of theological discussion and disagreement—but it also contains a blessed spiritual truth that Maltbie Babcock helped me to see when he wrote: "Circumstances do not make character. The noblest character can emerge from the worst surroundings, and moral failures come out of the best. Just where you are, take the things of life as tools and use them for God's glory; so the Master will use the things of life in cutting and polishing you so that there shall someday be seen in you a soul conformed to his likeness." Without going into the theological ramifications of this verse, we can take from it the marvelous truth that God is at work in us to make us what he wants us to be! Not one of us is too small or insignificant to receive his attention.

16

That the trial of your faith, being much more precious than of gold that perisheth, though it be tried with fire, might be found unto praise and honour and glory at the appearing of Jesus Christ.

1 Peter 1:7

TRIALS TEST, but they also deepen and intensify the spiritual temper of the believer just as the furnace strengthens steel, and the fire purifies gold.

Testing inevitably produces a better person—or a bitter person. In a sense, the outcome is up to the individual and his attitude toward testing.

The courageous quadriplegic woman, Joni Eareckson, contrasts the individual reactions to pressure as taking one of two courses. One person, under pressure, can react as does a marble—splintering into sharp pieces of glass, hurting anyone with whom he comes in contact. Or one can handle pressure as does the grape—yielding sweet and refreshing wine as the pressure is applied.

In our scripture today, Peter goes on to give the secret of reacting like the grape. In verse 8, referring to Jesus Christ, he says, "Whom having not seen, ye love; in whom, though now you see him not, yet believing, ye rejoice with joy unspeakable and full of glory." This is the secret of being a "grape" Christian. If we can rejoice under trial, if we can yield submissively under pressure, we can give forth the sweetest fragrance and the sweetest wine.

This is not a call to compromise or lack of conviction. It is a call to submissiveness and yieldedness to whatever the heavenly Father allows to come into your life. Dare the clay say to the sculptor, "Don't touch me"? If the shapeless lump of clay is to be made into something beautiful and meaningful, it must yield to the sculptor's pressure and shaping.

May God help each one of us as his children to praise him through the trials of life as well as in the high places.

17

No, in all these things we are more than conquerors through him who loved us. For I am sure that neither death, nor life, nor angels, nor principalities, nor things present, nor things to come, nor powers, ... nor anything else in all creation, will be able to separate us from the love of God in Christ Jesus our Lord.

Romans 8:37–39, RSV

WE AREN'T ALWAYS responsible for the circumstances in which we find ourselves. However, we *are* responsible for the way we respond to them. We can give up in depression and suicidal despair. Or, we can look to a sovereign God who has everything under control, who can use the experiences for our ultimate good by transforming us to the image of Christ (2 Cor. 3:18).

God engineered circumstances. He used them to prove Himself as well as my loyalty. Not everyone had this privilege. I felt there were only a few people God cared for in such a special way that He would trust them with this kind of experience [paralysis]. This understanding left me relaxed and comfortable as I relied on His love, exercising newly learned trust. I saw that my injury was not a tragedy but a gift God was using to help me conform to the image of Christ, something that would mean my ultimate satisfaction, happiness—even joy.

JONI EARECKSON

Quoted from Joni Eareckson and Joe Musser, *Joni* (Grand Rapids: Zondervan, 1976), p. 154.

18

Hezekiah received the letter . . . and Hezekiah went up unto the house of the Lord, and spread it before the Lord.

Isaiah 37:14

THAT WAS HEZEKIAH'S WAY of laying his troubles in the Lord's hands. He could not do anything, and so he gave the matter to God. We all have our cares. Sometimes it is a business perplexity, sometimes it is a temptation; or it may be a combination of circumstances that seems about to crush us.

What is our duty? What is our privilege? We may take the matter directly to God. We may cast the burden upon him. That is what Paul tells us to do with all our anxieties; and he says the peace of God shall then guard our heart and thoughts in Christ Jesus.

J. R. MILLER

19

Sing, O heavens; and be joyful, O earth; and break forth into singing, O mountains: for the Lord hath comforted his people, and will have mercy upon his afflicted.

Isaiah 49:13

IT'S NATURAL, I guess, to wish for a life in which everything goes right. None of us knowingly asks the Lord for problems and afflictions. But the prophet here reflects upon an aspect of adversity that we should not overlook—in fact he advises us to sing and be joyful in the face of affliction because God is in it. An anonymous writer has said: "No man is more unhappy than the one who is never in adversity; the greatest affliction in life is never to be afflicted." The starlit night sky is never more brilliant than when seen from the pitch darkness. The blind and deaf genius, Helen Keller, wrote: "I thank God for my handicaps, for through them, I have found myself, my work and my God." An old

Chinese proverb has it: "The gem cannot be polished without friction, nor man perfected without trials." Young people may well ask for 'life on a silver platter"—but it is far better to "sing . . . and rejoice" in whatever comes, knowing that our God is in it.

And we know that all that happens to us is working for our good if we love God and are fitting into his plans. **20**

Romans 8:28, LB

WHEN I BROKE MY BACK and thought that I was going to be paralyzed from the neck down, when my parental family was destroyed by sickness and accident, and when I did not get a certain crucial promotion, such tragedies seemed so meaningless and wasteful. Yet these and other disappointments provided the only doorways I now have into the hearts and lives of struggling men and women. For many of them live with tragedy and disappointments and are also afraid to make decisions which involve risk. Finally, it was my inability to be able to control my circumstances which led me to begin to turn my life over to God. . . . And I have found a good bit of release from the fear of failure in this discovery that nothing has to be wasted in a life with God.

KEITH MILLER

Quoted from *Habitation of Dragons* (Waco, TX: Word Books, 1970).

For I reckon that the sufferings of this present time are not worthy to be compared with the glory which shall be revealed in us. **21**

Romans 8:18

SUFFERING IS NOT a theme often thought about in a book for young people. Even as an older person, I don't like to think about it. Somehow for many years the very idea was repugnant to me—and yet I was struck with Paul's positive attitude toward suffering evident in this verse and others in his Epistles. Why couldn't I feel that way about it? I felt guilty because I didn't. And then I met Joni Eareckson, whom I have quoted elsewhere in this book, and a whole new understanding of suffering began to grow in me. It didn't spring up full-blown, and I still rebelled at the idea—but Joni's experience helped me immensely. Her acceptance of suffering didn't happen overnight either, but gradually she saw God in her dilemma of complete physical helplessness. As Leo Tolstoy, the Russian novelist, so perceptively stated: "It is by those who have suffered that the world has been advanced." Because of her growth through the experience of suffering, Joni has indeed made a great contribution to her world. Another word from Cardinal Mercier, Belgian patriot who died in 1926, describes Joni's spirit: "Suffering accepted and vanquished . . . will give you a serenity which may well prove the most exquisite fruit of your life." May that be my attitude toward suffering!

22

Blessed are all they that put their trust in him.

Psalm 2:12

THE BLESSEDNESS OF LIFE is found in making the most of unfavorable circumstances and overcoming conditions by transforming them. A tree may be made into a canoe to carry a savage into battle, or it may furnish medicine for curing chills and fevers. Thus it is with all the experiences of life: they become for us the thing for which we use them. The grace of God, the enablement of the Holy Spirit, will turn our fears into fountains, and will make our sorrows a source of refinement.

O. G. WILSON

WE CHRISTIANS have a joy that cannot be destroyed by our circumstances, a joy that not only lasts, but continually increases, a joy that is real and deep in health or sickness, in life or death. Even after death our joy will be as lasting as eternity, "for if the living God is our Friend, our joy in Him will never end."

JOHN ROBERTS

23

The eternal God is thy refuge, and underneath are the everlasting arms: and he shall thrust out the enemy from before thee.

Deuteronomy 33:27

"AN ATHEIST is a man who has no invisible means of support," says Bishop Fulton Sheen. I never read the words, "underneath are the everlasting arms," but what I pause to give God thanks that he is my "invisible means of support." I have never seen God, but I have, many times, seen what he has done and is in the process of doing. As Jesus told Nicodemus, "The wind bloweth where it listeth, and thou hearest the sound thereof, but canst not tell whence it cometh, and whither it goeth: so is every one that is born of the Spirit" (John 3:8). In the *Living Bible* the verse reads, "Just as you can hear the wind but can't tell where it comes from or where it will go next, so it is with the Spirit. We do not know on whom he will next bestow this life from heaven." We see the evidences of his work and presence—that's how we know he's been there! I can look at my own life and note the changes he has made there in the years since I first began walking with him. I can recall the countless miracles he has performed for me personally, and for so many others I know—and there is no room for doubt in my mind that, indeed, "underneath are the everlasting arms." He has been my refuge, my salvation, and he remains so today. And, someday, I am going into his very presence, this One of whom Moses said in Psalm 90, "Lord, thou hast been our dwelling place in all generations. Before the mountains were brought forth, or ever thou hadst formed the earth and the world, even from everlasting to everlasting, thou art God" (vv. 1–2). This eternal God is my "invisible means of support"!

A wicked man earns deceptive wages, but one who sows righteousness gets a sure reward.

24

Proverbs 11:18, RSV

READ PAUL'S STATEMENT in Galatians 6:7–9, "Be not deceived; God is not mocked: for whatsoever a man soweth, that shall he also reap. For he that soweth to his flesh shall of the flesh reap corruption; but he that soweth to the Spirit shall of the Spirit reap life everlasting. And let us not be weary in well doing: for in due season we shall reap, if we faint not." It is so familiar to us that we consider it almost a cliché—but Paul reflected the wisdom of the ages in his sweeping statement. The prophet Hosea, too, warned his people: "Sow to yourselves in righteousness, reap in mercy; break up your fallow ground: for it is time to seek the Lord, till he come and rain righteousness upon you" (10:12). Every true act of righteousness may be looked at from two points of view. First, it may be regarded as the fruit of an inner spiritual life, of a divine principle within the man. Or it may be looked at as the seed which is to bring forth fruit in the lives of others. Righteousness brings its own reward, even if we think of it only in terms of the joy and peace that fill the heart of the one who thus sows. But on top of this reward is the divine approval that rests upon the righteous soul now—and the pleasant prospect of ultimate heavenly reward: "And, behold, I come quickly; and my reward is with me, to give every man according as his work shall be" (Rev. 22:12). The years of youth are not too early to think about it!

25

The pillar of cloud moved from before them and stood behind them.

Exodus 14:19, RSV

IT IS NOT always guidance that we most need. Sometimes we must stand still, with danger all around us, and then God goes behind us to shelter us. He always suits himself to our need. When we require guidance, he leads us. But when we need protection, he puts himself between us and the danger.

There is something very striking in this picture—the divine presence moving from before, and becoming a wall between Israel and their enemies. There are some mother-birds—storks, for instance—which cover their young with their own body in time of peril, to shield them, receiving the dart themselves. Human love often interposes itself as a shield to protect its own. On the cross, Jesus bared his bosom to receive the storms of wrath, that on his people no blast of the awful tempest might strike.

But not only does Christ put himself between us and our sins; he puts himself also between us and danger. The Lord God is our shield. Many of our dangers come upon us from behind. They are stealthy, insidious, assaulting us when we are unaware of their nearness. The tempter is cunning and shrewd. He does not meet us full-front. It is a comfort to know that Christ comes behind us when it is there we need the protection.

J. R. MILLER

26

He knoweth the way that I take.

Job 23:10

IN A WORLD as complicated and complex as ours, it's a comfort to count upon such a promise as this. God knows every detail of my day, every circumstance of my life. He also knows my imperfections and my weaknesses: "For he knoweth our frame; he remembereth that we are dust" (Ps. 103:14). This should not be considered an excuse for sinning but as the blessed ground for his compassion toward us. If we admit our helplessness and dependence, he will undertake for us. He will be our Guide. He will be our strength in the midst of duty and difficulty alike. He will be everything to us our circumstances require. On the other hand, if we are complacent in our own self-righteousness, we shut ourselves off from his gracious provision. Our ruling principle for life becomes self rather than Christ. God has not called us to himself that we should be our own guides or masters. The only true life is the life of self-renunciation—the life that depends entirely upon God and looks to him to supply every need. As Paul says, "When I am weak, then am I strong" (2 Cor. 12:10). It is in our conscious admission of weakness that we tap into the divine strength available to us.

I pray not that thou shouldest take them out of the world, but that thou shouldest keep them from the evil. **27**

John 17:15

HAVE YOU EVER wondered why the Lord should leave his children here on earth, when he has saved them from so many dangers and pitfalls? It might have seemed best that he should at once remove them from scenes of such painful conflict and alluring temptations. But our Lord has a gracious purpose in keeping his children still in the world for a while. "I pray not that thou shouldest take them out of the world." What would this world be like without Christ's witnesses on the earth? "I pray," says the Lord, "that thou shouldest keep them from the evil," and emphatically from the *Evil One*. Satan is behind all temptations; he is the worker in every subtle plot. "That *thou* shouldest keep them." Blessed is the man who is thus divinely kept. We cannot keep ourselves: "The Lord is thy keeper" (Ps. 121:5). How slow some of us are to learn that fact! This is the privilege of everyone whom he has saved—to be "kept by the power of God through faith unto salvation" (1 Peter 1:5).

EVAN H. HOPKINS

Thou art my hope in the day of evil. **28**

Jeremiah 17:17

AS A YOUNG PERSON (and then as an older one as well) all of us encounter evil in one form or another. Perhaps it's a subtle temptation.

March

Or it may be some form of affliction or trouble. Sometimes one's faith is tempted and tested severely as the enemy makes a frontal attack on our souls. What is the answer? Look at today's verse. The RSV says, "Thou art my *refuge* in the day of evil," and the NIV has "refuge in the day of disaster." The key is not to wait till disaster strikes to find your refuge. Many rejoice in the Lord at the beginning of their Christian walk, and then lose their peace when the testing comes, because they didn't really *hide in* or trust in the refuge. David said, "Thou art my hiding place; thou shalt preserve me from trouble; thou shalt compass me about with songs of deliverance" (Ps. 32:7). That's what we need to do at the outset of our Christian experience, so as to be ready for whatever comes. After all, it's not the outward trial that "blows our cover." The real danger lies in the inner evil that can strike us in the secret place when our back is turned. Only in finding refuge from evil can we be kept from it. That's what Jeremiah is telling us here.

29

Be not far from me; for trouble is near; for there is none to help.

Psalm 22:11

IT'S VERY EASY for me to identify with David! I can recall more than once calling upon God when trouble was near. Please understand that I'm not advocating calling upon God only when you are in trouble—but isn't it great to know that you can? It's in the hour of trouble that the believer realizes the value and preciousness of the promises of God. They are not intended to allow us to dispense with our prayers. It is true God does not need our information or our persuasion to be merciful. But he has specified that if we would know the fulfillment of his promises we must make our requests "known unto" him (Phil. 4:6). In Psalm 91:15 God says, "He shall call upon me, and I will answer him: I will be with him in trouble; I will deliver him, and honor him." To cry unto God and to seek his presence is not to doubt the truth of his promise. It is to plead it. It's like bringing a check to the bank to be cashed. The presence of the Lord as a fact revealed to the soul includes every possible spiritual blessing. We need to pray as David did: "Say unto my soul, I am thy salvation" (Ps. 35:3), and sing as David sang in Psalm 62:2, "He only is my rock and my salvation; he is my defense." The key is to get this "head-knowledge" down into the heart!

Call upon me in the day of trouble: I will deliver thee, and thou shalt glorify me.

Psalm 50:15

30

HERE'S A VERSE we should never forget! It contains a command, a promise, and a privilege. The command is God's direction to us when we face trouble: "Call upon me." When we call upon him, we throw ourselves at his feet for strength, comfort, deliverance—whatever. We may be facing trouble at any moment, any day. If so, God commands us to come to him for deliverance. Then comes the promise to encourage our expectation and strengthen our faith: "I will deliver thee." Our responsibility is to pray and trust; his is to fulfill his own promise! We may count on him to do it (1 Thess. 5:24). Then comes the privilege, one of the greatest we can possibly experience: "Thou shalt glorify me." We can't accomplish this in ourselves—we lack both the power and the wisdom to do it. But, says God, we *shall* glorify him. By becoming the people of his pardoning mercy and redeeming grace, we may glorify him. By being examples of his freeing power, we may bring glory to his name (John 15:8; Isa. 61:3; Ps. 50:23).

With long life I will satisfy him, and show him my salvation.
Psalm 91:16, RSV

31

WHEN I ENTERED the army in 1944, my home church gave me a pocket New Testament with Psalms as a going-away memento, and I remember that Psalm 91 was inscribed on the flyleaf as a scriptural motto for a fledgling soldier. As I read the psalm, I well remember the comfort it gave me to know that God was "my refuge and my fortress" (v. 2) and to be reminded that "he will give his angels charge of you to guard you in all your ways" (v. 11, RSV). But, do you know that it was only recently, more than thirty years later, that I read with real appreciation and understanding the last verse of the Psalm, the verse for today. My perspective has changed. As a young man, I was concerned with the immediate and could not see down the corridor of time. Now I suddenly realize what "long life" (relatively speaking) is. My God was not only with me in the immediate dangers of World War II, he has been with me daily down through the years since then. And, young man or young woman reading these pages, he will be with you, too, in every walk and way of life, if you can say to him, "My God, in whom I trust" (v. 2, RSV).

April

Trusting in God

1

So Abraham called the name of that place The Lord will provide; as it is said to this day, "On the mount of the Lord it shall be provided."

Genesis 22:14, RSV

THE EARLIER we learn this tremendous lesson the better! It should be the doorway through which we enter every day of our lives. But Abraham didn't learn it overnight! He was well on in years, the ancient father of a teenage son, when he made this powerful statement of faith. He had learned it by living it—and he wanted his boy to realize it as early in his life as possible. In the New Testament Paul told the young Christians in the Philippian church, "My God shall supply all your need according to his riches in glory by Christ Jesus" (Phil. 4:19). This is, in the final analysis, how God "will provide"—through his Son, our Savior. Whatever your need has been or can be, God has foreseen it and made full provision for it in Christ!

2

The barrel of meal wasted not, neither did the cruse of oil fail.

1 Kings 17:16

THERE WAS ALWAYS just a little meal and a little oil, but the supply never grew any less. After each day's food had been taken out, there was another day's left. There was never a month's supply ahead, nor even two days' supply. The added provision came only as there was need. Thus there was in that household a continuous lesson in faith. But the food of no day failed.

The lesson is, that God wants us to live by the day. The same truth is taught us in the prayer Christ gave: "Give us this day our daily bread." Enough for the day is all we are to ask. God does not promise supplies in advance. If we have only bread for today and are doing our duty faithfully we may trust him till tomorrow for tomorrow's food. And it will surely come, for God's word fails not.

Charge not thyself with the weight of a year,
Child of the Master, faithful and dear;
Choose not the cross for the coming week,
For that is more than he bids thee seek.
Bend not thine arms for tomorrow's load;
Thou mayest leave that to thy gracious God.
"Daily," only, he saith to thee,
"Take up thy cross and follow me."

It is well that we get this lesson fixed in our heart at this time of the year. As the days come, each one will bring with it its own little basket, carrying a day's supplies, but no more.

J. R. MILLER

Let everyone bless God and sing his praises, for he holds our lives in his hands. And he holds our feet to the path.

Psalm 66:8–9, LB

3

AS ONE MOVES ON in the school of faith one of the most difficult lessons to learn is that of trust—of "letting go and letting God." Our natural inclination is to trust God for our ultimate salvation, but not for our daily situation. Sometimes we say we don't want to bother him with our little problems, so we try to struggle through on our own. Or we say, "I got myself into this mess. I'll get myself out." But what an enormous blessing we miss out on when we fail to turn over all of life, the little as well as the big, to our Lord. A man with an unusual name and a striking grasp of spiritual truth, Hammer William Webb-Peploe, once said: "Don't try to hold God's hand; let him hold yours. Let him do the holding, and you the trusting." That's a lesson I need to learn!

The name of the Lord is a strong tower; the righteous runneth into it, and is safe. . . . Neither is there salvation in any other: for there is none other name . . . whereby we must be saved.

Proverbs 18:10; Acts 4:12

4

SOME PIONEERS were making their way across one of the central states toward a distant territory that had been opened for homesteading. They traveled in covered wagons drawn by oxen, and progress was necessarily slow. One day they were horrified to note a long line of smoke in the west, stretching for miles across the prairie. It was a grass fire and it was coming toward them rapidly. They had crossed a river the day before, but it would be impossible to get back to it before the flames overtook them. Only one man seemed to realize what should be done. He gave command to set fire to the grass behind them. Then when a space was burned over, they all moved back upon it.

As the flames roared on toward them from the west, a little girl cried out in terror, "Are you sure we shall not all be burned?"

The man replied, "My child, the flames cannot reach us here, for we are standing where the fire has been!"

H. A. IRONSIDE

5

Blessed be the God and Father of our Lord Jesus Christ, which according to his abundant mercy hath begotten us again unto a lively hope by the resurrection of Jesus Christ from the dead.

1 Peter 1:3

BETTER TO BE without anything else than without hope. We may be in great present distress, but if we have a good and sure hope for the future, it matters little. We may have present prosperity, but if we have no hope for the future it is of little worth. I would rather be the poorest man who walks the streets and have a good hope for the future, than to be the richest millionaire and have none. Spiritually, all hope is centered in Christ, who is centered in God.

The resurrection of Jesus Christ is the truth which, made living in our hearts by the Holy Spirit, results in the new birth unto a living hope, and an incorruptible inheritance. Through our believing in a risen and living Christ, Christ begins to live in us. The resurrection of Christ also forms a firm foundation of fact, upon which to build our hope for the future.

R. A. TORREY

6

And I tell you that you are Peter, and on this rock I will build my church, and the gates of Hades will not overcome it.

Matthew 16:18, NIV

THE PEOPLE OF GOD, filled with his power, literally outlived, outprayed and outthought the pagan world. They overcame the Roman Empire's effort to destroy them, and finally won the pagan world to their faith. They were the one light of the dark ages. They kept learning, art, and morals alive when the barbaric hordes from the North and East threatened to destroy all the inherited culture of the past. In some of humanity's most turbulent days, St. Augustine, St. Jerome, St. Francis, St. Thomas Aquinas, Erasmus, Luther, and millions of other dimly remembered saints, wise men, and prophets, carried the golden thread of pure faith through the centuries down to our time. These men and women have spread the light into every corner of the world. This is the great miracle of history.

Wars cannot destroy the power of this faith, dictators cannot suppress it. It is beaten out in one spot only to burst into a brighter flame in another. . . . History testifies that spiritual force must always win in the end, because spiritual force issues from the Lord of life himself.

HELEN SMITH SHOEMAKER

Now faith is the assurance of things hoped for, the conviction of things not seen.

Hebrews 11:1, RSV

7

THE AMPLIFIED translation of this verse sheds more light on the nature of faith: "Now faith is the assurance (the confirmation, the title-deed) of the things [we] hope for, being the proof of things [we] do not see and the conviction of their reality—faith perceiving as real fact what is not revealed to the senses." James Freeman Clarke says on the subject: "All the strength and force of man comes from his faith in things unseen. He who believes is strong; he who doubts is weak. Strong convictions precede great actions." As I look back upon my own life, it has been those times when I believed in something strongly enough to risk action that I accomplished something "above and beyond the call of duty." But I'm afraid that most of the time I'd rather play it safe and maintain the status quo. Faith involves a willingness to risk with God. How often do I take the plunge? Another Clarke, William Newton by name, put it well: "Faith is the daring of the soul to go farther than it can see."

Faith is the substance of things hoped for, the evidence of things not seen.

Hebrews 11:1

8

IF THIS MAY BE CALLED a definition, it is the only definition of faith we have in the Bible. Before he gives us its working, and its results in the lives of men, the inspired writer puts before us its nature. He thus describes it: "Faith is the substance [or confidence] of things hoped for." It substantiates the *promises* of God; and not the promises only, but the *present facts* or realities of revelation, which are to sight, for the most part, unseen. What we cannot see with the natural eye, what we cannot touch and realize with physical sense, faith enables us to grasp as actually present and true. Faith must not be confounded with fancy. God does not say, "*Imagine* these blessings in your heart, and believe them, *as if* they were really true." No, God begins by declaring their actual existence, that they are already true, and *because* they are true, commands us to believe. He never bids us believe without providing a foundation of *promise* or of *fact* on which to rest our faith. And so faith becomes to us "the evidence" or demonstration—the convincing proof—of things not seen.

EVAN H. HOPKINS

---

9   *Jesus said unto him, If thou canst believe, all things are possible to him that believeth.*

Mark 9:23

I DARE TO SAY THAT—*it is possible,* for those who are willing to reckon on the power of the Lord for keeping and victory, to lead a life in which His promises are taken as they stand and are found to be true.

It is possible to cast all your care upon Him daily and to enjoy deep peace in doing it.

It is possible to have the thoughts and imaginations of the heart purified, in the deepest meaning of the word, through faith.

It is possible to see the will of God in everything, and to receive it, not with sighing, but with singing.

It is possible, by taking complete refuge in divine power, to become strong through and through; and where previously our greatest weakness lay, to find that the things which formerly upset all our resolves to be patient or pure or humble, furnish today an opportunity—through Him who loved us, and works in us an agreement with His will and a blessed sense of His presence and His power—to make sin powerless.

These things are *divine possibilities,* and because they are His work, the true experience of them will always cause us to bow lower at His feet and to learn to thirst and long for more. We cannot possibly be satisfied with anything less than—each day, each hour, each moment, in Christ, through the power of the Holy Spirit—*to walk with God.*

H. C. G. MOULE

Watch ye, stand fast in the faith, quit you like men, be strong.
1 Corinthians 16:13

10

WHOEVER THOUGHT the Christian life was for "softies" didn't know what he was talking about! Paul's admonition here calls for real men and women of God to stand firm in their faith in the face of whatever opposition might come. The "prince of preachers," Charles H. Spurgeon, has a choice word here: "Pray God to send a few men [and women] with what is called 'grit' in them—men, who when they know a thing to be right, will not turn away, or turn aside, or stop; people who will persevere all the more because there are difficulties to meet or foes to encounter; who stand all the more true to their Master because they are opposed; who, the more they are thrust into the fire, the hotter they become; who, just like the bow, the further the string is drawn the more powerfully it sends forth its arrows, and so the more they are trodden upon, the more mighty will they become in the cause of truth against error." Yes, the Christian life is a challenge, but let it be said of us, as it was of the early disciples, "These men are the servants of the most high God" (Acts 16:17).

Jesus saith unto him, Thomas, because thou hast seen me, thou hast believed: blessed are they that have not seen, and yet have believed. . . . But these are written, that ye might believe that Jesus is the Christ, the Son of God; and that believing ye might have life through his name.

John 20:29, 31

11

EVIDENCE WEIGHED and knowledge gained lead up to faith. It is true that faith in Jesus is the gift of God; but yet He usually bestows it in accordance with the laws of mind, and hence we are told that "faith cometh by hearing, and hearing by the Word of God." If you want to believe in Jesus, hear about Him, read about Him, think about Him, know about Him, and so you will find faith springing up in your heart,

April

like the wheat which comes up through the moisture and the heat operating upon the seed which has been sown. The Bible is the window through which we may look and see the Lord. Read over the story of His suffering and death with devout attention, and before long the Lord will cause faith secretly to enter your soul. If you are anxious to give up every evil way, our Lord Jesus will enable you to do so at once. His grace has already changed the direction of your desires; in fact, your heart is renewed. Therefore, rest on Him to strengthen you to battle with temptations as they arise, and to fulfill the Lord's commands from day to day.

CHARLES H. SPURGEON

12

And Thomas answered and said unto him, My Lord and my God.

John 20:28

LEW WALLACE was a general in the U.S. Army and a novelist *(Ben Hur,* 1880). His original purpose as he researched his novel of the time of Christ was to disprove the deity of Christ—to prove that he was nothing more than a mere mortal. But something happened to him on the way to that goal. Let him tell about it: "After six years given to impartial investigation of Christianity, as to its truth or falsity, I have come to the deliberate conclusion that Jesus Christ was the Messiah of the Jews, the Saviour of the world, and my personal Saviour." What a statement of faith!

Apparently Thomas, who spoke the words of our text for the day, must have come through a similar experience of conviction and convincing. Earlier he had said, "Except I shall see in his hands the print of the nails, and put my finger into the print of the nails, and thrust my hand into his side, I will not believe." How much conviction will it take to convince us of who Jesus is? How long will we wait to commit ourselves to him? Like Lew Wallace, we must confess him as our own "personal Saviour"!

13

Be careful for nothing; but in every thing by prayer and supplication with thanksgiving let your requests be made known unto God.

Philippians 4:6

AS I BEGAN to pray and depend on Him, He did not disappoint me. Before, I'd say, "Lord, I want to do Your will—and Your will is for me to get back on my feet, or, at least, get my hands back." I was deciding His will for me and rebelling when things didn't turn out as I planned.

Now I wept for all those lost months filled with bitterness and sinful attitudes. I prayed for an understanding of His will for my life. What was God's will for my life? To find out, I had to believe that all that had happened to me was an important part of that plan. I read, "In everything, give thanks, for this is the will of God concerning you." God's will was for me to be thankful in everything? Okay. I blindly trusted that this was truth. I thanked God for what He did, and what He was going to do.

As I concentrated on His positive instruction from the Bible, it was no longer necessary to retreat from reality. Feelings no longer seemed important. Fantasies of having physical feeling and touch were no longer necessary because I learned that I was only temporarily deprived of these sensations. The Bible indicates that our bodies are temporal. Therefore, my paralysis was temporal. When my focus shifted to this eternal perspective, all my concerns about being in a wheelchair became trivial.

JONI EARECKSON

Quoted from Joni Eareckson and Joe Musser, *Joni* (Grand Rapids: Zondervan, 1976), p. 142.

For I know the plans I have for you, says the Lord, plans for welfare and not for evil, to give you a future and a hope.
Jeremiah 29:11, RSV

14

IT IS BETTER we should not know our future. If we did, we should often spoil God's plan for our life. If we could see into tomorrow and know the troubles it will bring, we might be tempted to seek some way of avoiding them, while really they are God's way to new honor and blessing. God's thoughts for us are always thoughts of love, good, promotion; but sometimes the path to the hilltop lies through dark valleys or up rough paths. Yet to miss the hard bit of road is to fail of gaining the lofty height. It is better, therefore, to walk, not knowing, with God, than it would be to see the way and choose for ourselves. God's way for us is always better than our own.

J. R. MILLER

April

15

But God gives it a body as he has chosen, and to each kind of seed its own body.

1 Corinthians 15:38, RSV

SMALLNESS doesn't necessarily mean insignificance. Many of us look down on ourselves as being small or insignificant in the plan and purpose of God. God wants us to be humble, but he doesn't want us to live below our potential simply because we downgrade our value in his eternal plan. Paul is telling the Corinthians here to be realistic in their appraisal of what God can do. As G. Campbell Morgan says: "Take a seed and hold it in the hand—strange little seed, without beauty, the very embodiment of weakness. But within that husk, in which the human eye detects no line of beauty or grace, no gleam or flash of glory, there lie the gorgeous colors and magnificent flower itself. From that seed, through processes of law, plant and bud proceed, until at last the perfect blossom is formed." We Christians are in process: "It does not yet appear what we shall be." But, praise God, he is at work in us—on us!

Let your conversation be without covetousness; and be content with such things as ye have; for he hath said, I will never leave thee, nor forsake thee.

16

Hebrews 13:5

HERE'S A PROMISE to hang your hat on! It's an exact quote from the Old Testament: Deuteronomy 31:6, 8; Joshua 1:5; and 1 Chronicles 28:20. It was a promise to Old Testament saints, but it applies as well to believers in New Testament times, and today. The writer says, "Be content with such things as ye have; for *he hath said.* . . ." It is the word of God himself upon which we rest our confidence. Because of that confidence we can go on and boldly say, "The Lord is my helper, and I will not fear what man shall do unto me" (Heb. 13:6). Not one spiritual blessing is left out of that promise. With Paul we can pray, "Not that I speak in . . . want: for I have learned, in whatsoever state I am, therewith to be content" (Phil. 4:11). We don't have to pray, "Lord, be with me." Rather, with the psalmist we can pray, "Yea, though I walk through the valley of the shadow of death, I will fear no evil: for thou *art* with me" (Ps. 23:4). That's what it means to stand on the promises!

And he said, The God of our fathers hath chosen thee, that thou shouldest know his will, and see that Just One, and shouldest hear the voice of his mouth.

17

Acts 22:14

THESE WERE THE WORDS of Ananias to Paul following the apostle's conversion on the road to Damascus. They point up the fact that nothing happens by chance in the world of the Christian. Our God is a God of order and purpose. Everything that happens to us is arranged according to definite precepts. In the life of the Christian there is no such thing as happenstance. Notice that Ananias emphasized Paul's selection by the Divine Hand and assured him that he would know God's will, that he would actually see him and hear the words that come from his mouth. All this happened for Paul—and it can happen for you. This is God's doing—the Christian is simply to use his eyes and ears to "tune in" to the heavenly vision.

It is better to trust in the Lord than to put confidence in man.

18

Psalm 118:8

THE NEW INTERNATIONAL VERSION translates this verse: "It is better to take refuge in the Lord than to trust in man." Have you ever realized how much we trust our fellowmen? When I hit the freeway I'm trusting the physical condition and judgment of every person I meet along the way. When I stop to buy groceries I'm trusting the integrity of the supplier and the merchant with whom I deal. If I consult a doctor, I'm entrusting myself to his professional skill and ability. Ours is a world of relationships—and every day calls for me to place my trust in others. But as the psalmist says here, how much better it is "to take refuge in the Lord than to trust in man." "His banner over me is love" (Song of Sol. 2:4, NIV). Sooner or later man will fail me—perhaps I'll encounter a drunken driver or one whose physical condition is otherwise impaired, and have an accident. I'll buy spoiled or imperfect merchandise. I may even get a wrong diagnosis or faulty treatment from the doctor I consult. But the Lord will never fail me. No matter what the circumstances he will not fall down on the job. The Lord is the One in whom I will trust!

April

19

Wait on the Lord: be of good courage, and he shall strengthen thine heart: wait, I say, on the Lord.

Psalm 27:14

WE ARE OFTEN waiting *for* the Lord, as if he were not willing or ready to bless, when all the while we should rather wait *on* the Lord, because he is waiting to be gracious unto us. To wait on the Lord is to seek his face, to hear his voice, to contemplate his character. There is no circumstance in life in which we may not continue in this attitude of restful confidence and holy expectation. None ever waited upon the Lord in vain. Let us encourage ourselves, not in our attainments or successes, but in the Lord. It is he who shall strengthen our hearts. There is a promise to this effect: "They that wait upon the Lord shall renew their strength" (Isa. 40:31). That is, they shall *change* their strength. They shall have it perpetually renewed. It will be continually grace upon grace. And it is true in another sense: they shall give up their own strength and take God's in exchange. That is a strength that shall never disappoint. It is not followed by exhaustion, and it can never be exhausted!

EVAN H. HOPKINS

20

The king . . . hurried to the lions' den. When he came near the den, he called to Daniel in an anguished voice, "Daniel, servant of the living God, has your God, whom you serve continually, been able to rescue you from the lions?" Daniel answered, "O king, live forever! My God sent his angel, and he shut the mouths of the lions. They have not hurt me, because I was found innocent in his sight. Nor have I ever done any wrong before you, O king."

Daniel 6:19–22, NIV

THE CHARACTER OF DANIEL has always fascinated me. Somehow, he comes through as "larger than life," almost legendary in his impact upon his world. He was a real person, however, and was quoted by Jesus in the New Testament (Matt. 24:15; Mark 13:14). I think the reason Daniel so intrigues me is the heroic faith he showed—probably the best known instance of that faith is found in his lions' den experience. As we see him cast into the den, we get the impression that the king was much more concerned than Daniel was! Apparently the king spent a sleepless night and ended up rising at the break of day to rush to the den to see how his friend Daniel had fared. Nowhere are we told that Daniel had missed any sleep or worried about his plight. A quote from *Missionary Tidings* might reveal the secret of Daniel's inner strength: "The faith that will shut the mouths of lions must be more than a pious hope that they will not bite." I think Daniel had faced the fact that he might not live to walk out of the lions' den—but he had complete faith that, regardless of what might happen, he was in God's hands. May a little of that kind of faith rub off on me!

Wherefore, seeing we also are compassed about with so great a cloud of **21**
witnesses, let us lay aside every weight, and the sin which doth so
easily beset us, and let us run with patience the race that is set before
us, Looking unto Jesus the author and finisher of our faith. . . .
Hebrews 12:1–2

TOO OFTEN we make the mistake of thinking that our faith depends on ourselves, and most translations of this passage encourage that misconception. The New English Bible translates the key words of this sentence: "our eyes fixed on Jesus, on whom faith depends from start to finish." Christ is the Completer of our faith. He is the Author and Finisher, the Leader and Perfecter of the life of faith. He's been there before us, and knows the way we must take. He's our Great Guide on the way.

I can't help but contrast his perfect Example with that of the "cloud of witnesses" mentioned here. Even though these men and women of faith were exemplary, not one of them was perfect. All of them broke down at some part of the course of faith. As we run our race (and like it or not, all of us are in one), let's not look at the "saints" around us, or the ones mentioned in the Old Testament. Let us not look at mere human examples—but upon Jesus, the only Perfect Example, who can lead and guide us through the maze of modern living.

So Abram went, as the Lord had told him. . . . **22**
Genesis 12:4, RSV

ABRAM BEGAN his journey without any knowledge of his ultimate destination (Heb. 11:8). He obeyed a noble impulse without any discernment of its consequences. He took "one step," and he did not ask "to see the distant scene." And that is faith, to do God's will here and now, quietly leaving the results to Him. Faith is not concerned with the entire chain; its devoted attention is fixed upon the immediate link. Faith is not knowledge of a moral process; it is fidelity in a moral act. Faith leaves something to the Lord; it obeys His immediate commandment and leaves to Him direction and destiny. And so faith is accompanied by serenity and self-control. "He that believeth shall not make haste"—or more literally, "shall not get into a fuss." He shall not get into a panic, neither fetching fears from his yesterdays nor from his tomorrows. Concerning his tomorrows, faith says, "Thou hast beset me before." Concerning his today, faith says, "Thou hast laid Thine hand upon me." That is enough, just to feel the pressure of the guiding hand.

J. H. JOWETT

23

When they [the high priests] heard these things, they were cut to the heart, and they gnashed on him [Stephen] with their teeth. But he, being full of the Holy Ghost, looked up steadfastly into heaven, and saw the glory of God, and Jesus standing on the right hand of God, and said, Behold, I see the heavens opened, and the Son of man standing on the right hand of God.

Acts 7:54–56

WHAT AN INSPIRATION to real manhood Stephen is. Because his outlook and attitude were adjusted to eternity, he was able to take the "upward look." Looking "steadfastly into heaven," he was able to handle anything that came to him on earth. This kind of courage isn't *attained*, it's *obtained*, through the power of the Holy Spirit. Somehow the saint moving in the glory of the Spirit is prepared for just about anything. *Until* his work for God is done, he's inviolable and invulnerable. When his work is done, he can depart and be with God—which is far better. I can't help but think that a great deal of the credit for the conversion of the apostle Paul must be laid at the feet of this courageous young martyr Stephen, for Paul was an eyewitness to this glorious homecoming of one of the saints.

24

And therefore will the Lord wait, that he may be gracious unto you. . . . Blessed are all they that wait for [upon] him.

Isaiah 30:18

THE IDEA of "waiting upon the Lord" is a theme that recurs over and over in the Scriptures. Elsewhere Isaiah says, "But they that wait upon the Lord shall renew their strength . . . mount up with wings . . . run, and not be weary . . . walk, and not faint." In Lamentations 3:25 Jeremiah affirms, "The Lord is good unto them that wait for him, to the soul that seeketh him." The Psalms, too, are replete with admonitions to wait upon the Lord and promises to those who do so.

This posture of patience is particularly difficult for young people who are accustomed to rapid movement and instant solutions. But here is a lesson we must learn if we are to really discover what it means to depend upon God. We want to move ahead of God even when he "waits for us," but our proper place is on our knees before him. And this is where the rub comes in. How difficult it is to remain on our knees when we want to be moving! We want immediate action rather than patient waiting. But God in his wisdom knows what is best for us. Today and tomorrow are the same to him. The past, present, and future are all "now" to him, so we can confidently rest in his timing and his answers to our prayers.

After all, as Isaiah points out, he wants to "be gracious" to us. The *Living Bible* says he wants to "show [us] his love," but in our impatience, we don't give him the opportunity to do what is best for us. Instead, too often we settle for second-best because we can get that sooner. If we want his best, we must wait for his best timing as well. Our seeking must be patient rather than pushy. Then our waiting will be rewarded.

Jesus was asleep at the back of the boat with his head on a cushion. Frantically they wakened him, shouting, "Teacher, don't you even care that we are all about to drown?"

25

Mark 4:38, LB

THERE IS A REMARKABLE contrast here between the anxious, even panic-stricken, attitude of the disciples and the striking serenity of the Savior. Look behind the lines a little. Jesus had been teaching all day, and (though we tend to overlook it) because he had a human body undoubtedly he was tired, if not exhausted. He had the same physical needs for rest and food that you and I do, so he was sound asleep in the stern of the boat, despite the noise and confusion around him. In calm and restful assurance of his Father's care, he slept "the sleep of the just." His disciples, on the other hand, were uptight and afraid. They expected the storm to do its worst and petulantly complained to the Master because he wasn't awake and worrying like they were. I've often wondered why they didn't awake Jesus to warn him of the danger *he* was in. Rather, their entire concern seems to be for themselves: "Carest thou not that *we* perish?" The good news for today is that Jesus is *always* aware of our dangers and ready to protect us from whatever threatens us. With Solomon we can exult: "Trust in the Lord with all thine heart; and lean not unto thine own understanding" (Prov. 3:5).

26

I know that my Redeemer liveth.

Job 19:25

THIS WAS JOB'S TESTIMONY to a personal interest or involvement in God's salvation. He says, "*My* Redeemer." Many have a faith in Christ as the Redeemer of men generally. But religion has little power in our lives until it becomes an individual matter. It is when we can thus appropriate God's unspeakable Gift, and say from our hearts, "You are *my* Savior, 'my Lord and my God,'" that the comfort and strength of his redemption are realized. It is then, but not before, that we can take our stand as witnesses to his saving grace.

Job speaks, too, without doubt or hesitation. He does not say, "I hope," but "I *know* that my Redeemer liveth." There are some who would regard such expressions as too presumptuous for sinful men. Well, it depends upon what our confidence is based. Is it confidence in what we have done, or are, or upon what we have attained? Then, most certainly, such language is utterly unsuitable for creatures such as we to use. But if it is confidence *in the Lord*—in his Word of assurance, in his promise, in what he has done or undertakes still to do—then it is impossible to trust too confidently.

EVAN H. HOPKINS

27

Thou wilt keep him in perfect peace, whose mind is stayed on thee: because he trusteth in thee.

Isaiah 26:3

THIS HAS ALWAYS BEEN one of my favorite verses of Scripture. If I were a preacher, I'd look at it under three headings:

The Keeper is God himself. No one else could handle the task of providing for our salvation. This involves not only *saving* us, it also includes his power to *keep* us from falling. We must make no mistake and take no credit upon ourselves: we are kept by the power and presence of God (Jude 24).

The *keeping* involved is described in the phrase, "in perfect peace." Only in the Prince of Peace, Jesus Christ, is *perfect* peace found—peace at its fullest and most complete, inwardly and outwardly, of conscience as well as relationships. Perfect peace is peace *with* God and the peace *of* God.

Isaiah also describes the *kept:* those "whose mind is stayed on thee." The word *mind* here is translated "heart" or "imagination" in other Old Testament passages. The imagination can be our downfall, that place where we begin to slide or go astray, if it is not "stayed" or centered on and trusting in God—which implies reposing or resting in him. The New International Version translates this verse: "You will keep in perfect peace him whose mind is steadfast, because he trusts in you." The only sound mind is the mind stayed on God.

For unto you it is given in the behalf of Christ, not only to believe on him, but also to suffer for his sake. 28

Philippians 1:29

I AM ACTUALLY EXCITED at these opportunities "to suffer for His sake" if it means I can increase my capacity to praise God in the process. Maybe it sounds glib or irresponsible to say that. Yet, I really do feel my paralysis is unimportant.

Circumstances have been placed in my life for the purpose of cultivating my character and conforming me to reflect Christlike qualities. And there is another purpose. Second Corinthians 1:3–7 explains it in terms of our being able to comfort others facing the same kinds of trials.

Wisdom is *trusting* God, not asking "Why, God?" Relaxed and in God's will, I know He is in control. It is not a blind, stubborn, stoic acceptance, but getting to know God and realize He is worthy of my trust. Although I am fickle and play games, God does not; although I have been up and down, bitter and doubting, He is constant, ever-loving.

JONI EARECKSON

Quoted from Joni Eareckson and Joe Musser, *Joni* (Grand Rapids: Zondervan, 1976), p. 227.

April

29

*"Do you finally believe this?" Jesus asked. "But the time is coming—
in fact, it is here—when you will be scattered, each one returning to
his own home, leaving me alone. Yet I will not be alone, for the
Father is with me. I have told you all this so that you will have peace
of heart and mind. Here on earth you will have many trials and
sorrows; but cheer up, for I have overcome the world."*

John 16:31–33, LB

IF YOU'RE NORMAL, you've already noticed that being a Christian
doesn't mean automatic avoidance of life's dangers and difficulties. In
fact, as a Christian, your primary concern must not be the avoidance of
difficulties, but remaining cheerful in the midst of them. Speaking
realistically, no Christian is freed from affliction because of his faith.
Faith makes no such promise but rather affirms, "Here on earth you will
have many trials and sorrows; but cheer up, for I have overcome the
world." The child of God, therefore, cannot hope for the absence of
trials and difficult circumstances. There's no way! But there is something the Savior expects us to achieve far more worthwhile than the
avoidance of trials—and that's *radiance in the midst of them!* He wants
us to have the kind of optimism that flourishes *in spite of* outward
circumstances, for that is a thousand times better than the enthusiasm
that comes *because of* them. Blessed is that person who can rejoice over
the harvest when the snow is on the ground, or who can sing if there's no
harvest at all!

30

*The light of the body is the eye: therefore when thine eye is single, thy
whole body also is full of light; but when thine eye is evil, thy body
also is full of darkness.*

Luke 11:34

THIS "SINGLE EYE" passage has been translated in many ways: "your eye
is sound" (RSV); "a pure eye lets sunshine into your soul" (LB); "when
your eyes are good" (NIV), but I still like the way the KJV handles it. A
"single eye" speaks to me of simplicity, of clear vision, an eye that does
not see double, but concentrates on one object at a time. It implies
concentration and focus as opposed to generality and fuzziness. When
the eye of the conscience is clear, then the whole person is full of light.
The heart is at rest and faith is able to function freely. This is what Jesus
is saying. And it is what James was talking about when he referred to the

"double-minded man . . . unstable in all his ways" (1:8). The one who tries to serve both God and mammon (the world) is setting himself up for frustration and failure. There is nothing more necessary in our walk with God than a singleness of aim and simplicity of purpose. He must be the Supreme Object of our love and life. If we seek him first, then "all these things shall be added unto" us (Matt. 6:33; Luke 12:31). Lord, give me a single eye!

May

Giving Your Life to God

1
I press on toward the goal for the prize of the upward call of God in Christ Jesus.

Philippians 3:14, RSV

MANY A CAREER of brilliant possibilities is marred by a wrong beginning. It is of the utmost importance that we start well. Many Christians walk in dark and shadow all their days, never entering into rich joy and peace because at the beginning they failed to realize the blessedness of the privileges to which, as children of God, they are entitled. Many others never attain anything noble and beautiful in Christian life and character because at the beginning they did not wholly disentangle themselves from their old life and fully consecrate themselves to Christ.

Many fail because they have no settled purpose, no goal set before them which with all their energies they strive to reach. They merely drift with the current. Multitudes never give one earnest thought to such questions as: "What is my life? For what purpose is it entrusted to me? What ought I to do with it? What should be the great aim of my existence? What should I strive to be and do?" An immortal life should have its aim ever shining before it bright and clear. Men with undying souls and measureless possibilities should have a purpose worthy of eternal life, and should strive with heroic energy to attain it. Our knowledge must be brought into life.

J. R. MILLER

2

*Stand fast in one spirit, with one mind striving together for the faith
of the gospel. . . . I press toward the mark for the prize of the high
calling of God in Christ Jesus.*

Philippians 1:27; 3:14

THANK GOD for goals! To quit trying is to stagnate, to become obese and
sluggish physically, dull and lethargic mentally. If we think we've
arrived spiritually as well, and "lean back on our laurels," we'll find the
same thing happening to our souls that I have described as happening to
our bodies and minds.

The apostle Paul was very goal-conscious. He never felt he had
arrived spiritually, but he went on striving for mastery of the inner man
until the day of his death, if we are to judge by his writings which
apparently continued almost to the day of his martyrdom. We know that
he wrote some of his most victorious and unforgettable epistles in prison.
And at that time in his life when he was literally behind bars, his
constant theme was victory and freedom (see the Book of Galatians). So
Paul didn't believe in rest and relaxation. He believed in constant
exercise, taking his cue from the successful athlete who steadfastly
pressed forward seeking the prize, never slacking in his effort to be first.

And what Paul practiced in his personal life, he urged upon the
Philippian Christians as well. He admonished them to strive "together
for the faith of the gospel." Does faith come by striving? In the sense
Paul is writing about it does. He considered the gospel, and unity in it, a
worthy goal for his spiritual children, and for Christians today. Don't
"ease up" just because you may have reached a certain goal previously
established. Set new goals! And don't be afraid to reach a little. If your
goals are too easy, you may find yourself slowing to a walk, then sitting
down in the shade while the rest of the church passes you by. Ask God to
give you a goal to strive for—then count on him for strength to reach it.

3

*He brought him to Jesus. Jesus looked at him, and said, "So you are
Simon the son of John? You shall be called Cephas" (which means
Peter).*

John 1:42, RSV

"YOU ARE . . . you shall be." We live in an extraordinary age! A man
walked across the United States in seventeen minutes recently—*a
hundred miles in the air!* Others have walked on the moon. Someone
described a computer that will make 100,000 computations per minute.

May

New planes are in the making that will fly twenty-one-hundred miles an hour with a payload of more than four hundred passengers. In medicine, in communications, in home building, in cooking, in just about every area of life there has been a revolution, making this the most extraordinary age man has ever known. A doctor told me recently that medical knowledge will be doubled in the next five years. I hope I live to the year 2000. It will be an amazing thing! We have watched miracles take place before our very eyes, things undreamed of even by a Jules Verne in the wildest science fiction books.

Great as these miracles are, there is yet a greater one—you can be more than you are. While we have done such marvelous things in science and manufacturing and the conquest of space, we have left the spirit of man the greatest undeveloped area in all of life. The dark country of earth is the soul of man. . . . We can be more than we are.

T. Cecil Myers

Quoted from *You Can Be More Than You Are* (Waco, TX: Word Books, 1976), p. 15.

---

4   *But grow in grace, and in the knowledge of our Lord and Saviour Jesus Christ. To him be glory both now and for ever.*

2 Peter 3:18

ELSEWHERE IN THIS BOOK we have likened life to a journey, but it's also like a garden. A garden is for growing, and so is life! A garden gives back what is put into it, and so does life. A garden rewards the labor of the gardener by producing more and better fruit—and life is like that too. The marvelous thing about the Christian life is that our Divine Gardener has the answers to our problems of growing and can defeat all the foes of our life-garden, whether they be discouragement, despair, or even the greatest foe of all, Satan. All of this isn't automatic, however. As S. D. Gordon says, "The best work in this garden is done down on our knees." If we are to fulfill "Peter's principle" as expressed in today's verse, we'll need some outside help from Jesus, our Divine Gardener.

---

5   *That he would grant you . . . to be strengthened with might by his Spirit in the inner man.*

Ephesians 3:16

THE STORY IS TOLD of how Fritz Kreisler, the famous violinist, secured his treasured violin, which he called "Heart Guarnarius." One day he was in an antique shop and heard someone playing a violin in the room behind the shop. Charmed with the pure liquid, penetrating tone of the violin, he asked if he could buy it. The dealer told him it was not for sale, that it had already been sold to a collector. After handling the violin, Kreisler said, "I must have this: I will give you all I have for it." Then he asked, "What will this collector do with the violin?"

"Oh," said the dealer, "I suppose he will put it in a glass case and keep it for people to look at."

"This is not an antique to look at," said Kreisler, "but an instrument to bless the world with."

Still determined to get the violin, he went to see the man who had bought it. Week after week he called on him to plead with him to sell it. Then one day the owner let Kreisler play it. "I played that violin," said Kreisler, "as one condemned to death would have played for a ransom." When he finished playing, the collector was so moved that he said, "I have no right to keep it; it belongs to you. Go out into the world and let it be heard." And Kreisler used it as a medium for his wonderful music.

Our lives can be useless or useful—it all depends on whether we allow the Lord Jesus Christ to use us. It is only when we become instruments in His hands that the finest music is heard in our lives, and blessings are brought to other people.

THE WESLEYAN METHODIST

Know this, my beloved brethren. Let every man be quick to hear, slow to speak, slow to anger.

6

James 1:19, RSV

WE MISS A GREAT DEAL by not being good listeners. The world is full of sweet music—bird songs, the chirping of insects, the sweet murmur of all nature, the breathing of the wind through the trees, the splashing of waters; and yet some people never hear one melodious sound as they go through the fields and forests. God is ever speaking in our ears—in conscience, in his Word, in the gentle voice of his Spirit; but many of us miss all this wonderful divine speech. We ought to train ourselves to listen, to hear, to be "quick to hear." We learn by hearing. Truth comes to us from all sides. There is nothing so mean, so lowly, that it may not have some message for us. Wordsworth says—

> To me the meanest flower that blows can give
> Thoughts that do often lie too deep for tears.

May

Unless we go about ever listening we may miss many a rich lesson, turning away unaware many an angel who comes from God with a message for us.

J. R. MILLER

7   *Do to others as you would have them do to you.*

Luke 6:31, NIV

THE PHOENIX FLAME put this thought into a more modern setting: "Live every day as if it were your last. Do every job as if you were the boss. Drive as if all other vehicles were police cars. Treat everybody else as if he were you." While this doesn't touch all the bases of life today, it does hint at some of the areas where we moderns spend the bulk of our lives: at work, in our cars, and at home. When Jesus said, "Do to others as you would have them do to you," he had in mind *every* area of life! The way we treat those with whom we come in contact, whether family, friends, or fellow-workers, reveals unerringly what kind of persons we are. The Christian life is relational. By that I mean we cannot escape relationships with others—and our commitment to Christ is bound to reflect itself in the way we treat others. If my lifestyle is shallow and slipshod, you have a right to wonder about my Christian commitment. If I run roughshod over others in my effort to move ahead in this life, then I'm failing to live as Christ commanded.

8   *And [Jesus] said unto them, Verily I say unto you, There is no man that hath left house, or parents, or brethren, or wife, or children, for the kingdom of God's sake, who shall not receive manifold more in this present time, and in the world to come life everlasting.*

Luke 18:29–30

AT THE BEGINNING of life we are under the illusion that the days before us are unlimited, and we squander our time accordingly. In our verse for today, Jesus is telling Peter (and us) after the encounter with the rich young ruler where to place our priorities. If we look at time in the light of eternity, we will not "kill" it. Rather, we will "seek first the kingdom of God," making the most of every moment, living each day to the hilt as if it were our last. This will add a dimension of intensity to our lives that will assure life at its best, lived above the limitations of petty pursuits. This is the kind of life that is truly "everlasting."

The fear of the Lord prolongeth days: but the years of the wicked shall be shortened. **9**

Proverbs 10:27

HE WASN'T A CHRISTIAN, but he was an astute observer of life. And the late Gabriel Heatter, prominent news commentator during World War II, said, "Mere longevity is a good thing for those who watch Life from the sidelines. For those who play the game, an hour may be a year, a single day's work an achievement for eternity." Someone else said, "It isn't whether you win or lose, it's how you play the game." Both of these concepts are involved in Solomon's wise saying here in Proverbs. In it I think he might have been echoing something his father, King David, said in Psalm 55:23, "But you, O God, will bring down the wicked into the pit of corruption; bloodthirsty and deceitful men will not live out half their days. But as for me, I trust in you" (NIV). In the living of life it's not the *quantity* that matters—it's the *quality*. It is my prayer that my life might count for something eternal. That's what Solomon was saying in Proverbs 9:11 when he wrote, "For by me [true wisdom] thy days shall be multiplied, and the years of thy life shall be increased."

Remember also your Creator in the days of your youth, before the evil days come. **10**

Ecclesiastes 12:1,RSV

IT IS EASIER to begin a Christian life in youth than at any other time. It is easy to train the heart's affections about the cross before they have learned to cling to earth's sordid things. It is easy to teach young fingers to play on the piano or organ, but it is next to impossible to train the stiff fingers of age to do it. So it is easy for the young to learn to strike the harps of heaven. It is easier to keep the heart pure and tender, than to get back its purity and tenderness when once they have been lost.

J. R. MILLER

May

11

Therefore, as we have opportunity, let us do good to all people, especially to those who belong to the family of believers.

Galatians 6:10, NIV

THE THRUST of this verse at first seems to be self-centered. Shouldn't we major on doing good to those outside "the family of believers" as a means of witness to unbelievers? Yes, Paul makes it clear we are to do good to all people, but he adds this phrase, *"especially* to those who belong to the family of believers." I think Paul knew what it meant to live in a family, and as so many of us do, take that family for granted. So often we put on our "best front" when we are meeting those outside our immediate family, and we're at our worst at home. This should not be! We are to evidence the fruits of the Spirit *especially* at home. Otherwise our "goodness" is nothing but a hypocritical cloak pulled on to impress others with our spirituality. We should live the same kind of transparent lives wherever we are, but especially among "those who belong to the family of believers."

12

Separate me Barnabas and Saul for the work whereunto I have called them.

Acts 13:2

I DON'T UNDERSTAND WHY—but God chooses to do his work through men and women. He could call upon regiments of angels, but he uses people. He could command the elements to rage and the seas to roll, but instead he employs people to work out his will in the world. G. Campbell Morgan points out: "God is seen choosing men fitted to the times for the accomplishment of work, the full value of which the rolling centuries alone declare. Let us take heart, knowing that perhaps the deepest meaning of what we do today will only be known and felt in the distant future." As one begins his adult life, those years of intense accomplishment and driving purpose, it is humbling and uplifting as well to know that God calls—and it is ours to answer.

13

Seest thou a man diligent in his business? he shall stand before kings.

Proverbs 22:29

MEN LIKE TO RISE in the world; but there are different kinds of elevation. One is that which money gives. Then, there is elevation which comes through social recognition. But true elevation is of character and worth. It can be obtained only by being diligent. We are not to wait idly for promotion, but are to be busy at our lowlier duty till the larger is ready for us. Because Moses could not be an emancipator at once, he did not spend his time in idleness, but was faithful as a shepherd; and when God wanted him, he found him at his work. Jesus found Peter, James, and John fishing. The way to make sure of being wanted for a greater work is to do well your plainer work. Diligence makes men ready to go up higher. Do well today's work, however lowly; perhaps tomorrow God will have something larger for you.

J. R. MILLER

Be strong, all ye people of the land, saith the Lord, and work: for I am with you, saith the Lord of hosts. **14**

Haggai 2:4

OURS IS A DAY of commitment and contracts—and it's also a day when people are looking to get "something for nothing." As God's spokesman, Haggai gives God's contract with his people. If they will commit themselves to work, God will supply the power. God's commands are assurances of power. He knows we cannot make ourselves strong. In effect he says, "Allow yourself to be empowered. You have no *ability*, but I have given you *capacity*. Your emptiness and need are your capacity to receive. Power is mine, and I have the ability to accomplish." He who bids us work is ready, in his own might, to make us strong.

His encouragement is based on his presence: "I am not only for you, I am *with* you—close at hand, ready to sustain and strengthen." This is his promise to you, too, if you are his child. It covers three aspects of your life: the call to service; the work or sphere of service; and the power or equipment for service. A pretty good place to start!

Then said Ahimaaz the son of Zadok, Let me now run, and bear the king tidings. . . . And Joab said, Wherefore wilt thou run, my son, seeing that thou hast no tidings ready? But howsoever, said he, let me run. And he said unto him, Run. Then Ahimaaz ran . . . And the king said unto him, Turn aside, and stand here. **15**

2 Samuel 18:19, 22–23, 30

DON'T TELL ME God doesn't have a sense of humor! What a picture this is! Ahimaaz, legs pumping like pistons, running to the king with

May

"tidings"—but he had no message! We've written about many members of Faith's Hall of Fame, but here's a candidate for the comedy section. But wait a minute—we've all made the same mistake. Before we laugh at Ahimaaz, we'd better take a hard look at ourselves in the Bible mirror. Haven't we been guilty of trying to do God's work without delivering God's Word? Our motive may be good (to serve the Lord!) but our method is weak (in our own strength). May our King Jesus never say of us, "Turn aside, and stand here." Rather, may he say, "Well done, good and faithful servant."

16　*For thus says the high and lofty One who inhabits eternity, whose name is Holy: "I dwell in the high and holy place, and also with him who is of a contrite and humble spirit, to revive the spirit of the humble, and to revive the heart of the contrite."*

　　　　　　　　　　　　　　　　　　　　　　　　　Isaiah 57:15, RSV

THE GREAT NATURALIST-PHILOSOPHER Henry David Thoreau once said, "You cannot kill time without injuring eternity." Realizing the truth of this observation puts a new urgency and importance into my daily routine. Despite our hectic modern pace, I don't suppose man has ever lived in a day in which he had more leisure time at his disposal. For decades we have heard talk about the possibility of a shorter work week with its accompanying ration of additional time for the things "we want to do." But when we view time in the light of eternity (and the One who inhabits and dominates eternity), suddenly individual moments of time take on new significance and seriousness. Wasting time becomes a criminal offense—and making every moment count takes on new worth. It's great to know that we have a direct line to that One who made us, and that all we have to do is acknowledge our need of his wisdom to have it at our disposal.

In Isaiah 40:28 the prophet says, "Have you not known? Have you not heard? The Lord is the everlasting God, the Creator of the ends of the earth. He does not faint or grow weary, his understanding is unsearchable" (RSV). In the next verses he goes on to say, "He gives power to the faint, and to him who has no might he increases strength. Even *youths* shall faint and be weary, and *young men* shall fall exhausted; *but* they who wait for the Lord shall renew their strength, they shall mount up with wings like eagles, they shall run and not be weary, they shall walk and not faint" (RSV, italics mine). Lord, let that be my discovery as I seek to make every day count for you!

May

17

We must work the works of him who sent me, while it is day; night comes, when no one can work.

John 9:4, RSV

WE ARE ALL in this world on divine missions, all sent from God to take some specific part in blessing the world. To do this we have just a day of time. A day is a brief time. It is a fixed time. When the sun comes to his going down, no power in the universe can prolong his stay for one minute.

Yet the day is long enough for God's plan. The sun never sets too soon for his purpose. Each life is long enough for the little part of the world's work allotted to it. This is true even of the infant who lives only an hour, merely coming into this world, smiling its benediction, and flying away. It is true of the child, of the young man or young woman, of him who dies in the maturity of his powers with his hands yet full of unfinished tasks. No one can ever offer as an excuse for an unfinished life-work that the time given to him was too short. It is always long enough, if only every moment of it be filled with simple faithfulness.

To have our work completed at the end, we must do it while the day lasts, for there will be no opportunity afterward. If we are living earnestly, we shall live all the time under the pressure of the consciousness that the time is short. We must not waste nor lose a moment. Soon it will be night, when we cannot work.

J. R. MILLER

18

I am writing to you, little children, because your sins are forgiven for his sake. I am writing to you, fathers, because you know him who is from the beginning. I am writing to you, young men, because you have overcome the evil one. I write to you, children, because you know the Father.

1 John 2:12–13, RSV

THE CHRISTIAN LIFE is always beginning, constantly adventuring, forever secure. It is for each of us to decide where we are in the Christian life. Some of us may still be babes and need to grow up. Others are in the thick of the battle to be faithful and obedient as Christ's disciples. Still others are enjoying the security of having grown to maturity in Christ. I want to keep the best of all three stages for all years. If we can never lose the initial joy, keep a daring discipleship, and become more mature in every day we are privileged to live, we will have the abundant

May

life Christ lived, died, and is with us now to make maximum. The new life in Christ will be exciting all the way up if we put him first in our lives.

LLOYD OGILVIE

Quoted from *When God First Thought of You* (Waco, TX: Word Books, 1978), p. 45.

19

Ye have compassed this mountain long enough: turn you northward.
Deuteronomy 2:3

WE OUGHT NEVER to be willing to live any year just as we lived the last one. No one is striving after the best things who is not intent on an upward and a forward movement continually. The circular movement is essential too—the going around and around in the old grooves—routine work, daily tasks; yet, even in this treadmill round, there should be constant progress. We ought to do the same things better each day. Then in the midst of the outward routine our inner life ought to be growing in earnestness, in force, in strength, in depth.

Yet there are some people whose life year by year is only a going around and around in the old beaten paths, with no onward movement. They are like men who walk in a circular course for a prize, covering a thousand miles, perhaps, but ending just where they began. Rather, our daily walk should be like one whose path goes about a mountain, but climbs a little higher with each circuit, until at last he gains the clear summit, and looks into the face of God. While we must do in a measure the same things every day, we should do them a little better with each repetition.

J. R. MILLER

20

Whereas you do not know about tomorrow. What is your life? For you are a mist that appears for a little time and then vanishes.
James 4:14, RSV

JAMES AND JOB sing a duet on this note, for the Old Testament wise man also said, "Remember that my life is a breath; my eye will never again see good" (7:7, RSV). The psalmist also realized the fleeting quality of earthly life when he wrote, "For my days are consumed like smoke, and my bones are burned as an hearth" (102:3). You and I make two mistakes in our estimate of life: first, we tend to regard this visible scene as if that were all there is—living only for and in the present. Second, and at the other extreme, we regard life as of little importance, as being comparatively worthless. And we also take for granted, especially in youth, that our lives will be prolonged: "Go to now, ye that say, Today or tomorrow we will go into such a city, and continue there a year, and buy and sell, and get gain" (James 4:13). How foolish and presumptuous we are! We should say: "If the Lord will, we shall live, and do this, or that" (James 4:15). A life lived on that level will reflect the wisdom God alone can give.

Not to be ministered unto, but to minister. **21**

Matthew 20:28

THE ART OF PHOTOGRAPHY is now so perfect that the whole side of a great newspaper can be taken in miniature so small as to be carried in a little pin or button, and yet every letter and point be perfect. So the whole life of Christ is photographed in one little phrase—"not to be ministered unto, but to minister." He came not to be served—if this had been his aim he would never have left heaven's glory, where he wanted nothing, where angels praised him and ministered unto him. He came to serve. He went about doing good. He altogether forgot himself. He served all he met who would receive his service. At last he gave his life in uttermost service—giving it a ransom for others. He came not to be ministered unto, but to minister.

You say you want to be like Christ. You pray him to print his own image on your heart. Here then is the image. It is no vague dream of perfection that we are to think of when we ask to be made like Christ. The old monks thought that they were in the way to become like Christ when they went into the wilderness, away from men, to live in cold cells or on tall columns. But that is not the thought which this picture suggests. "To minister"—that is the Christlike thing. Instead of fleeing away from the world we are to live among men, to serve them, to seek to bless them, to do them good, to give our life for them.

J. R. MILLER

May

22

Ye know . . . after what manner I have been with you at all seasons, serving the Lord with all humility of mind, and with many tears, and temptations, which befell me by the lying in wait of the Jews.

Acts 20:18–19

THE CHRISTIAN LIFE is a life of service—but not of servitude! This is what Paul was telling the elders of the church at Ephesus in this passage. In so doing, he sets out a gem of spiritual truth for us to examine and profit from. The kind of service Paul is talking about here represents perfect freedom rather than slavery, as Zechariah, the father of John the Baptist, said in his song: "That we, being delivered out of the hand of our enemies, might serve him without fear . . ." (Luke 1:74). Paul further describes this freedom in Romans 6:22, "But now being made free from sin, and become servants to God, ye have your fruit unto holiness, and the end everlasting life."

Not only *freedom* but also *sonship* is implied here. We don't serve *for* our salvation; we serve *from* or *out of* it. As God's children we are automatically servants: "Obey God because you are his children; don't slip back into your old ways—doing evil because you knew no better" (1 Pet. 1:14, LB).

Another condition of our service involves humility, as Peter further points out: "Clothe yourselves, all of you, with humility toward one another, for 'God opposes the proud, but gives grace to the humble'" (1 Pet. 5:5, RSV). Self is the greatest hindrance to service. As Dr. Bill Bright of Campus Crusade for Christ so often points out, self or ego on the throne of the heart makes it impossible to serve God successfully, for pride and self-confidence are our biggest obstacles to success in the Christian experience. Jesus provided the pattern in Luke 18:13–14: "The tax collector . . . would not even lift up his eyes to heaven, but beat his breast, saying, 'God, be merciful to me a sinner!' I tell you, this man went down to his house justified rather than the other; for every one who exalts himself will be humbled, but he who humbles himself will be exalted" (RSV).

23

. . . the greatest among you should be like the youngest, and the one who rules like the one who serves. For who is greater, the one who is at the table or the one who serves? Is it not the one who is at the table? But I am among you as one who serves.

Luke 22:26–27, NIV

OUR LORD is our example in all things, but especially in this matter of serving others. It's too bad that our human natures are so inclined to be served that we really resist this command of Christ. Our natural bent is to be served rather than to volunteer to serve others—and yet this kind of dedication is exactly what Christ is demanding of his followers. Peter was asking for the same dedicated service when he wrote: "Likewise you that are younger be subject to the elders. Clothe yourselves, all of you, with humility toward one another, for 'God opposes the proud, but gives grace to the humble'" (1 Pet. 5:5, RSV). Dr. Ray Stedman has written two books dealing with this very attitude of service demanded by the New Testament, *The Ruler Who Serves* and *The Servant Who Rules.** Both of these deal with the life of Christ as set forth in Mark's Gospel, where Christ is pictured in the active role of servant (Isaiah in the Old Testament also sets him forth in that light). If Jesus placed so much importance on serving others, shouldn't we? Some anonymous word-smith has put it in modern terms for us: "Life is like a game of tennis; the player who serves well seldom loses." Serving in life and in tennis may not be exactly alike—but this kernel of truth applies to both!

*(Waco, TX: Word Books, 1976).

Yet now, be strong . . . be strong, all ye people of the land, saith the Lord, and work: for I am with you, saith the Lord of hosts.
Haggai 2:4

24

WHAT A PROMISE for a lifetime: "Be strong . . . and work, for I am with you." Someone might say, "Yes, but that is a promise only for those who are in the Lord's work. It's not for the rank and file." Not so. These words were for "all the people of the land," the Lord's *people*, not just his priests. All the Lord requires from us is our willingness. We must allow ourselves to be filled with power from above, to be infilled from the Lord's limitless capacity. If we empty our lives of ourselves, he can move in with his tremendous power to work through us. It is his responsibility to equip us for the task—not ours. Our responsibility is to come for filling and to remain at his disposal all the days of our lives.

Three things are here intimately associated: the call to service; the work or area of involvement; and the empowerment for service. Each of these comes from God—and he can use us wherever he calls and places us. We must submit to that calling and placement.

May

25

Let the beauty of the Lord our God be upon us: and establish thou the work of our hands upon us; yea, the work of our hands establish thou it.

Psalm 90:17

WHAT DO YOU KNOW about the work of the Lord that gives you the right to say that your power is little? God may have some most critical use to put you to as soon as you declare yourself his servant. Men judge by the size of things; God judges by their fitness. You can see something of your size, but you can see almost nothing of your fitness until you understand all the wonderful diverse work that God has to do. It is most reckless presumption and pride for any man to dare to be sure that there is not some important and critical place which just he and no one else is made to fill. It is almost as presumptuous to think you can do nothing as to think you can do everything. The latter foolish assumption supposes that God exhausted himself when he made you; the former supposes that God made a hopeless blunder when he made you, which is quite as irreverent for you to think.

PHILLIPS BROOKS

26

Jesus said unto him, Judas, betrayest thou the Son of man with a kiss? . . . Hereafter shall the son of Man sit on the right hand of the power of God. Then said they all, Art thou then the Son of God? And he said unto them, Ye say that I am.

Luke 22:48, 69–70

HERE AGAIN WAS A CASE of Jesus dealing with "religious" people, people who nonetheless failed to grasp who Jesus really was. Both Judas and the Pharisees claimed to know God and to serve him—but they totally missed the fact that Jesus was the Son of God. As Oswald Chambers has said, "Beware of worshiping Jesus as the Son of God, and professing your faith in him as the Savior of the world, while you blaspheme him by the complete evidence in your daily life that he is powerless to do anything in and through you." We don't like to place ourselves in this kind of company, but the truth is that by our unbelief and lack of faith, we sometimes render God's power inoperative in our lives. My prayer is that I might be made more aware of this treacherous tendency in my own life—and really be in close contact with my Savior, daily!

He that is faithful in that which is least is faithful also in much; and **27**
he that is unjust in the least is unjust also in much.

Luke 16:10

THE MAN who missed his opportunity and met the doom of the faithless servant was not the man with five talents, or the man with two, but the man who had only one. The people who are in the most danger of missing life's great meaning are the people of ordinary capacity and opportunity, and who say to themselves, "There is so little I can do that I will not try to do anything." One of the finest windows in Europe was made from the remnants an apprentice boy collected from the cuttings of his master's great work. The sweepings of the British mint are worth millions. So God places a solemn value and responsibility on the humble workers. Our littleness will not excuse us in the reckoning day.

A. B. SIMPSON

You do not know what a day may bring forth. **28**

Proverbs 27:1, RSV

SOLOMON IS GIVING VOICE to an awesome truth in these words. If we approached each day of our lives with a consciousness of the day's unique qualities perhaps our attitude toward life would be different. Maltbie Babcock once said: "Opportunities do not come with their values stamped upon them. Everyone must be challenged. A day dawns, quite like other days; in it a single hour comes, quite like other hours; but in that day and in that hour the chance of a lifetime faces us. To face every opportunity of life thoughtfully and ask its meaning bravely and earnestly is the only way to meet the supreme opportunities when they come, whether open-faced or disguised." What would happen in your life and mine if we looked at each day in this light and lived it accordingly?

I glorified thee on the earth, having accomplished the work which thou **29**
gavest me to do.

John 17:4, RSV

JESUS IS THE ONLY MAN who has ever lived so as to be able to say this. The best lives are but fragments, leaving many things unfinished. Yet we ought to take a lesson from Christ's finishing of his work. He did it, simply by doing each day the will of his Father for the day.

He was a young man when he died—only thirty-three. We think of those who die young as dying before their work is completed. We learn, however, that even a young man, dying, may leave a finished work. The truth is, everyone's life is a plan of God. Years enough are given in which to do the work allotted. Even a baby who lives only a day, merely looking into the mother's eyes and then going away, does the work that was given it to do. The young man who dies at thirty-three with his hands full of tasks, if only he has lived faithfully, has finished the work which God gave him to do. Not years, but faithfulness, counts with God.

J. R. MILLER

30

For ye have not received the spirit of bondage again to fear; but ye have received the spirit of adoption, whereby we cry, Abba, Father.

Romans 8:15

SOME RECEIVE CHRIST as a sin-bearer and thus find pardon, but do not get beyond that, and their lives are daily failures. Others receive him as their risen Savior also, and thus enter into an experience of victory over sin. But we must also take him as our Deliverer from the power of sin, the keeper of our souls. Thus shall we achieve daily victory over sin.

A spiritual life, governed by a lot of rules, is a life of bondage. Sooner or later one is sure to break one or another of these man-made rules, and to get into condemnation. The true Christian life is the life of a trusting, glad, fear-free child; not led by rules, but by the personal guidance of the Holy Spirit, dwelling in the heart and directing every movement of the outward life.

R. A. TORREY

31

He ascends the heights, leading many captives in his train. He receives gifts for men, even those who once were rebels. God will live among us here.

Psalm 68:18, LB

SIN AND HOLINESS are not in things, but in souls; and all things are beautiful in the time when a soul uses them for holy uses with a loving, humble, and obedient life. The human soul sits at the center of everything, and Christ sits at the center of the human soul. If *he* changes us, then everything will be changed to us. "He that sat upon the throne said, Behold, I make all things new" (Rev. 21:5). If the world is ugly and bitter and cruel to you; if circumstances taunt and persecute you; if everything you touch is a strain and a temptation—do not stand idly wishing that the world were changed. The change must be in you. To the new heart all things shall be new. The new person shall see already the new heaven and the new earth. "If any man be in Christ, he is a new creature . . ." (2 Cor. 5:17); and the new creature is immediately in the new creation. Some of you know already by daily experience what that means. And for all of you it waits to be revealed if you will let Christ do his work in you.

PHILLIPS BROOKS

June

Living for God

1

Yes, Adam's sin brought punishment to all, but Christ's righteousness makes men right with God, so that they can live.

Romans 5:18, LB

GOD IS THE ONLY final dream of man. Door after door opens; there is no final room till we come where he sits. All that ought to be done in the world has a right to know itself as finally done for him; it is God, and the discovery of him in life, and the certainty that he has plans for our lives, and is doing something with them, that gives us a true, deep sense of movement, and lets us always feel the power and delight of unknown coming things.

The unity of life is never lost. There must not be any waste. How great and gracious is the economy of life which it involves! Neither to dwell in any experience always, nor to count any experience as if it had not been, but to leave the forms of our experiences behind, and to go forth from them clothed in their spiritual power, this is what God is always teaching us is possible, and tempting us to do. To him who does it come the two great blessings of a growing life—faithfulness and liberty: faithfulness in each moment's task and liberty to enter through the gates beyond which lies the larger future. "Well done, thou good and faithful servant: thou hast been faithful over a few things . . . enter thou into the joy of thy lord" (Matt. 25:21).

PHILLIPS BROOKS

No, *dear brothers, I am still not all I should be but I am bringing all my energies to bear on this one thing: Forgetting the past and looking forward to what lies ahead, I strain to reach the end of the race and receive the prize for which God is calling us up to heaven because of what Christ Jesus did for us.*

Philippians 3:13–14, LB

WHAT DOES IT MEAN to live a life like this—a life that is straining to "receive the prize," or as the King James Version has it, to "press toward the mark for the prize of the high calling of God in Christ Jesus"? Whatever kind of life it is, the apostle Paul, who wrote these words, lived it! Is it living with a "one-track mind," concentrating on one thing to the exclusion of all others? In a sense, I guess, it is—but it is a life concentrating on a certain goal while attending to the multitude of duties that press in upon us from all sides. It reminds me of being in a long-range sailboat race. The goal is to win the race, but all kinds of tasks must be carried out on a daily basis to keep the ship on an even keel, taking full advantage of every wind that blows and every current that flows. Every decision made affects the outcome of the race. So it is with the Christian "race"—and the key is "what Christ Jesus did for us."

Neither yield ye your members as instruments of unrighteousness unto sin: but yield yourselves unto God, as those that are alive from the dead, and your members as instruments of righteousness unto God.

Romans 6:13

SUPPOSE WE DELIBERATELY made up our minds as to what things we were henceforth to allow to become our life? Suppose we selected a given area of our environment, and determined once for all that our efforts should go to that alone, fencing in this area all around with a morally impassable wall? True, to others we should seem to live a poorer life; they would see that our environment was circumscribed and call us narrow because it was narrow. But, well-chosen, this limited life would really be the fullest life; it would be rich in the highest and worthiest, and poor in the smallest and basest.

HENRY DRUMMOND

June

4

. . . that ye may prove what is that good, and acceptable, and perfect, will of God.

Romans 12:2

IT'S AN OLD STORY with many variations, but let me share my version. A tourist was watching a beautiful young lady hard at work treating some of the worst cases of leprosy in a leper colony. "Ugh!" he said, "I wouldn't do what you are doing for a million dollars!" Her cheerful reply: "Neither would I!" Why was she involved in a task money couldn't pay her to do? Her desire was to be pleasing to her Lord—she was trying to do his will.

For some reason, many of us feel that God's will is somehow second-best—that he doesn't want us to know real happiness in our work. How wrong we are. Like Paul, we have to learn by experience that his will is "good . . . acceptable . . . perfect." Before Paul yielded himself to God's will for his life, he probably thought he had it made. But instead, after he launched out into the life of sacrifice and danger that God had in mind for him, he discovered true contentment in the will of God for him: "I have learned, in whatsoever state I am, therewith to be content" he wrote the Philippians (4:11). That's the lesson we need to learn as well. If we're following God's will for our lives, we can't go wrong.

5

I will send thee to Jesse . . . I have provided me a king among his sons.

1 Samuel 16:1

THE LORD is never at loss for a man. When one fails he has another ready. His plans and purposes go on in spite of human failure, and through all seeming disaster.

Here was a boy, keeping the sheep in the fields, probably not dreaming of greatness, and yet God had him marked out to be king. The boys do not know what God has in mind for them. They may be sure, however, that for everyone of them he has some plan. It may be a great place or a small one, as the world rates greatness or smallness; but every boy should feel that to be just what God made him to be is the grandest, noblest, best thing possible for him. If God made him to be a carpenter, and by his own restless strivings he gets to be a member of Congress or Parliament, or President of the United States, his place is not half so high and great in the angels' sight as if he had been the carpenter he was meant to be.

The greatest place anyone can attain is the place God intended him to fill. How can we know what God wants us to do and to be? By doing his will, day by day, with quiet fidelity, wherever we find ourselves. God's will for each day is God's plan for us for that day. Thus God will lead us continually to that which he has for us to do. Failure in the lowlier duties will hinder our promotion to the higher.

J. R. MILLER

We who are strong ought to bear with the failings of the weak, and not to please ourselves; let each of us please his neighbor for his good, to edify him.

Romans 15:1–2, RSV

6

PAUL'S MEANING here comes a little clearer to me in J. B. Phillips's translation: "We who have strong faith ought to shoulder the burden of the doubts and qualms of the weak and not just go our own sweet way. We should consider the good of our neighbor and help to build up his character." Paul is calling for a spirit of self-denial and selflessness—something generally contrary to our natural bent. But he has put his finger on the secret of happy living: living for others rather than self. Carl W. McGeehon, writing in *Link* magazine, put it this way: "No one is happy or free who lives only for himself. Joy in living comes from immersion in something one recognizes to be bigger, better, worthier, more enduring than he himself is. True happiness and true freedom come from squandering one's self for a purpose." Since ours is a world filled with needy people, what better way to "squander" ourselves than in service to others rather than self?

For physical training is of some value, but godliness has value for all things, holding promise for both the present life and the life to come.

1 Timothy 4:8, NIV

7

THE PHILOSOPHER WILLIAM JAMES once said, "The great use of life is to spend it for something that outlasts it." This, I think, is the quality of life Paul is calling for here in his fatherly challenge to his spiritual son, Timothy. In *The Greatest Thing in the World* Henry Drummond says: "Keep in the midst of Life. Do not isolate yourself. Be among men, and among things, and among troubles and difficulties and obstacles. You remember Goethe's words: 'Talent develops itself in solitude, character in the stream of life.'" This, it seems to me, is the call of the Christian in today's world. He is to be involved, not isolated; he is called to the front lines, not the rear echelon! His is a call to conflict, not complacency.

8

Whatsoever ye do, do it heartily, as to the Lord.

Colossians 3:23

CHRIST NEVER ASKS for anything we cannot do. But let us not forget that He always does expect and require of each of us the best we can do. The faithfulness Christ wants and approves implies the doing of all our work, our business, our trade, our toil, as well as we can. Let no one think that the Christian faith does not apply to private life, the life between Sundays. Whatever your job is, you cannot be altogether faithful to God unless you do your best. To slur any task is to do God's work badly; to neglect it is to rob God. The universe is not quite complete without your work well done, however small that work may be.

J. R. MILLER

9

The disciple is not above his master.

Matthew 10:24

A DISCIPLE is a learner—a learner not only of the Lord's truth, but also of the Lord's humility. He has to follow his Master both in doctrine and in suffering. He must always be at his Master's feet. He must never be above his Master. And so the true disciple finds that in following he has perpetually to descend. For his Master is the very embodiment of humility. He "made himself of no reputation"—emptied himself. And the disciple must not seek for himself anything above that which his Master sought for himself. "It is enough for the disciple that he be as his master, and the servant as his lord" (v. 25). The Master was among us as one who served. Though Lord of all, he took the place of a servant. It was as such he glorified his Father. It is as such that we shall glorify our Lord. O for this spirit of self-surrender, this mind which was in Christ Jesus! There is no real following until we know what it is to ignore or surrender self: "If any man will come after me, let him deny himself, and take up his cross, and follow me" (Matt. 16:24). This denial of self is not the end, but the beginning or condition of following the Master.

EVAN H. HOPKINS

But God forbid that I should glory, save in the cross of our Lord Jesus Christ, by whom the world is crucified unto me, and I unto the world.
Galatians 6:14

10

IT HAS BEEN SAID THAT the cross is an I crossed out. That's a way of restating Paul's words to the Galatians about the cross. Thomas à Kempis, whose writings unfortunately are little known today, said, "Carry the cross patiently, and with perfect submission; and in the end it shall carry you. If you bear the cross unwillingly, you make it a burden, and load yourself more heavily; but you must of necessity bear it. If you cast away one cross, you will certainly find another, and perhaps a heavier." He was voicing a principle as true today as when he first verbalized it back in the fourteenth century. Might I also realize, in these last decades of the twentieth century, that in bearing the cross my Lord has for me I am fulfilling his will and purpose in my life. And, really, it is not I who carry it at all, but "Christ in me, the hope of glory."

No man taketh it [my life] from me, but I lay it down of myself. I have power to lay it down, and I have power to take it again. This commandment have I received of my Father.
John 10:18

11

"THIS COMMANDMENT RECEIVED I of My Father." The great center around which the life of Jesus moved was the will of His Father and devotion to Him. It is easy to work ourselves up into a passion of sacrifice, but that is not the true element in dedication. As a saint I have power to refuse to give my sanctification to God; I can use that sanctification for my own selfish ends, with unutterable ruin to my own soul and to others. Our only guide is our Lord Himself: "For their sakes I sanctify Myself." In full possession of His powers Jesus dedicated Himself to God, and His call to those of us who are His disciples is to

June

dedicate ourselves to Him with a clear knowledge of what we are doing, free from the plaintive, the sad, and the emotional. Can we only serve God when He thrills us? Can we only speak for Him when we feel His conscious touch? Cannot we have all the deep passion of our heart and spirit ablaze for God, our whole personality under control for one purpose only—to dedicate ourselves to the Lord Jesus Christ as He dedicated Himself to His Father?

Let Him make our lives narrow; let Him make them intense; let Him make them absolutely His!

OSWALD CHAMBERS

12

I am not saying this because I am in need, for I have learned to be content whatever the circumstances. I know what it is to be in need, and I know what it is to have plenty. I have learned the secret of being content in any and every situation, whether well fed or hungry, whether living in plenty or in want. I can do everything through him who gives me strength.

Philippians 4:11–13, NIV

FOR SOME REASON, this last verse has always struck me as the perfect verse on which to build a life. It is strikingly appropriate for the young—or the young at heart. I have some gray in my hair now, but I still get a thrill when I hear this ringing declaration of our faith similar to that which I feel when I see the flag go by. It has a sort of militant ring—and I think it's time again for us Christians to become more militant in our stand for Christ. Satan's soldiers were never more vocal and visible than they are today, and we need to counteract their cause with our own victorious chant, "I can do everything through him who gives me strength!" The dynamic German poet-philosopher Johann Fichte (1762–1814) once cried out in his native tongue, "Give me a great thought that I may *live!*" That's my cry today.

13

. . . take hold of the life which is life indeed.

1 Timothy 6:19, RSV

WILLIAM JENNINGS BRYAN, great lecturer and editor of the early twentieth century, once said, "Destiny is not a matter of chance. It is a matter of choice." The apostle Paul is saying something like that here to Timothy, and his words ring down through the centuries to us today with clarity and conviction. Some anonymous sage has written, "The final test of our lives will not be how *much* we have lived but *how* we have lived, not how tempestuous our lives have been, but how much bigger, better and stronger these trials have left us. Not how much money, fame, or fortune we have laid up here on earth, but how many treasures we have laid up in heaven!" In Paul's words for today is a treasure to be had and a goal to move toward.

Where are you going? What are your goals? A recent survey showed that nine out of ten people had no clear goals. Every person must have some definite goals in life to accomplish anything. Otherwise one only drifts and dreams.

So teach us to number our days, that we may get a heart of wisdom.
Psalm 90:12, RSV

14

THERE ARE SEVERAL WAYS of numbering our days. One way is merely to count them off as we tear off the daily leaves of our calendar. Each evening a man has one day less to live. But that is not true numbering. Another way is merely to count the days into the aggregate of life. A man is one day older—but that is all. He is no better. He has left no worthy record on the day's page. The true numbering is that which fills the days as they pass with records of good and beautiful living, and with lines of growth in character.

What have we given the days to keep for us? What lessons of wisdom have we learned from them, as one by one they have passed? There is little good in worrying over the failures of the years, but we ought to learn from our past. He is the wise man, not who makes no mistakes, but who does not repeat his mistakes.

J. R. MILLER

It is appointed unto men once to die, but after this the judgment.
Hebrews 9:27

15

THESE ARE SOBERING WORDS. In this book we have sought to be positive or at least optimistic in our tone and outlook. Most of you who read these words are young and relatively healthy, looking forward to a long and happy life. But none of us can be assured that long life is God's plan for us. Here in the Epistle to the Hebrews God sounds a note we need to hear: one day you and I will die and face the judgment, and of that day and hour "knoweth no man." I don't remind you of this fact so that will worry your way through the rest of your life, but I do remind you of the *brevity* of life so that you will concentrate on the *quality* of life rather than its *quantity*. Make the most of today, for you may not have tomorrow. The best you can do with today is to live it for him! Then this verse will not hang over your head like a threat. Rather, the words of verse 28 will characterize your lifestyle: "So Christ, having been offered once to bear the sins of many, will appear a second time, not to deal with sin but to save those who are eagerly waiting for him" (RSV).

16 *And let us consider how to stir up one another to love and good works.*

Hebrews 10:24, RSV

WHEN JESUS CHRIST walked this world we are told that he "went about doing good" (Acts 10:38). When he left us in the world, that mission of goodness was part of our assignment. Indeed, one of the fruits of the Holy Spirit is goodness (Gal. 5:22). It may sound trite, but Jesus "has no hands but our hands" to do his work in the world today. We Christians are an indispensable link in the chain to accomplish his will. We are "God with skin on," the only contact some people will have with the God of the universe. This is an awesome responsibility—but thank God we don't have to accomplish all this in our own strength. God gives the commandment, but he also gives the strength to carry out the commission: "Lo, I am with you alway, even unto the end of the world" (Matt. 28:20)

17 *Walk in newness of life.*

Romans 6:4

BOTH LIFE AND LIBERTY are needed before we are ready to "walk." The life is secured to us in Christ. He is our life. So too is liberty. Deliverance from sin's power, as well as from sin's penalty, is the fruit of

Christ's death. "Stand fast . . . in the liberty wherewith *Christ hath made us free*" (Gal. 5:1). We are set free, not for idle contemplation or personal enjoyment, but for practical service. Walking in newness of life embraces the whole of that life that glorifies God. It is the apostle's favorite term for moral conduct. He says *"newness* of life" instead of *"new* life," because he would make prominent the idea of the new nature of this second life. The old life terminates at the cross. If we died with Christ, then the life that belongs to the "man of old" has been brought to an end; and if we are risen with Christ, we have entered into the life of the "new man." That is a life of freedom and power. Walking in this life is not a hard, irksome struggle, but free and joyous action. What physical exercise is to the man who is in robust health, "walking in newness of life" is to the soul who is in the power of Christ's resurrection.

EVAN H. HOPKINS

And Hezekiah commanded to offer the burnt offering upon the altar. And when the burnt offering began, the song of the Lord began also with the trumpets, and with the instruments ordained by David king of Israel.

18

2 Chronicles 29:27

CONDUCT is the mouthpiece of character. What a man is declares itself through what he does. Character without conduct is like the lips without the trumpet, whose whispers die upon themselves and do not stir the world. Conduct without character is like the trumpet hung up in the wind, which whistles through it and means nothing. The world has a right to demand that all which claims to be character should show itself through conduct which can be seen and heard. The world has a right to disallow all claims of character which do not show themselves in conduct. "It may be real, it may be good," the world can say, "but I cannot know it or test it; and I am sure that however good and real it is, it is not shown unless there are positive signs of activity." James said it another way: "What does it profit, my brethren, if a man says he has faith but has not works? Can his faith save him? If a brother or sister is ill-clad and in lack of daily food, and one of you says to them, 'Go in peace, be warmed and filled,' without giving them the things needed, . . . what does it profit? So faith by itself, if it has no works, is dead. But some one will say, 'You have faith and I have works.' Show me your

faith apart from your works, and I by my works will show you my faith"
(James 2:14–18, RSV).

PHILLIPS BROOKS

19

*Do everything without complaining or arguing, so that you may
become blameless and pure, children of God without fault in a
crooked and depraved generation, in which you shine like stars in the
universe as you hold out the word of life—in order that I may boast on
the day of Christ that I did not run or labor for nothing.*

Philippians 2:14–16, NIV

I PARTICULARLY LIKE the way this new translation renders the phrase,
"shine like stars in the universe." James Moffatt phrased it, "Where ye
shine like stars in a dark world." That is saying we Christians are God's
luminaries in an age of darkness. What a remarkable way to put it.
Scripturally, the stars, which represent the children of God, are
imperfect in his sight: "Yea, the stars are not pure in his sight" (Job
25:5). Still, to encourage us in our Christian walk, the "Father of lights"
has appointed the imperfect, faulty "stars for a light by night" (Jer.
31:35). This is just another place where God is calling for our human
best clothed in his Spirit. As God's luminaries, we are to radiate a
reflected light—holding out "the word of life." And to put it mildly, *one
can't glow if he's grouchy.* That's why those whom God honors as his
night lights, as his stars, must be faultless, innocent, and unblameable
when covered with his Spirit (see the Amplified translation for the
various shades of meaning in the words *blameless* and *pure* in our text).
What a challenge this is to a life that glows for God along the way.

20

*And Jesus said to them, "Follow me and I will make you become
fishers of men." And immediately they left their nets and followed
him.*

Mark 1:17–18, RSV

MY CHERISHED BROTHER in Christ, Dr. Robert Munger, said recently
in a covenant group we share with a group of pastors, "It is more

effective to spend time talking to Christ about a person than talking to a person about Christ, because if you are talking to Christ about a person seriously, earnestly, trustingly, in the course of time you cannot help talking to the person effectively about Christ." That challenged me to consider if I had spent as much time talking to Christ about people as I had spent talking to people about Christ. Prayer without sharing is ineffective, but sharing without prayer is futile.

All this boils down to our willingness. A decision is necessary to follow Christ and allow him to make us become fishermen who take men alive. Mark tells us that in response to Jesus' call the disciples immediately left their nets and followed him. Some translations read, "Forsook their nets." Either way, the idea is that it was a once and for all action. Our challenge is to leave a privatism and an inverted piety and follow the Lord in his central activity of communicating love to others. If we try to follow him without becoming fishers of men we will not follow for long. If we want to be with him, we must join him in doing what is ultimately crucial to him and the people he died to save.

LLOYD OGILVIE

Quoted from *Life Without Limits* (Waco, TX: Word Books, 1975), p. 40.

Thou hast given a banner to them that fear thee, that it may be displayed because of the truth.

21

Psalm 60:4

BANNERS ARE OFTEN MENTIONED in the Scriptures—and we speak of them in other meditations. In this case the psalmist is speaking of a banner as a rallying point or assurance of victory. The gospel itself is the Christian's banner. It is important that we, first of all, take our stand beneath *this* banner. After all, we certainly cannot proclaim it to others if we have not experienced it for ourselves. Any hesitancy or uncertainty on our part will nullify our testimony. To display the banner faithfully and to proclaim the message effectively, we must know of a certainty that the gospel is indeed God's power unto salvation (Rom. 1:16) and his answer to life's deepest needs. Because of its truth, its practicality in the marketplace of life, we can offer this gospel to a world in need, confident that our God is great enough to handle every situation life can hand us.

June

22 *You are the light of the world. A city on a hill cannot be hidden. Neither do people light a lamp and put it under a bowl. Instead they put it on a stand, and it gives light to everyone in the house. In the same way, let your light shine before men, that they may see your good deeds and praise your Father in heaven.*

Matthew 5:14–16, NIV

TOO MANY OF US Christians think of witnessing as a purely verbal exercise. And, like Moses, we excuse ourselves because we are not of ready tongue (Exod. 4:10). But the great Charles H. Spurgeon, one of history's greatest and most eloquent preachers, put mere verbal witness in perspective when he said, "I would not give much for your religion unless it can be seen. Lamps do not talk, but they do shine." The apostle James had this "faith in action" approach in mind when he said, "faith by itself, if it is not accompanied by action, is dead" (2:17, NIV). While I don't agree with Ramakrishna's theology, I think the Hindu reformer and mystic was on the right track when he said, "Common men talk bagfuls of religion but act not a grain of it, while the wise man speaks little, but his whole life is a religion acted out." May both my words *and* my actions bear out my relationship to Jesus Christ.

23 *Be very careful, then, how you live—not as unwise but as wise, making the most of every opportunity, because the days are evil.*

Ephesians 5:15–16, NIV

THIS TRANSLATION adds a different dimension to the traditional KJV rendering of today's verse: "See then that ye walk circumspectly . . ." Truly there is here a double idea—"See *how* you walk" (or "live") and "*that* ye walk circumspectly." Both the manner of the walk and the act of walking, or living, are included in the thought. It is of primary importance that we be careful of the way we live before our fellowmen: "Walk in wisdom toward them that are without, redeeming the time" (Col. 4:5). At one point I planned to title this book *Timelines*, so important do I feel is this subject of "redeeming the time." Let us walk accurately, correctly, in relation to unbelievers, so that we give no occasion or cause for stumbling. "Make the most of every opportunity," Paul says to the Ephesians here—and that admonition is equally applicable to all of us today who are serious about living as Christians before a hostile and misunderstanding world.

24

Once you were alienated from God and were enemies in your minds because of your evil behavior. But now he has reconciled you by Christ's physical body through death to present you holy in his sight, without blemish and free from accusation.

Colossians 1:21–22, NIV

THESE ARE WEIGHTY WORDS, a portion of Scripture which we usually pass over lightly since the concept expressed is so difficult to grasp. It is probably the type of passage Oswald Chambers had in mind when he wrote: "Profoundly speaking, it is not sufficient to say, 'Because God says it' or 'Because the Bible says it,' unless you are talking to people who know God and know the Bible to be his Word. If you appeal from the authority of God or of the Bible to a man not born again, he will pay no attention to you because he does not stand on the same platform. You have to find a provisional platform on which he can stand with you, and in the majority of cases you will find the platform is that of moral worth. If Jesus Christ is proved worthy on the plane men are on, they will be ready to put him as the Most Worthy One, and all the rest will follow." In our witnessing to others, we must start where they are and lead them gently and lovingly to where we are. We can't drive or push others into the kingdom, but by our loving attitude and gentle spirit we can *attract* them there.

25

This is the third time I am coming to you. In the mouth of two or three witnesses shall every word be established.

2 Corinthians 13:1

IN NEW TESTAMENT TIMES, as now, witnesses were the core of courtroom procedure. The word *witness* is an interesting one with several meanings and connotations in the legal world: "one who tells what he knows"; "to see or know by personal presence or perception"; "to be present at an occurrence as a formal witness, spectator, bystander"; "to bear witness to, testify to, give or afford evidence." These definitions make the individual Christian's designation as a "witness" doubly significant—and also remove a monkey from our back. For years I labored under the impression that a Christian witness needed to take responsibility for the whole course of another's conversion. Not only was I responsible to testify of what Christ meant to me, but I also had to "call all the plays and run for the touchdown"! Only in recent years have I made the blessed discovery that I must tell what I know, but it is God

June

who gives the increase. Nathaniel Emmons says, "Any fact is better established by two or three good testimonies than by a thousand arguments." That's my cue. I don't have to argue another into the kingdom—I simply have to tell what Jesus Christ means to me and let the Holy Spirit take it from there.

26

And my being in prison has given most of the brothers more confidence in the Lord, so that they grow bolder all the time to preach the message fearlessly.

Philippians 1:14, TEV

WE SHOULD KEEP QUIET about our faith until we can't keep still! What I mean is—when the experience of our Lord's unchanging love is the confidence of our lives, we will be bold and not bland. People who have been healed by a miracle drug are not reluctant to tell you what saved their lives. Someone who is convinced of a political candidate doesn't have to be asked twice to tell you why. When we are wondrously in love, we want to talk about our lover. Possibly the reason we find it difficult to talk about what's happened to us in our faith is because so little has happened.

Most of the problems and frustrations of life we face are also troubling other people. If we share our faith as a theory, we touch no one where he is living. But when we talk about life and the confidence Christ has given us, there is communication. The burden to convince is replaced by the desire to care.

LLOYD OGILVIE

Quoted from *Let God Love You* (Waco, TX: Word Books, 1974), p. 34.

27

As ye have therefore received Christ Jesus the Lord, so walk ye in him.

Colossians 2:6

WE ALL LIVE in relationships. Most of us live in families, or at least grew up in one. We also rub elbows with our own wider circle of friends and acquaintances. Many of these relationships develop within the context of a school or working situation, as well as in the church. We cannot completely avoid others, although some people try to do so (we

112

call them hermits). Paul is aware of the fact of interaction and urges us to "walk in" Jesus so that we won't be negative in our influence on others. As G. Campbell Morgan points out, "Every one of us exerts influences which will have their effect upon other lives, and the generations yet unborn will be lifted nearer God or thrust into deeper darkness, because we have lived and moved and had our being on the earth." Our influence on others (for good or ill) is a solemn responsibility to consider. Without the Lord we couldn't cope—but with him we can "walk" as we should.

They couldn't get to Jesus through the crowd, so they dug through the clay roof above his head and lowered the sick man on his stretcher, right down in front of Jesus.

Mark 2:4, LB

28

THERE IS A RICH LESSON in this story of healing for those of us who consider ourselves just average Christians with no particular talent c r gift to expend for the kingdom of God. Four men were instrumental in bringing this palsied ("paralyzed," LB) man to Jesus, and their names are not even given! We only know that they had enough love and simple faith to bring a helpless cripple to Jesus—and enough boldness to rip off the roof above Jesus' head when that proved to be the only way they could get to him. Their unsophisticated faith was amply rewarded when Jesus said, "Son, your sins are forgiven!" (v. 5, LB). There are people who will not come to Christ if you and I don't carry the message to them. Tremendous talent and unusual ability are not required. Just a little faith blended with sincere love can expose the unbeliever to the transforming power of Jesus and his Word.

"You are a king, then!" said Pilate. Jesus answered, "You are right in saying I am a king. In fact, for this reason I was born, and for this I came into the world, to testify to the truth. Everyone on the side of truth listens to me."

John 18:37, NIV

29

HAVE YOU EVER asked yourself, "Why was I born?" This is one of the most penetrating questions a person could ask himself. For the

June

Christian, there is only one adequate answer, the one given here by Jesus to Pilate: "to testify to the truth." If you have been saved by grace, this must be your answer, too. Every commission Jesus received (except his atoning death on the cross) has been transferred to his disciples: "As the Father has sent me, even so send I you." Why was *I* born? To bear witness to Jesus, the One who said, "I am the Truth." Am I a witness for Christ every day of my life? Someone has said, "Witnessing is the whole work of the whole church for the whole age." That means now!

30

He destined us in love to be his sons through Jesus Christ, according to the purpose of his will, to the praise of his glorious grace which he freely bestowed on us in the Beloved.

Ephesians 1:5–6, RSV

GOD HAS A PLAN for our lives, for each individual life. There is something special that He made us for; He has a thought in mind for us, something He wants us to be and to do. Now we can never be what God wants us to be except by doing His will day by day. Disobedience or lack of submission at any point will mar the perfection of His plan for us. We know that whatever He wills for us is for us the highest possible good. God's will for us is always blessing. It will lead us at every step in the best way home. It will fashion in us each day a little more fully the image of Christ.

J. R. MILLER

July

Guidance from God

Show me thy ways, O Lord; teach me thy paths. Lead me in thy truth, $\qquad$ **1**
and teach me: for thou art the God of my salvation; on thee do I wait
all the day.

Psalm 25:4–5

MANY OF YOU reading these pages are just starting out in the Christian experience. You're just getting your feet wet in the river of life, as it were. This prayer of David's makes a grand motto as one launches out. As you leave on life's trip, make this your prayer: "Show me . . . teach me . . . lead me. . . ." It covers every aspect of the trip. To begin with, "Show me thy ways . . ." Give me a preview of your will for me, O Lord. I want to follow it—so I have to know it first. Then, "Teach me thy paths." Spend time with me, Lord, that I might learn my lessons well and be equipped for the journey. Finally, "Lead me in thy truth. . . ." Go right along with me Lord, while I'm on the journey. Don't just prepare me, but accompany me as well. Only a great God could answer all of David's petitions—and did. And he is just as ready to go with each of us, too. All we need to do is open our lives to him and he will come in—and fill our lives with his gracious presence.

Now when they had gone throughout Phrygia and the region of $\qquad$ **2**
Galatia, and were forbidden of the Holy Ghost to preach the word in
Asia, after they were come to Mysia, they assayed to go into Bithynia:
but the Spirit suffered them not.

Acts 16:6

IT IS POSSIBLE for us to have the unerring guidance of the Holy Spirit at every turn of life. For example: in personal work it is manifestly not

July

God's intention that we speak to everyone we meet. There are some to whom we ought not to speak. Time spent on them would be taken from work more to God's glory. Doubtless Philip met many as he journeyed toward Gaza before he met the one of whom the Spirit said: "Go near, and join thyself to this chariot" (Acts 8:29). So is God ready to guide us also.

Do you know the companionship of the Holy Spirit, the partnership of the Holy Spirit, the fellowship of the Holy Spirit, the comradeship of the Holy Spirit? To put it into a single word—and I say it reverently—do you know my *Friend*, the Holy Spirit? "And thine ears shall hear a word behind thee, saying, This is the way, walk ye in it, when ye turn to the right hand, and when ye turn to the left" (Isa. 30:21).

R. A. TORREY

3
He keepeth the paths of judgment [the just], and preserveth the way of his saints.

Proverbs 2:8

A PERFECT EXAMPLE of this preservation of the faithful is found in Hannah's prayer after Samuel's birth: "He will guard the feet of his saints, but the wicked will be silenced in darkness" (1 Sam. 2:9, NIV). God keeps both the *way* and the *feet* of the faithful! How well I remember how my wife and I laid claim to these and similar promises as our teenage sons began their independent travels first in the family car and later on their own wheels. But I wonder if we fully realized (then or now) our need to rely upon God's protective and preserving grace. Like Hannah we *believed* that he guards "the feet of his saints," but we couldn't grasp the full meaning of that promise. The promise is good not because of who we are, but because of who *he* is. We may think of the way as the path along which we have to travel, but God is the One who prepares and preserves it. We need not be anxious as to our future, as to marking out our path and planning our ways. We have but to seek his guidance daily to be taught his way concerning us. He will assuredly say to us, "This is the way; walk ye in it."

4
And he said, My presence shall go with thee, and I will give thee rest.

Exodus 33:14

THIS IS A BOOK of guidelines—and we might think of "guidelines" as a map showing us the way to go. Being "on the way" implies that we are on a journey—and that's a pretty apt description of what life is all about. It *is* a journey, and all of us, young and old, need some guidelines. Moses was on a journey, too, when in Exodus 33:13 he prayed to the Lord, "Show me now thy way"—tell me what to do! John MacDuff analyzes the way God answered that prayer: "Moses asked to be shown 'the way.' Here is the answer: The way is *not* shown—but better than this, God says, 'I will go with thee!' The way may be very different from what *we* would have chosen, but the choice is in better hands." You and I need to ask God to show us the way as well, and then bask in his presence on that way. We may not know the way he is leading us, but we know the One who is with us on that way!

Thou shalt guide me with thy counsel, and afterward receive me to glory. **5**

Psalm 73:24

THE UNDERLYING THEME of this book has been guidance. When one thinks of guidance, he expects to find a map or a set of blueprints to follow. What better guidance than the "counsel" of God? Lawyers and other knowledgeable people are important in the scheme of things, but they are mere mortals and make mistakes. I'd rather rely on the "Wonderful Counsellor," God himself. The Psalms have come down to us from centuries ago, but their advice is timeless. Even though they came out of a culture that was much simpler than ours, they deal with the stuff of life—realistically and practically. I'm glad the "God who lived in David's time is just the same today"! He guides me today—and glory comes "afterward"!

I will instruct thee and teach thee in the way which thou shalt go: I will guide thee with mine eye. **6**

Psalm 32:8

IF WE HAVE absolute confidence in God's judgment and God's willingness to guide us, and are absolutely surrendered to His will, whatever it may be, and are willing to let God choose His way of guidance, and will go on step by step as He does guide us, and are studying His Word to know His will, and are listening for the still, small voice of the Spirit, going step by step as He leads, He will guide us with His counsel to the end of our earthly pilgrimage, and afterwards receive us into glory.

R. A. TORREY

A WALK is made up of steps. Though a man circle the globe, yet he must do it one step at a time; and the character of the steps will determine the character of the walk. So life is made up, for the most part, of trifles, of commonplaces, or the reiteration of familiar and simple acts. And what we are in those, that will determine the color and value of our lives in the verdict of eternity. Life is not made by the rapturous but brief moments which we spend on the transfiguration mount but by the steps we take along the pathway of daily duty, and of sometimes monotonous routine.

F. B. MEYER

7

What man is he that feareth the Lord? him shall he teach in the way that he shall choose.

Psalm 25:12

THE WISDOM OF THE AGES, it seems to me, is wrapped up in the Psalms. Or perhaps it would be more accurate to say, "the wisdom of God." And here the psalmist gives us a key to unlock that wisdom: if we "fear" the Lord, he will teach us the way he wants us to go. The NIV says, "He will instruct him in the way chosen for him." The wise man lets the Lord choose his way for him. This doesn't mean God wants us to be robots—he just wants us to think Godward. We hear a lot about "thinking positively" and "possibility thinking"—but our real need is for "godly" thinking and the kind of living that takes the path of God's choosing. As he leads his child, God will continue teaching him, says the psalmist—a divine "on-the-job" training. It's possible to know the way of salvation without walking in it. Sometimes God's children wish for and follow their own way. Salvation is a transition from the power of Satan to the power of God. This is but one aspect of it, however. Salvation is also a lesson in perpetual submission to God in all things. That's what it means for a Christian to walk in the "way chosen for him."

And the word of the Lord came unto him, saying, Get thee hence. . . . 8

1 Kings 17:2–3

I LIKE THAT PHRASE, "the word of the Lord came to him." He did not need to go to search for it; it *came* to him. And so it will come to you. It may come through the Word of God, or through a distinct impression made on your heart by the Holy Spirit, or through circumstances; but it will find you out, and tell you what you are to do. "Lord, what wilt thou have me to do? And the Lord said unto him, Arise, and go into the city, and it shall be told thee what thou must do" (Acts 9:6).

It may be that for long you have had upon your mind some strong impression of duty; but you have held back, because you could not see what the next step would be. Hesitate no longer. Step out upon what seems to be the impalpable mist: you will find a slab of adamant beneath your feet; and every time you put your foot forward, you will find that God has prepared a stepping-stone, and the next, and the next—each as you come to it. The bread is by the day. The manna is new every morning. He does not give us all the directions at once lest we should get confused.

F. B. MEYER

The steps of a good man are ordered by the Lord: and he delighteth in his way. 9

Psalm 37:23

THIS VERSE would make a good, a great motto for life. The "he" in the last phrase refers to God, and if we live life in the light of causing *him* delight, it should make a difference in our priorities and goals. Recent translations of the verse delete the word *good* and that troubles, but at the same time encourages, me. The New International Version has: "The Lord delights in the way of the man whose steps he has made firm." What a relief! I don't have to drum up "goodness" in order to have my steps ordered by his hand. No, that hand "delights in the way of the man whose steps *he* has made firm." It's all of God—and not of me. I can relax in the knowledge that he cares, that he loves me in spite of what I am. In fact, I'm important to God—important enough that he sent his only Son to die for me that my steps might be "ordered"!

July

10

For this God is our God for ever and ever: he will be our guide even unto death.

Psalm 48:14

MANY OF THE VERSES quoted in this book speak directly of God's guidance, but none more specifically and forcefully than this one. The psalmist's choice of language here implies *fact* and *promise*, both of which are wonderful to contemplate. When God declares something as a fact, it is ours to accept it and rest upon it. When God gives us a promise, it is ours to claim it and confidently expect its fulfillment.

Many of us have been actively *seeking* God when we should have been *resting* in his promises and confident of our place in his plan. In Isaiah 41:10 he says, "I am thy God." With the psalmist we should say, "This God is our God for ever and ever." Realizing that God is *our* God allows us to fully trust him as our Guide. And a further truth expressed in this verse probably doesn't strike most young people: "He will be our guide even unto death." The psalmist David wrote, "Yea, though I walk through the valley of the shadow of death, I will fear no evil: for thou art with me . . ." (Ps. 23:4), and this realization blesses me in what I assume is the latter half of my life: my Lord and I will walk *through* the valley, not merely up to it. I like the way the New English Bible translates today's verse: "he shall be our guide eternally." Isn't that neat?

11

To give knowledge of salvation unto his people by the remission of their sins . . . to guide our feet into the way of peace.

Luke 1:77, 79

GOD'S GUIDANCE is the privilege of the believer in Jesus Christ, and of him alone. By believer, I do not mean the one who merely has an orthodox faith about Jesus Christ, but one who has that living faith in Jesus Christ which leads him to receive Jesus Christ as Lord and Savior, and to surrender his life to his service and control.

But there is another side to this coin. If God's guidance is a fact of life, so is his surveillance. There is nothing that anyone does in any part of the universe, there is not one slightest act, good or evil, that God does not keep watch upon. We all do well to keep that solemn fact in mind day and night, and to remember that we cannot hide one thing we do from God. This is the other side of guidance!

R. A. TORREY

He led them on safely, so that they feared not: but the sea **12**
overwhelmed their enemies.

Psalm 78:53

PSALM 78 is a psalm which speaks throughout of God's guidance of his people, tracing that leading throughout Israel's history. Here in verse 53 the writer reminds his readers of how the Lord led his people safely out of Egypt. Our God is our Guide! And he leads us in the way we should go. But before we are ready to consider the "way," we must be sure as to the destination. "Where am I going?" is the first question. Then comes the inquiry as to the road we are taking. Our destination is not a place merely, but a Person: "Christ also hath once suffered for sins, the just for the unjust, that he might *bring us to God*" (1 Pet. 3:18). The right way is the way that leads to God. He brings us now into God's presence. We have access through him into the Holiest, and he will go on to present us "faultless before the presence of his glory with exceeding joy" (Jude 24). Psalm 107:7 says, "He led them straight to safety and a place to live" (LB).

This perpetual presence of Christ as the Guide of his people is a great and blessed reality: *He led them.* Though pardoned and redeemed, inspirited and set free, they are not able to guide themselves. The people are as helpless in the journey as they were in the "horrible pit" (Ps. 40:2): "He brought me up also out of a horrible pit, out of the miry clay, and set my feet upon a rock, and established my goings." As David said in Psalm 56:13, "You have saved me from death and my feet from slipping, so that I can walk before the Lord in the land of the living" (LB).

He led them forth by the right way, that they might go to a city of **13**
habitation.

Psalm 107:7

IN THIS BOOK we are sharing guidelines for life's journey. Nothing is more important at the beginning of a trip than a right start. And to be in "the right way" requires that we follow the right Guide: "He led them forth." Yet when a person has fallen into a deep hole, it is not safe *leading* he needs, but complete deliverance out of that pit! In Psalm 40:1–2, David says, "I waited patiently for the Lord; and he inclined unto me, and heard my cry. He brought me up also out of an horrible pit, out of the miry clay, and set my feet upon a rock, and established my goings." This is what you and I need!

The reason we fail to know or to follow the Guide is that we allow too great a distance to come between us. This is a perfect time to draw close to our Guide. His guidance is not only safe, but it is happy, for it is fellowship with him. "The right way" spoken of here by the psalmist is not a generalized route—it is the right way for *me*. I could never find it on my own, nor continue in it apart from my Guide. With the psalmist I pray, "Teach me thy way, O Lord."

14

And the Lord shall guide thee continually. . . . My presence shall go with thee, and I will give thee rest.

Isaiah 58:11; Exodus 33:14

THE GUIDANCE OF GOD is essential if we are to successfully reach our destination. Just as we do not set out on a journey (if we are wise) to a strange land without a road map, we should not start on the "trip of life" without a map—the Word of God. But anyone going into unknown territory would be even wiser to hire a guide who was familiar with the area, in addition to the map. God is ready to guide you. Scores, even hundreds of times, he stated that willingness to the children of Israel. Our passages for meditation today chronicle just two of those promises. The Psalms, in particular, are full of references to his guidance and his presence with his children. As you move through the "unknown territory" of life, don't make the mistake of trying to go it on your own. Admit that you need guidance—and then go to the right Guide. He will guide you not just intermittently, but continually! And along with his constant guidance will come the "rest" of knowing you are on the right road, and the great privilege of his presence on your daily path!

15

And now, behold, I go bound in the spirit unto Jerusalem, not knowing the things that shall befall me there: save that the Holy Ghost witnesseth in every city, saying that bonds and afflictions abide me. But none of these things move me. . . . And finding disciples, we tarried there [Tyre] seven days: who said to Paul through the Spirit, that he should not go up to Jerusalem.

Acts 20:22–24; 21:4

THERE'S A STRANGE inconsistency here that intrigues me—and I just wonder if there isn't a lesson here for us. It appears in Acts 20 that the

Spirit is telling Paul to go to Jerusalem, but in Acts 21 he's telling certain disciples that Paul *shouldn't* go to Jerusalem. The New English Bible gives a marginal reading for Acts 20:22, "under an inner compulsion." I can't help but wonder whether Paul may have been running ahead of God here, in view of what later happened to him on this trip. And running ahead of God gets one's human best beyond the beam of God's light. Does it make any difference if one, out of unguided human ego, embarks upon a good work for God? In Paul's case, if I'm right in my interpretation of this verse, his single-minded journey ahead of God resulted in difficulties he might have otherwise avoided. Might it have been better if he, with David, had "waited patiently for the Lord" (Ps. 40:1)? Even if I'm wrong here (and I could well be), there's still a real lesson in *guidance* to be learned in this startling experience of the apostle Paul.

And when he putteth forth his own sheep, he goeth before them, and **16**
the sheep follow him: for they know his voice.

John 10:4

WE HERE in the United States have the wrong picture of a shepherd in our minds. The oriental shepherd, the shepherd of the Holy Land, did not simply sit on a hillside with his dog and "keep an eye" on the sheep in his care. No, in the Holy Land the shepherd *led* his sheep. He actually went before them in the difficult and dangerous places to make sure that the way was plain and safe. As John says in verse 3, "He calls his own sheep by name and leads them out" (RSV). As Theodore Cuyler brings out in his commentary on this verse: "Through every step in life the Shepherd offers to guide us if we will but hear his voice and follow him. He never promises us smooth paths but he does promise *safe* ones. When we obey his voice, we may often be called to toil and self-denial; but we shall never be called to go ahead of him, for 'he goeth before.'" With such a Guide, how can we go wrong?

The angel of God . . . went before the camp of Israel. **17**

Exodus 14:19

THIS ANGEL was revealed in the form of cloud and fire. It was wonderful guidance which God gave to his people in their marches. By day the pillar of cloud sheltered them, and then by night the same cloud was light. By day it was shelter, by night it was light. And always it was guidance. When they were to move, it lifted and went in advance, to lead them. When they were to halt and rest, it settled down, thus giving them the signal to pitch their tents.

This was miraculous guidance; but we have God's presence just as really, though without a visible pillar to lead us. God guides his people by his word, by his providence, by his Spirit. If we are willing to follow unquestioningly, we shall never be left long in perplexity as to the way we should take. Our guidance is given to us only as we will accept it and shape our course by it.

Nor is the guidance given in maps and charts, showing us miles and miles of the road; it is given only step by step as we go on.

J. R. MILLER

18

Order my steps in thy word: and let not any iniquity have dominion over me.

Psalm 119:133

WHEN I SEE these words they create a picture in my mind—or rather, several pictures. I sometimes see a flight of steps leading upward, and know that the best way to climb them is a step at a time, beginning at the bottom. I can't see all the way to the top, so I'd like to have a guide to show me the way. As a youth I might want to climb two or more steps at a time, but the idea of "order" does not seem to indicate that kind of haste. I also see a winding path through an otherwise pathless jungle—a path that might become faint farther on—so I need someone who's been there before to guide me. I believe both aspects of guidance are expressed in these pictures—guidance *upward* and guidance *through.* Isn't it great that the One who guides me, who "orders my steps," has been there before and knows the way? This verse in the New International Version has a slightly different flavor that I like: "Direct my footsteps according to your word; let no sin rule over me." There's a connection here between the way I live and the kind of guidance I can expect. Let me live in the Word!

19

Order my steps in thy word. . . .

Psalm 119:133

BURIED IN THE HEART of the longest psalm is this short but powerful phrase of only six words, but what worlds of wisdom they contain. If only we modern-day Christians would look to our God in simple faith and pray these words! R. A. Torrey, a deeply perceptive preacher from another generation, has this to say: "A very large share of our perplexity about the will of God stems from the fact that we are troubled because God has not shown us what he wants us to do next year, or, it may be, next month. All we need is God's guidance for today. Follow on, step by step, as he leads you, and the way will open as you go." How applicable this admonition is to young people today. Much is said and written about finding or living in "the will of God," but practical help in discovering that will is sometimes lacking. The secret of spiritual guidance lies in the Word of God—read and applied to your life and mine.

I will instruct thee and teach thee in the way which thou shalt go: I will guide thee with mine eye.

Psalm 32:8

20

READING THIS PASSAGE in the King James Version, one is impressed with the majestic cadence of these sentences but puzzled by the real meaning of "I will guide thee with mine eye." Here is the way the RSV renders it: "I will counsel you with my eye upon you." Sounds a little more contemporary, doesn't it? Looking at some of David's other references to God's guiding activity in the Christian's life opens up other facets of this exciting truth:

"Good and upright is the Lord; therefore he instructs sinners in the way" (Ps. 25:8, RSV).

"Behold, the eye of the Lord is on those who fear him, on those who hope in his steadfast love" (Ps. 33:18, RSV).

In this complex and troubled world, we desperately need guidance—guidance that includes "counsel." In fact, human counselors have never been busier than they are today—and more subject to error when they ignore the spiritual dimension. What greater Guide and Counselor could we ask for than God himself, who over and over in his Word expresses his willingness to guide and care for his children? Guidance includes the concept of trust, for a guide will do us no good if we do not take him at his word and follow him unquestioningly. Thomas Benton Brooks points out: "We trust as we love, and where we love. If we love Christ much, surely we will trust him much."

Where is your trust today? If it is in the divine Guide, you will enjoy divine guidance!

July

21

Thy word is a lamp unto my feet, and a light unto my path.

Psalm 119:105

A LOCAL COMMUTER AIRLINE has the slogan, "Your first step to everywhere." In a sense this is what the psalmist is telling us here. From our meditation on the Word we don't necessarily gain guidance for next month or next year, but we do for today and sometimes for tomorrow. Our heavenly Father through his Word guides us a step at a time. He reveals our immediate needs so that we know how "to pray as we ought." As we take that first step, he reveals his plan a step or a day at a time. His Word is a lamp that lights our immediate path. In Texas in some areas during the heat of summer, it is not too wise to walk about in the dark because snakes often like to lie on the warm pavement. But one need not be afraid to walk in the night if he has a good flashlight to illuminate his immediate path. This is the way we should use the light of God's Word—a step at a time. He will lead us through this life personally!

22

They . . . were forbidden of the Holy Ghost to preach the word in Asia . . . They assayed to go into Bithynia: but the Spirit suffered them not . . . A vision appeared to Paul . . . a man . . . saying, Come over into Macedonia, and help us.

Acts 16:6, 7, 9

WHENEVER YOU ARE DOUBTFUL as to your course, submit your judgment absolutely to the Spirit of God, and ask Him to shut against you every door but the right one. In the meanwhile continue along the path which you already have been treading. His way lies in front of you; pursue it. Expect to have as clear a door out as you had in; and if there is no indication to the contrary, consider that you are on the track of God's will. The Spirit of God awaits to be to you, O pilgrim, what He was to Paul. Only be careful to obey His least prohibitions, and if there are none go forward with a happy heart. When doors are shut right and left, an open road is sure to lead to Troas. There Luke awaits, and visions will point the way where vast opportunities stand open, and faithful friends are waiting.

F. B. MEYER

O God, thou art my God; early will I seek thee.

Psalm 63:1

23

DAVID IS SUCCINCTLY STATING a tremendous spiritual principle here—
a secret of spiritual strength for daily living and effectiveness in the all-
important pursuit of prayer. If one were to single out one common
denominator in the lives of great people of God, that single ingredient
would be a strong and effective prayer life. Says S. D. Gordon, "When a
man has a heart-to-heart talk alone with God daily, he's pretty apt to talk
with both life and lip in the crowd for God. Keep the inner heart-touch
with God fresh, and the outer touches are sure to be true and winsome.
The outer hinges on the inner. Your prayer contacts control your
contact with your fellows and with commonplace things. The knees
decide the language of the lips." It would appear that David sought his
Lord early in the morning. There's no better way to start the day—and
no better Person to walk with!

*Thus saith the Lord God, I will yet for this be inquired of by the house
of Israel, to do it for them.*

Ezekiel 36:37

24

THE NIV HAS HERE, "This is what the Sovereign Lord says: Once again I
will yield to . . . the house of Israel." That's our Lord's attitude toward
our heartfelt prayers. Once again it shows the connection between
promise and prayer—the promise that God gives, and the prayer that he
honors. It is his will that we should "ask" if we are going to "receive." I
don't think that he holds back simply that we might plead more for his
blessings. No, I think we "plead in prayer" so that we won't look on his
blessings as common things and receive them lightly, as a matter of
course. I could say I don't think many young Christians know what it
means to "plead in prayer"—but I'm afraid the condemnation must be
much broader than that. Most Christians do not know how to really
pray. Ezekiel is giving us the key here—we must care enough to *plead*.
Prayer is more than a privilege—it's a discipline!

I desire then that in every place the men should pray. . . .

1 Timothy 2:8, RSV

25

IN EPHESIANS 6:17 Paul calls the Word of God "the sword of the
Spirit," and in the same "Christian soldier" passage, he urges the use of

prayer as a spiritual weapon (see v. 18). This is one aspect of prayer not often called to our attention. Indeed, we are usually counseled to leave the battlefield to do our praying. That's not what Paul is telling Timothy here. G. Campbell Morgan puts it rather succinctly when he says: "When men retire from the conflict to pray, they cut the nerves of prayer. Men only pray with prevailing power who do so amid the sobs and sighing of the race." All of us, young and old alike, need to sharpen our prayer weapons and, with Paul, "pray at all times in the Spirit." Make prayer your partner in every walk of life—and discover the greatness of God's power unleashed in your life.

26 *Lord, teach us to pray. . . .*

Luke 11:1

MARTIN LUTHER once said, "The fewer the words, the better the prayer." I think Jesus would have endorsed that, for that model prayer which we call the Lord's Prayer has in it only sixty-six words in Matthew's version, and just fifty-eight in Luke's rendering. Yet this is the pattern prayer our Lord left to guide us into the realm of proper prayer. It is not our many or beautiful words that win us a hearing with our heavenly Father, as Jesus pointed out in Matthew 6:7: "Use not vain repetitions, as the heathen do: for they think that they shall be heard for their much speaking." What a freeing experience it is to know that my heavenly Father isn't impressed by my choice of words, or the number of them. He "looketh on the heart" (1 Sam. 16:7). He is mainly interested in my motivation for prayer, my attitude of heart. Some of the most effective prayers recorded in the Bible have been but a few short words: from the father of the demon-possessed boy, "Lord, I believe; help thou mine unbelief" (Mark 9:24); the Philippian jailer, "What must I do to be saved?" (Acts 16:30); the disciples in the storm, "Lord, save us" (Matt. 8:25). Lord, teach me to pray sincerely and concisely, as you did!

27 *For my thoughts are not your thoughts, neither are your ways my ways, saith the Lord.*

Isaiah 55:8

GOD SOMETIMES ANSWERS our prayers in surprising and unexpected ways. In an old book on prayer, James H. McConkey describes an experience he had one summer vacationing at one of the Great Lakes. He fell ill, and found that the only thing he could do to take advantage of his location was sailing. He was too weak for any other recreation. One day he was sailing in the bay when the wind suddenly died. With no movement of air, the boat remained motionless, and the hot summer sun beat down on him. He prayed that the Lord would send a breeze to push him back to shore. But no wind arose, and his faith was really tested. Suddenly he noticed another boat bearing down on him. An old fisherman, correctly assessing the situation, was coming out to tow him back to shore.

Mr. McConkey saw an important lesson in this—one that all God's children need to learn. Though he apparently had denied *the words* of Mr. McConkey's prayer, God answered the petition in his *own way*. The sick man was rescued, albeit not in the way he had asked.

This is reminiscent of another such experience many centuries ago. Monica, mother of St. Augustine, prayed for the conversion of her son, asking that he not go to Rome where so many temptations lay. But God allowed the profligate young man to go to that wicked city, and there in Rome God met him in a marvelous way. God's ways, indeed, are not our ways. "He that is perfect in knowledge is with thee" (Job 36:4).

Hear my cry, O God; attend unto my prayer. From the end of the earth will I cry unto thee, when my heart is overwhelmed: lead me to the rock that is higher than I.

28

Psalm 61:1–2

DR. E. LEE PHILLIPS has said, "We pray no larger than our trust in God, no deeper than our walk with the Savior." As I read the opening words of David's prayer in Psalm 61, I'm convinced that David, had he lived in New Testament days, would have echoed Dr. Phillips's sentiments. How true it is. The character of our prayer life is governed by our daily walk with Jesus. If our walk is close with him, then our talk with him in prayer will be warm and intimate, as is the conversation of very dear friends. But David is emphasizing another facet of the truth here; we limit God's power in our lives that can be unleashed by prayer. How do we limit it? By our small faith. Our prayers rise no higher than our faith, in a sense. Expect great things from God, and you will experience them. In fact, Paul says, "Now glory be to God who by his mighty power at work within us is able to do far more than we would

July

ever dare to ask or even dream of—infinitely beyond our highest prayers, desires, thoughts, or hopes" (Eph. 3:20, LB). Prayer is infinitely more than words, as this verse makes clear. Prayer includes our dreams, our desires, our thoughts and hopes. Our inner life controls and motivates our prayer life. With David I cry to God, "Lead me to the rock that is higher than I!" That's Jesus for me.

---

29 *Because he hath inclined his ear unto me, therefore will I call upon him as long as I live.*

Psalm 116:2

A PRAYER does not have to be eloquent or contain the language and terms of a theologian. When you made your decision for Christ, you were given the privilege of addressing God as Father. You pray to him as a child talking to his loving and gracious father. In the beginning you may not be fluent, but it's important to begin. . . .

When Paul said we should pray without "ceasing," he chose a term used in his day to describe a persistent cough. Off and on, throughout our day we should be turning quickly to God to praise and thank him, and to ask for his help. Prayers should be specific. God is interested in everything you do and nothing is too great or too insignificant to share with him.

BILLY GRAHAM

Quoted from *How to Be Born Again* (Waco, TX: Word Books, 1977).

---

30 *The Lord is nigh unto all them that call upon him, to all that call upon him in truth. He will fulfil the desire of them that fear him: he also will hear their cry, and will save them.*

Psalm 145:18–19

IN THIS PSALM David is praising God for his ability and willingness to answer the prayers of his people. Helen Smith Shoemaker has this to say on the subject: "Prayer is a force as vital as electricity, a force that can be utilized only by those who love and trust God, and who let the stream of their life purpose run along in the stream of his great will. When we put the drop of our tiny will into the stream of his deathless purpose, we may ask anything and it shall be done for us. When we abide in Christ, our tiny will becomes an atom in his almighty will, and in his name we speak spiritual continents into being." If we really believed in the power of our prayers to unleash the might of the infinite God, I wonder if our practice of prayer would be different? In *The Way to Power and Poise* Dr. E. Stanley Jones wrote, "In prayer you align yourself to the purpose and power of God and he is able to do things through you that he couldn't do otherwise. . . . For this is an open universe, where some things are left open, contingent upon our doing them. If we do not do them, they will never be done. So God has left certain things open to prayer—things which will never be done otherwise."

Pray without ceasing. **31**

1 Thessalonians 5:17

IN THE FIELD of religious publishing there seems to be no end to the books being written on the subject of prayer. One would think that nothing new or earth-shaking could be said about prayer after all this time—but still new insights (or old insights in new dress) are continually coming to the forefront. One thing hasn't changed, however, and that is the nature of prayer. G. Campbell Morgan said it well when he pointed out: "Prayer is the voice of man in his need speaking to God; prophecy is the voice of God in His power speaking to man." Only in Jesus were these two gifts combined in a unique fashion. As very man he sought God's help on a daily basis, providing a striking example of what it means to walk by prayer; as God's spokesman and representative, he delivered a vital message to his generation. Indeed, Jesus himself is our best example of what it means to "pray without ceasing."

August

Learning from God

1

When you pray, go into your room and shut the door and pray to your Father who is in secret; and your Father who sees in secret will reward you.

Matthew 6:6, RSV

THERE IS NO POWER like prayer. Dr. Alexis Carrel once said, "The most powerful form of energy one can generate is prayer. Prayer is a force as real as terrestrial gravity. Prayer like radium is a luminous and self-generating form of energy." There is a power greater than the atom locked up in the human heart. That power can control the atom. It is spiritual power and is released through prayer. We work, we think, we push, we shove. These are the commonly accepted ways of getting ahead. Prayer is thought of as something special, to be used at funerals, weddings, and baptisms, and made by the pastor in the pulpit. It is something special for special days . . . saved for the sanctuary. The elimination of prayer from man's common daily experience is tragic. It compels us to bear the burdens of life alone. . . . Prayer drives us beyond ourselves.

T. CECIL MYERS

Quoted from *You Can Be More Than You Are* (Waco, TX: Word Books, 1976), pp. 22, 30.

2

Call to me and I will answer you and tell you great and unsearchable things you do not know.

Jeremiah 33:3, NIV

TOO MANY OF US have a misconception concerning prayer. We think of it as one-way communication—our prayers going up to God. We forget that prayer is two-way communication. Not only do we speak to God in prayer, but he answers us if we are in real contact with him. The North Carolina *Christian Advocate* puts prayer in perspective for us: "The most important thing in any prayer is not what we say to God, but what God says to us. We are apt to pray and then hurry away without giving God a chance to answer." Hurry and heedless haste are signs of the day in which we live—and unfortunately this characterizes our prayer lives too. The gospel song says, "Take time to pray." And some of that time we should remain silent so that God can communicate with us, and we'll hear even when he whispers.

But we will give ourselves continually to prayer.

3

Acts 6:4

THE MIGHTY MEN of prayer in the Bible, and the mighty men of prayer throughout all ages of the church's history have been men who were much given to thanksgiving and praise. David was a mighty man of prayer, and how his Psalms resound with thanksgiving and praise! The apostles were mighty men of prayer; of them we read that "they were continually in the temple, praising and blessing God." Paul was a mighty man of prayer, and how often in his Epistles he bursts out in definite thanksgiving to God, for definite blessings and definite answers to prayer.

Jesus, too, was a man of prayer. The words *prayer* and *pray* are used at least twenty-five times in connection with Jesus, and there are many instances in which the fact of his praying is implied, where the actual words do not occur. The life of Christ had many marked characteristics, but nothing is more marked than his prayerfulness. His was a life of work and prayer—and so should ours be.

R. A. TORREY

Likewise the Spirit also helpeth our infirmities: for we know not what we should pray for as we ought: but the Spirit itself maketh intercession for us with groanings which cannot be uttered.

4

Romans 8:26

THE DEEPEST OF ALL SOURCES of spiritual power is prayer; and the greatest personal hindrance to it is the lack of prayer. I *know* that when I send up my aerial it catches power, thoughts, direction (according as God sees my need) from on high. I need longer times for prayer, especially in the early morning. I need to cultivate awareness of "the presence of God" at all times. But most particularly, I need the momentary, frequent prayer that simply calls out to Him a hundred, a thousand times a day for light, for power, for understanding, for guidance. Sometimes it is not a request, just a "Lord, I love You," or "God, use me now." I have never got so very far in achieving a continuous mystical sense of God's Presence, but I have learned a little about asking for working directions from Him and receiving them when and as they are really needed. Frequently there is no great sense of God at the time, nor even of guidance nor power. But I try to keep the situation before Him, lifting it or the person to Him again and again. And I find that, when the time comes to act, guidance is there—I often do better than I deserve, or could possibly do without frequent short prayers. One can be clear out of the stream one minute, and back in it the next, because he is honest and asks God's forgiveness and calls on Him to be restored and put in touch again. Without prayer, lots of it, carried on more and more of the time, we can neither get into the stream of power nor stay there. None of us stays there all the time; but there can be a growth in the amount of time when we are available to God. Prayer is the principle secret.

SAM SHOEMAKER

5   *I will therefore that men pray every where, lifting up holy hands, without wrath and doubting.*

1 Timothy 2:8

THIS WORD from the apostle Paul to his son in the faith, Timothy, opens up more than one channel of thought for me. Paul begins the chapter by telling Timothy, "I exhort therefore, that, first of all, supplications, prayers, intercessions, and giving of thanks, be made for all men" (2:1). All of these words describe aspects of prayer—and Paul was definitely pro-prayer! In fact, his lifestyle was permeated by prayer. He would have agreed with Thomas Brooks who wrote: "God hears no more than the heart speaks; and if the heart be dumb, God will certainly be deaf." And then, Paul says we are to pray "every where," echoing the psalmist who wrote, "Lift up your hands in the sanctuary" (134:2), but also intending that wherever the Christian goes he is to be in a spirit of prayer. That's what it means to "pray every where." May our God guide us into this kind of a relationship with him and with others!

Moreover as for me, God forbid that I should sin against the Lord in ceasing to pray for you: but I will teach you the good and the right way.

6

1 Samuel 12:23

WE SIN AGAINST OUR FRIEND when we do not pray for him. Of all the ways of doing good and showing kindness to others, prayer is the best. Sometimes we catch ourselves saying to one who is in sore trouble: "I am sorry I cannot do anything to help you; I can only pray for you." But if we really pray for him, we do the very best that we could possibly do. God knows better how to help him than we do. Ofttimes the help we would give would only harm him. We would lift away burdens he would better carry longer. We would make easy the path which would better be left rough. We are always in danger of hindering God's work in a man's life when we come in with our help. The best we can do is to pray for him.

J. R. MILLER

Because he hath inclined his ear unto me, therefore will I call upon him as long as I live.

7

Psalm 116:2

T. CECIL MYERS tells how at fourteen he learned the definition of prayer. His Sunday school teacher, Bob, took the class to hear Toyohiko Kagawa, the Japanese Christian and social reformer: "I shall never forget how Kagawa looked. He was very short of stature, wore very thick glasses, but he spoke in a positive way. When he had finished Bob thought we ought to meet him, so he took us backstage and we all shook hands. Several people were asking him questions, and one was simply, 'What is prayer?' This great man, honored by his own nation, revered by Christians everywhere, said simply, 'Prayer is surrender.' I'll never forget that simple, short definition of prayer. When we think of surrender we think of a yellow streak right up the back, or cowardice. But in this case,

August

surrender means the yielding of one's spirit to the spirit of God to cooperate with him in accomplishing his will for our lives. It is like the yielding of the flower to sun, rain, soil for growth and beauty, the yielding of the mind of the student to the process of education for learning, the yielding of the light bulb to the dynamo for brilliance. It is the yielding up of my spirit to the love and power of God for the strength I need for living every day."

Quoted from *You Can Be More Than You Are* (Waco, TX: Word Books, 1976), p. 26.

8
Wherewithal shall a young man cleanse his way? by taking heed thereto according to thy word.

Psalm 119:9

TO FALL IN LOVE with a good book is one of the greatest events that can befall us. It is to have a new influence pouring itself into our life, a new teacher to inspire and refine us, a new friend to be by our side always, who, when life grows narrow and weary, will take us into his wider and calmer and higher world. Whether it be biography, introducing us to some humble life made great by duty done; or history, opening new vistas into the movements and destinies of nations that have passed away; or poetry, making music of all the common things around us, and filling the fields and the skies and the works of the city and cottage with eternal meanings—whether it be these, or story-books, or religious books, or science, no one can become the friend even of one good book without being made wiser and better.

HENRY DRUMMOND

WHAT BOOK better fulfills Mr. Drummond's criteria than the Bible itself? Indeed it is the Book of books and stands alone in its influence upon mankind.

9
For whatsoever things were written aforetime were written for our learning, that we through patience and comfort of the scriptures might have hope.

Romans 15:4

LIFE is for learners! And those who never stop learning. That's the kind of person I'd like to be. In fact, in our fast-moving modern day, one must go on learning through all of life if he is to cope with the complexities of the twentieth century—especially these last two decades of it. But Paul is talking about much more than purely secular learning here, although what he says is applicable to all knowledge. A thorough familiarity with the scriptures equips the Christian to handle the labyrinth of life today, just as certainly as it met the needs of people in Paul's day. We think our problems are peculiar to our own day—but the early Christians were confronted with just as perplexing a panorama as we are. And God met their need. In fact, they were able to handle situations and problems even more complex (for them) than ours. Through the Scriptures, Paul says, we have hope—what a reassuring promise. What a guideline for living!

I will meditate on thy precepts, and fix my eyes on thy ways. I will delight in thy statutes; I will not forget thy word. . . . Thy testimonies are my delight, they are my counselors.

10

Psalm 119:15–16, 24, RSV

THE NEW INTERNATIONAL VERSION translates the latter part of verse 16, "I will not *neglect* your word." I'm afraid that's exactly our problem in this modern day, in spite of the fact that we might spend time in the Word even daily with a book such as this. Oswald Chambers has perceptively pointed out the subtle danger we are in: "The reasons some of us are not healthy spiritually is because we don't use the Bible as the Word of God but only as a textbook." He has also succinctly said, "Beware of reasoning about God's Word—obey it!" We sometimes get so hung up on the intellectual meaning or overtones of a passage that we completely miss its impact upon the heart, the inner core of our beings. That's what the psalmist was saying when he urged us to "delight" in the Word, to let it wash over our hearts and seep down into our lives in such a way that our very beings might be flooded by the blessed Presence of the Holy Spirit. If more of us Christians lived lives like that, our impact on the world around us would certainly be greater!

The unfolding of thy words gives light; it imparts understanding to the simple.

11

Psalm 119:130, RSV

AN ANONYMOUS WRITER has said, "The Bible is the Book by which you may know certainly the future; it is the only Book that satisfactorily answers the questions: Where did I come from? Why am I here? Where am I going?" These along with "Who am I?" are indeed the big, basic questions of life. In a sense, the psalmist was acknowledging the truth of this statement when he prayed the words of today's verse. Are you looking for answers to the puzzling questions of life? Do you have reservations as to your own independent ability to cope with the thorny problems? Be thankful that God's Book is there to answer your needs, to give "understanding to the simple." Be thankful, too, that God himself stands ready to enlighten you through his Word and his presence in your life.

12

. . . how from childhood you have been acquainted with the sacred writings which are able to instruct you for salvation through faith in Christ Jesus.

2 Timothy 3:15, RSV

JOSEPH COOK asks, "Do you know a book that you are willing to put under your head for a pillow when you are dying? Very well; that is the book you want to study when you are living. There is only one such book in the world." Is there any other book than the Bible that meets this stringent criterion? Even books *about* the Bible that glorify and expound it as the veritable Word of God do not reach its timelessness. I have been involved in religious book publishing for thirty years and have seen many good books come and go. Indeed, only a handful of books even outlive their authors. Yet the Bible lives on and achieves new heights of impact on each succeeding generation. Why? Because *its* Author is still living! God is alive and well in the midst of a wicked and perverse world. I'm glad I've had the "Sacred Writings" since my childhood. They are even more precious to me now!

13

For ever, O Lord, thy word is settled in heaven.

Psalm 119:89

THE UTTERANCES of Jesus Christ are not outgrown; they are as precious today, as when they were first spoken. They are as perfectly applicable to present-day needs as the needs of that day. They contain the solutions to all modern individual and social problems; they have perpetual youth. There is not one single point at which the teachings of Jesus Christ have been outgrown or become antiquated. The human mind has been expanding for nearly twenty centuries since Jesus Christ spoke here on earth, but it has not outgrown Him. Words that can endure twenty centuries of growth and still prove as thoroughly adequate to meet the needs of the race and each member of it as when first given, will stand for ever.

R. A. TORREY

. . . how from infancy you have known the holy Scriptures, which are **14**
able to make you wise for salvation through faith in Christ Jesus.
2 Timothy 3:15, NIV

I AM NOT a bibliolator—by that I mean I do not worship the Bible. At the same time I must confess a great attitude of reverence toward it. With James McClure I can say, "No word or words of man can ever for all time confine the meaning of the Bible, for the Bible is a living book, and therefore, an ever-enlarging book." But there is another side to this whole matter. If my reverence for the Word makes that Word impenetrable by me, if I'm afraid to study it and live by it because it is so great and above my comprehension, then I have an improper attitude of reverence. Rather, with Daniel Webster, I can confidently say: "I believe the Bible is to be understood and received in the plain and obvious meaning of its passages; since I cannot persuade myself that a book intended for the instruction and conversion of the whole world, should cover its true meaning in such mystery and doubt, that none but critics and philosophers can discover it." No, the genius of this grand Book is that it is for the marketplace, not the ivory tower!

Thy words were found, and I ate them, and thy words became to me a **15**
joy and the delight of my heart.
Jeremiah 15:16, RSV

THE WORD OF GOD is a constant and continuing source of joy for the Christian. I don't think I've ever met a joyless Christian who was regularly employed in searching the Scriptures. The result of such searching is to see beyond the words the One who inspired them. Of all the habits the Christian can cultivate, this is one of the most blessed and profitable. Some books are exhausting and exhaustible. The Bible is the only Book that rewards the student with increasing insight as he allows the Word of God to flow through and cleanse him. Indeed, it is the only Book that can cleanse and purify the life of its reader. Other books can inform, but only the Scriptures can transform, infill, and inspire. Are you taking advantage of this "divine diet"?

16

And I will pray the Father, and he shall give you another Comforter, that he may abide with you forever.

John 14:16

ONE OF THE MOST precious thoughts contained in the whole Word of God, for this present dispensation, is that during the absence of our Lord, until that glad day when he shall come again, another Person just as divine as he, just as loving and tender and strong to help, is by my side and dwells in my heart every moment, to commune with me, and to help me in every emergency that can possibly arise.

I know of no thought better calculated to put one in the dust and keep one in the dust than the great biblical truth of the Holy Spirit as a Divine Person coming to take up his dwelling in our hearts, to take possession of our life and use us as he, in his infinite wisdom, sees fit to do.

R. A. TORREY

17

Religion that God our Father accepts as pure and faultless is this: to look after orphans and widows in their distress and to keep oneself from being polluted by the world.

James 1:27, NIV

OUR WORLD is laboring under a misconception. Religion is not something you *do*—it is something you *are*. The real Christian is concerned for the whole man. Martin Luther King, Jr. said: "Any religion that professes to be concerned with the souls of men and is not concerned with the slums that damn them, the economic conditions that strangle them, and the social conditions that cripple them, is a dry-as-dust religion." The only problem with this statement is that he had only one type of people in mind. James would have us be concerned for *all* those downtrodden and less fortunate than we. The person who sets aside Sunday to worship the Lord, but doesn't let that worshipful spirit permeate the rest of his week is not living the Christian life in its ultimate dimension. Charles Kingsley once said, "What I want is, not to possess religion but to have a religion that shall possess me." That's it exactly. If I'm not so full of the Holy Spirit that my life overflows with that Spirit, there's something lacking. The original Martin Luther, whose grasp of the big picture was a bit firmer than was Martin Luther King's, said, "The heart of religion lies in its personal pronouns." True religion is a relationship—between me and my Savior, first of all, but also between me and those who need to experience his love as shed abroad in me, his witness.

I say also unto thee, That thou art Peter, and upon this rock I will build my church; and the gates of hell shall not prevail against it.
Matthew 16:18

18

IN THESE POWERFUL WORDS our Lord set forth his will for his church. Unfortunately, in too many instances, we equate the church with a building or a program as we know it—and forget that the church is an organism, not an organization; it is a Person and a power. Because we Christians too often fail to realize and recognize the true nature of the body of Christ, the church, we fail to be the power in the world we should be. In *The Secret of Effective Prayer* Helen Smith Shoemaker says, "If the Christian Church were a pillar of fire leading the peoples of the world, instead of an ambulance corps bringing up the rear as it so often seems to be, communism probably would never have been born." She could be right. Communism has come into our world to fill a vacuum that would never have existed if we in the church had completely fulfilled our mission outside the walls of the church, where the action is! Ernest Southcott in *Christian Herald* said, "The holiest moment of the church service is the moment when God's people—strengthened by preaching and sacrament—go out of the church door into the world *to be the Church*. We don't *go* to church; we *are* the Church."

August

19

Now when they saw the boldness of Peter and John, and perceived that they were uneducated, common men, they wondered; and they recognized that they had been with Jesus.

Acts 4:13, RSV

THIS IS A REMARKABLE VERSE that speaks to our needs as Christians today. I particularly like the way the *Living Bible* renders it: "When the Council saw the boldness of Peter and John, and could see that they were obviously uneducated non-professionals, they were amazed and realized what being with Jesus had done for them!" In the eyes of those around them, Peter and John were unschooled in theology and untrained in a professional or scholarly capacity. The "Council" consisted of the Sanhedrin, chief priests, elders, and scribes—the Establishment, as it were. Because of their wisdom and boldness, and Peter's remarkably well-argued and logical defense of the Christian faith before the Sanhedrin, they "marvelled" ("were amazed," LB; "wondered," RSV) and recognized that they had been with Jesus. Luke explains the phenomenal power of the apostles in Acts 4:31, "When they had prayed, the place in which they were gathered together was shaken; and they were all filled with the Holy Spirit and spoke the word of God with boldness" (RSV). Paul tells us what had happened: "God chose what is foolish in the world to shame the wise, God chose what is weak in the world to shame the strong" (1 Cor. 1:27, RSV). The secret strength of the apostles lay in their relationship to Christ; their astonishing wisdom came from the Holy Spirit who filled and controlled them. This same strength and wisdom is available to you from the same Source. As Richard Ellsworth Day says, "life's superlative endowment in a servant of God is an adequate experience of Christ."

20

As the body is one, and hath many members, and all the members of that one body, being many, are one body: so also is Christ.

1 Corinthians 12:12

WHEN WE HAVE SEEN the meaning of substitution (Christ *for* me), we have to go on and learn the meaning of union (I in Christ and Christ in me). We have to understand what this mystical union is in relation to ourselves individually, and in relation to believers collectively. Christ "is the head of the body, the church" (Col. 1:18). There can be only one head, but there are many members. Each member recognizes that head, and is under the control of that head. There is but one Center of wisdom and of will, and but one Source of life and power. That Center and that Source is Christ. But Christ is not only the name that belongs to the head—the man Christ Jesus. It is the name that belongs also to the members. All believers are included in that name. As the natural human body is one, so "also is Christ," i.e., the mystical body, of which the risen Lord is the head. A true understanding of our relationship to him as the head will bring us to a right knowledge of our relation to the members.

EVAN H. HOPKINS

Grieve not the Holy Spirit of God, whereby ye are sealed unto the day of redemption.

21

Ephesians 4:30

THIS IS ONE of the many passages of Scripture which point to the distinct personality of the Holy Spirit. He is not a mere quality in the divine nature, an emanation from God; he is a person. An influence may be checked, but not "grieved." None can be grieved but one who has understanding, and will, and affections. All these are asserted of the Spirit of God. That which proves the Father and the Son to be distinct persons is equally true of the Holy Spirit. The Holy Spirit is said to rule in and over the Church, to choose and appoint overseers, to discern and judge all things; to convince, to comfort, and to strengthen. It was as a person our Lord spoke of him: "I will send *him* unto you." We should mark the particular title that belongs to him—"the *Holy* Spirit of God." As such he comes to dwell in our hearts. It is by virtue of his presence that the temple in which he dwells is also holy. "Ye are the temple of God. . . . Your body is the temple of the Holy Ghost" (1 Cor. 3:16; 6:19).

EVAN H. HOPKINS

But we have the mind of Christ.

22

1 Corinthians 2:16

THE HIGHEST FORM of mastery in this world is self-mastery. This is the complete life, a life manifesting love, joy, peace, longsuffering, kindness, goodness, faith, meekness. These things are the *"fruit* of the Spirit,"* not fruits of the Spirit; they are the many delicious flavors of the one fruit. Wherever the Holy Spirit is given control, not some, but all of these will be seen to flourish.

The same Spirit by which Jesus was begotten is at our disposal for us to be begotten of him. The same Spirit by which Jesus Christ offered himself without spot to God is at our disposal for us to offer ourselves without spot, the same Spirit by which Jesus was anointed for service is at our disposal for us to be anointed for service, and so on through every phase of Christian experience.

R. A. TORREY

23

For as many as are led by the Spirit of God, they are the sons of God.

Romans 8:14

NOT MERELY does the Holy Spirit give us power to live a holy life, but he takes us, as it were, by the hand and leads us into that life. Our whole part is simply to surrender ourselves utterly to him to lead and mold us. Those who do this are not merely God's offspring (which all men are), they are *sons* of God.

The Holy Spirit was sent by the Father into this world to be to the disciples of our Lord in this present dispensation, just what Jesus Christ had been to his disciples during the days of his personal companionship with them on earth. Is he that to you? Do you know the communion of the Holy Spirit? "For he dwelleth with you, and shall be in you" (John 14:17).

R. A. TORREY

24

. . . To be spiritually minded is life and peace.

Romans 8:6

WHAT A GLORIOUS PROMISE! The Bible is a Book of promises, and this is one of the most striking and all-pervading. Earthly life is an entity given to all of us by God at our birth, so Paul must be talking about something different and deeper when he tells us "to be spiritually minded is *life*"—a special kind of life—"and peace." He is referring to a deeper dimension of life, I'm sure. I like what the New International Version says here: "the mind controlled by the Spirit is life and peace." The One who controls us determines our destiny, and also our day-to-day existence and lifestyle. As Paul goes on to point out in verses 7–9, "For the mind that is set on the flesh is hostile to God; it does not submit to God's law . . . those who are in the flesh cannot please God. But you are not in the flesh, you are in the Spirit, if the Spirit of God really dwells in you" (RSV). This Controller, the Holy Spirit, assures us of peace and the fulfillment of the deepest dimension which will be Godward if we are truly his.

That he would grant you, according to the riches of his glory, to be strengthened with might by his Spirit in the inner man.
Ephesians 3:16

25

THE SOURCE of spiritual power is God. More particularly, it is God the Holy Spirit. In the some three hundred times where He is mentioned in the New Testament, as Henry Drummond reminds us, He is almost invariably associated with power. We do not ourselves either generate or create the power; all we can do is to channel it. Why anyone should ever grow proud of spiritual power (and people sometimes do) is a mystery, for it is so clear that man cannot of himself make this power. That is for God alone to do. The Holy Spirit is like a vast reservoir with endless quantities of power waiting to be appropriated. Let men come to this reservoir with great prayers and great expectations; the supply is unlimited. But let them come humbly, knowing that while the Holy Spirit is infinitely open and accessible to us, it is His power, not ours, that does the wonderful things spiritual power accomplishes in this world. Anybody can be the recipient of it. Nobody can be either the origin or the control of it. That is God's alone.

When it comes to channels for spiritual power, the field is unlimited in possibility. Anybody can be a channel who is willing to *be* a channel, not a director. We must not tell God what to do, though we can ask and in a sense may be allowed to turn the power toward some desired object or some designated individual. To be a channel, we must be open— open to God's will and plan, not set upon one of our own. Pipes for water, wires for electricity, must only be open. They are quite passive in their service. We, being persons whom God allows to co-operate with Him in His creation, are more active than they, but we must in one sense be just as passive in our transmission of what the Holy Spirit gives to us.

SAM SHOEMAKER

26

Then was Jesus led up of the Spirit into the wilderness to be tempted of the devil.

Matthew 4:1

"THEN"—that is, immediately after his baptism by the Holy Spirit, Christ was anointed for service. This spiritual equipment was intended for work and for conflict, for trial and temptation. So it must be with us. Times of special blessing, of peculiar spiritual enlightenment or enduement, are not intended for lives of inactivity or ordinary duties. They are the preparation for special service, for fierce conflict, for greater usefulness. It is the Holy Spirit who must lead. Even our Lord did not place himself in these circumstances of trial. He was led of the Spirit. So we must be on our guard lest our trials or temptations be self-imposed. It is possible to run before the Spirit. We may find ourselves in places of alluring temptation into which the Holy Spirit has never brought us. We have come there ourselves. In this we tempt God. But where the Spirit leads us, there the Spirit clothes us. The whole armor of God is always available so long as we are led of the Spirit. And his is an impenetrable armor!

EVAN H. HOPKINS

27

Create in me a clean heart, O God, and put a new and right spirit within me.

Psalm 51:10, RSV

THE CREATION OF A NEW HEART, the renewing of a right spirit, is an omnipotent work of God. Leave it to the Creator, the One who made the heart originally, to accomplish this miracle. He alone is capable of the task. All of us must join David in his repentance prayer, for none of us manages to live his life perfectly, no matter how hard we try. Indeed, David goes on to plead, "Cast me not away from thy presence, and take not thy holy Spirit from me" (Ps. 51:11, RSV). By so doing he is not implying that the Holy Spirit will actually withdraw from him, he is merely facing the fact that we can so quench the Holy Spirit within us that we lose the living awareness of his presence—and the joy that awareness can bring.

Praying always with all prayer and supplication in the Spirit, and watching thereunto with all perseverance and supplication for all saints.

28

Ephesians 6:18

NO AMOUNT of mere human teaching, no matter who our teachers may be, will give us a correct apprehension of the truth. We must be taught of the Holy Spirit. And we may be thus taught—each of us. He who is thus taught will understand the truth of God better (even if he does not know a word of Greek or Hebrew) than a man who knows Greek and Hebrew and is not taught of the Spirit.

When we come into God's presence we should recognize our infirmity, our ignorance of what we should pray for, and in the consciousness of our utter inability to pray aright, look to the Holy Spirit, and cast ourselves utterly upon him, to direct our prayers, to lead our desires, and guide our utterance of them.

R. A. TORREY

Then Peter, filled with the Holy Spirit. . . .

29

Acts 4:8, RSV

WHAT DOES IT MEAN to be full of the Holy Spirit or "filled with the Holy Spirit"? One way of picturing this filling is to imagine your life as a bucket full of dirty water. Empty out that water, and the bucket is ready to be filled with the clear clean water of the Holy Spirit. But a picture I like even better is this: empty out the old water and then take the bucket down to the ocean of God's fullness (Eph. 3:19) and immerse it in that sparkling body of water. As soon as the bucket enters the sea it is filled to overflowing—in an instant, in the twinkling of an eye! That's the way God does it. That's the way it happened to Peter and to Paul, and that's the way it can happen to you and me!

August

30

Hereby know we that we dwell in him, and he in us, because he hath given us of his Spirit.

1 John 4:13

A GREAT BIBLE TEACHER of another generation often said that the secret of grasping the meaning of a particular portion of scripture lay in one simple practice which any Bible student, great theologian or beginner, could follow: whenever you see *therefore* in the Bible, check back to see what it's *there for*. I'd like to apply that same principle to our verse for today, but to a different word—*hereby*. Instead of looking back for the reason it is there, I look ahead in the same verse where I'm told that the reason I can know I dwell in Christ is that I have his Spirit. How do I know I have his Spirit? Verse 12 tells me, "If we love one another, God dwelleth in us, and his love is perfected [made complete] in us." Think of it—I, as an obedient, Spirit-filled believer, have a small part in presenting a "complete" picture of God's love!

But there's a greater truth here. As a believer, I am *in Christ*, so I am under his protection from anything *outside* of me. Christ is *in me*, so I have *inside* might and power to withstand any outward force of evil. I am completely impregnable in him!

Paul, too, gives us a solid checkpoint for determining the Spirit's ministry in our lives: "But ye are not in the flesh, but in the Spirit, if so be that the Spirit of God dwelleth in you." What part of you has the ascendancy in your life—the flesh or the spirit? Do not give place to the devil and fleshly pursuits. Rather, yield to his Spirit that the glorious fruit of that presence may be shown in your life—and that will result in spiritual fruit for you as you let your light shine before everyone, glorifying God in all that you do.

31

Not by might, nor by power, but by my spirit, saith the Lord of hosts.

Zechariah 4:6

GOD'S VICTORIES are not achieved by human energy or natural strength. They are won by a spiritual force. Not by an abstract power but a personal Spirit: "My spirit, saith the Lord of hosts." God is speaking not of a mere influence or emanation, but of the Third Person of the Trinity—the Holy Spirit. He is set forth in this chapter under a beautiful and striking emblem. The golden oil that flowed from the golden bowl, through the golden pipes, was the secret and illuminating power of the golden candlestick. So the Holy Spirit is the believer's secret of success in all work for God. He is the "unction"—the anointing that comes to us from the "Holy One" (1 John 2:20). How often do we forget where our true strength lies! How often have we laboriously struggled and put forth every energy to accomplish our work! And how miserably we have failed, because we have not honored God the Holy Spirit! "The Lord saveth not with sword and spear; for the battle is the Lord's" (1 Sam. 17:47).

EVAN H. HOPKINS

September

Looking at Life through God's Eyes

1

And as he sat at table in the house, behold, many tax collectors and sinners came and sat down with Jesus and his disciples.

Matthew 9:10, RSV

THERE IS A PROFOUND TRUTH about our own relationship with Jesus Christ today expressed in these few words. There were several kinds of people at the table with Jesus on this particular day, and there did not seem to be any dissension among them. It was the Pharisees on the sidelines who said, "Why does your teacher eat with tax collectors and sinners?" (v. 11, RSV). I wonder if Oswald Chambers had this scene in mind when he wrote: "The further we get away from Jesus the more dogmatic we become over what we call our religious beliefs, while the nearer we live to Jesus the less we have of certitude and the more of confidence in him." Somehow I think that we are in better company among the tax collectors and sinners than we are among the Pharisees. Too often, in our day as well as then, the "religious" people are farther from Jesus than those who have no particular religious affiliation, but are actively seeking to be "with Jesus."

2

Ye shall know the truth, and the truth shall make you free.

John 8:32

A MAN MAY TAKE a dollar or a half-dollar and hold it to his eye so closely that he will hide the sun from him. Or he may so focus his telescope that a fly on a boulder may be as large as a mountain. A man may hold a certain doctrine very intensely—a doctrine which has been looming upon his horizon for the last six months, let us say, and which has thrown everything else out of proportion, it has become so big itself. Now, let us beware of distortion in the arrangement of the religious truths we hold.

HENRY DRUMMOND

But seek first his kingdom and his righteousness, and all these things shall be yours as well.   3

Matthew 6:33, RSV

PEOPLE OFTEN TELL others that if they seek the kingdom of God, everything else is going to be *subtracted* from them. They tell them that they are going to become gloomy, miserable, and will lose everything that makes life worth living—that there will be no more fun and games, and they will have to become little old men and spend all their time in going to meetings and singing hymns.

Now, that is not true. Christ never said anything like that. He says we are to "seek first the kingdom of God," and everything else worth having is to be *added* unto us.

Religion does not tell us to give things up, but rather gives us something so much better that they give themselves up. Instead of telling people to give up things, we are safer to tell them to "seek first the kingdom of God," and then they will get new things and better things, and the old things will drop off of themselves.

HENRY DRUMMOND

The gates of hell shall not prevail against it.   4

Matthew 16:18

NO YOUNG CHRISTIAN, and no old Christian, can have real success in the Christian life without the fellowship of other believers. The church is a divine institution, built by Jesus Christ himself. It is the one institution that abides. Other institutions come and go; they do their work for, and in, their day, and disappear, but the church continues, and *will* continue to the end.

It is made up of imperfect men and women, and, consequently, is an imperfect institution; but none the less, it is of divine origin and God

September

loves it, and every believer should realize that he belongs to it and should openly take his place in it, and bear his responsibilities regarding it.

R. A. TORREY

5

Then he [the angel] answered and spake unto me, saying, This is the word of the Lord unto Zerubbabel, saying, Not by might, nor by power, but by my Spirit, saith the Lord of hosts. Who art thou, O great mountain? before Zerubbabel thou shalt become a plain: and he shall bring forth the headstone thereof with shoutings, crying, Grace, grace unto it.

Zechariah 4:6–7

SINCE THE DAWN of time, society has had the strange practice of saying to its youth, "The world is in a mess [some enlightened adults even admit that the older generation may have been partly responsible for the breakdown]. We're counting on you young people to set things right!" It's been going on for generations and I don't suppose it will change. Tomorrow's young people will go on paying the bills yesterday's adults have run up. Zechariah and Zerubbabel were paying yesterday's bills— and the remarkable thing here is that God was giving them the wherewithal to do it: "Not by might, nor by power, but by my Spirit!" Thank God for the tonic value that lies in youth disciplined to his will— and may this be the story of today's youth as it was in Zechariah's day.

6

For what is a man profited, if he shall gain the whole world, and lose his own soul? or what shall a man give in exchange for his soul?

Matthew 16:26

THE LAW OF REVERSION to type runs through all creation. If a man neglect himself for a few years, he will change into a worse man and a lower man. If it is his body that he neglects, he will deteriorate into a wild and bestial savage, like the dehumanized men who are sometimes discovered upon desert islands. If it is his mind, it will degenerate into imbecility and madness—solitary confinement has the power to unmake men's minds and leave them idiots. If he neglect his conscience, it will run off into lawlessness and vice. Or, lastly, if it is his soul, it must inevitably atrophy, drop off in ruin, and decay.

HENRY DRUMMOND

September

For what does it profit a man, to gain the whole world and forfeit his life?

7

Mark 8:36, RSV

OUR WORLD WORSHIPS at the altar of so-called success. Almost without exception success is measured in terms of wealth or power. Some will "sell their souls" to gain one or the other—or both. Indeed, the two do seem to travel together. It was the same in Jesus' day—and it was this spirit of striving after worldly success that Jesus was questioning when he asked, "What does it profit. . . ?" Such is the kind of success G. Campbell Morgan decries when he says, "There is no failure more heart-breaking and disastrous than success which leaves God out of the bargain. . . . If you are simply setting out in life to amass mere material success, fame created or position gained, then success will be the most dismal and disastrous failure." As Jesus said in another place, life doesn't consist in the accumulation of things. What are your goals—and what are you striving for?

Beware! Don't always be wishing for what you don't have. For real life and real living are not related to how rich we are.

8

Luke 12:15, LB

IN THE RSV, this verse reads: "Take heed, and beware of all covetousness; for a man's life does not consist in the abundance of his possessions." Today's concern for material possessions bothers me, for it permeates the Christian church just as surely as it does the world. In fact, I've succumbed to it myself and seen the same thing happen to others. Yet, here in Luke, Jesus condemns that spirit of covetousness. As I look around me at the possessions which surround me, I'm afraid that at times I'm at their mercy rather than making them my servant. When your possessions possess you, then you're in trouble. The ancient Greek philosopher Epicurus (341–270 B.C.) is usually remembered for his advocacy of a hedonistic lifestyle. But I think this cryptic saying might be closer to his true feelings: "Wealth consists not in having great possessions but in having few wants." More recently, Earl Riney said pretty much the same thing in *Church Management*: "A man's wealth does not depend so much on what he has as on what he can do without." One thing I'm learning is that possessions don't satisfy—they just create more wants. Maybe it's time we applied Jesus' evaluation of true riches to *our* lives!

153

September

9

He said to his disciples, "Therefore I tell you, do not be anxious about your life, what you shall eat, nor about your body, what you shall put on. For life is more than food, and the body more than clothing."

Luke 12:22–23, RSV

AS A YOUNG PERSON, what should this commandment from the lips of Jesus say to me? The Amplified expands the meaning of the verse: "do not be anxious and troubled [with cares] about your life." I'm not to be overly anxious, fretful, or worried. Does this mean I'm to hang so loose that I don't even bother to work to supply myself with bodily needs? Does it excuse me from doing all I humanly can to care for myself and my loved ones? Does following Jesus' command give me an excuse for physical laziness in the name of spiritual trust? To ask the question in those words is to answer it. What Jesus is demanding is that we Christians not be caught up in a spirit of worldliness—trying covetously to accumulate *things* to satisfy temporal hungers to the neglect of our spiritual selves. As Luke 12:15 makes clear, "A man's life consisteth not in the abundance of the things which he possesseth." Material wealth can have no effect on the duration or happiness of a man's life. Spiritual riches are not measured in dollars or possessions.

10

Why spend money on what is not bread, and your labor on what does not satisfy? Listen, listen to me, and eat what is good, and your soul will delight in the richest of fare.

Isaiah 55:2, NIV

SUCCESS IN THIS WORLD is the carrot we hold out to our young people. How often we mistakenly equate this with the accumulation of wealth and possessions. I have noticed this tendency to worship wealth even in the church of Jesus Christ—and I wonder what this materialistic philosophy is doing to our youth. Are we too late to stem the tide and change the direction? Elsewhere in this book I have quoted Phillips Brooks, clergyman of the last century, because he speaks so concisely to our understanding and tendencies today. On the subject of true success he has this to say: "To find his place and fill it is success for a man [or woman]." H. G. Wells, novelist and historian who lived until the mid-twentieth century, had an equally pithy estimate of success: "Success is to be measured not by wealth, power, or fame, but by the ratio between what a man is and what he might be." Both of these statements echo the words of our Savior when he said, "Do not labor for the food which perishes, but for the food which endures to eternal life, which the Son of man will give to you" (John 6:27, RSV). Wise words which point us on the path of real success—the discovery and fulfillment of God's will for our lives!

Love not the world, neither the things that are in the world.   **11**
                                                        1 John 2:15

SOME WISE WORDS from Henry Drummond have helped me get a handle on this verse: "The weight of a load depends upon the attraction of the earth—gravity. But suppose the attraction of the earth were removed? A ton on some other planet, where the attraction of gravity is less, does not weigh half a ton. Now Christianity removes the attraction of earth, and this is one way in which it diminishes men's burdens." In Romans 12:2, the apostle Paul writes: "Do not be conformed to this world but be transformed by the renewal of your mind, that you may prove what is the will of God, what is good and acceptable and perfect" (RSV). The NIV rendering is even clearer: "Do not conform any longer to the pattern of this world, but be transformed by the renewing of your mind. Then you will be able to test and approve what God's will is—his good, pleasing and perfect will." That's what it means to "love not the world"—and that's where the will of God for me lies.

[Jesus] said to them, "You are from below, I am from above; you are of   **12**
this world, I am not of this world."
                                                        John 8:23, RSV

THERE IS A GREAT DEAL in the world that is delightful and beautiful; there is a great deal in it that is great and engrossing; but it will not last. All that is in the world—the lust of the eye, the lust of the flesh, and the pride of life—are but for a little while. Love not the world therefore. Nothing that it contains is worth the life and consecration of an immortal soul. The immortal soul must give itself to something that is immortal.

HENRY DRUMMOND

September

13

Then Jesus answered, "I am not an earthly king. If I were, my followers would have fought when I was arrested by the Jewish leaders. But my Kingdom is not of the world."

John 18:36, LB

"MY KINGDOM is not of this world. . . ."—"You can have no notion of My kingdom from the kingdoms of this world." It is the duty of any upright man to oppose wrong, but Jesus Christ did not come to enable us to do that. He came to put within us a new spirit, to make us members of His Kingdom while we are in this world—not *against* the world, and not *of* it, but *in* the world, exhibiting an otherworldly spirit. The popular evangelical idea that we are to be against the world in the sense of a pitched battle with it, is simply an expression of the spirit of the world dressed up in a religious guise. Our Lord was not against the world in that sense; He submitted to its providential order of tyranny, but there was no compromise in His spirit, and the model of the Christian's spirit is Christ Himself. There is a religious cult which courts persecution. Jesus said, "Rejoice when men shall revile you, and persecute you, *for My sake.*" It is by our spiritual choices that we maintain a right relation to the world. When a man ceases conflicting the world by spiritual choices, he succumbs to it and becomes part of the world that needs saving instead of being a saviour in the world.

OSWALD CHAMBERS

14

As for the rich in this world, charge them not to be haughty, nor to set their hopes on uncertain riches but on God who richly furnishes us with everything to enjoy. . . . Tell those who are rich not to be proud and not to trust in their money, which will soon be gone, but their pride and trust should be in the living God who always richly gives us all we need for our enjoyment.

1 Timothy 6:17, RSV; LB

IT IS STRIKING and significant to me that Paul, in writing to Timothy, emphasizes that the Christian life is to be lived in joy—for that is the priceless commodity people are looking for, but in all the wrong places! Note the sharp contrast in this passage between what the world looks upon as joy-producing, and what is true joy. Outwardly, the "rich in this world" seem to have a corner on joy, according to the world's standards, but it is God alone "who richly furnishes us with everything to enjoy," or as the *Living Bible* has it, "all we need for our enjoyment." "All things are yours" says Paul in another letter (1 Cor. 3:21). How prone we are to forget that it is the God who redeemed us and supplies our spiritual needs who also showers us with our temporal blessings! He gives us all things to *enjoy*. He delights in his children's happiness. But when we take his gifts and forget to thank the One who gave them, we are like the foolish rich man who sets his hopes on his riches.

For we through the Spirit wait for the hope of righteousness by faith.   **15**
Galatians 5:5

THE ETERNAL VERITIES of life are what count when the chips are down. Dr. O. P. Kretzmann put it this way in the *Illinois Medical Journal:* "If we are to survive the atomic age, we must have something to live by, to live on, and to live for. We must stand aside from the world's conspiracy of fear and hate and grasp once more the great monosyllables of life: faith, hope and love. Men must live by these if they live at all under the crushing weight of history." As I survey the world around me, it seems to be on a pell-mell path to destruction, a collision course with destiny. It would be the height of foolishness to place our faith in the feeble fabric of this world, to harness our hope to what it can do, to squander our love at its temporary altar. How much better to lift our sights to a higher plane as the Holy Spirit fills and guides us toward life eternal! As Charles Mayes once said in *World Vision Magazine:* "Make sure the thing you are living for is worth dying for!"

[Joshua said:] As for me and my house, we will serve the Lord. . . .   **16**
And Crispus, the chief ruler of the synagogue, believed on the Lord
with all his house. . . .
Joshua 24:15; Acts 18:8

JOSHUA AND CRISPUS were responsible heads of families, and though they lived centuries apart, they responded similarly to the pressures around them. Their families were solid units, strong enough to face whatever came. The modern family is in trouble today, beset by enemies on every hand without the strength to face the battle effectively. As the fiber of family life weakens, the erosion of the "ties that bind" accelerates. Society itself cannot long survive without this strong inner fiber. The strong nuclear family unit is the very fabric of our world. As the family goes, so inevitably must the society follow. It was the breakdown of the family and the rise of antifamily forces that spelled the doom of the Greek and Roman Empires centuries ago. In more recent days this same inner erosion has weakened and well-nigh ruined the once great British Empire. And the lack of a solid family fiber will ultimately nullify the communist bloc of countries. When Sir John Bowring said, "A happy family is an earlier heaven," he was epitomizing society's strength. And the failure of the family unit is a trend in the United States that must be reversed—or our country, too, will go the way of past great societies. Let us join with Joshua and Crispus in commitment to our families—and to our God.

---

17 *May God our Father and the Lord Jesus Christ give you grace and peace.*

Philippians 1:2, TEV

GRACE TELLS US what God is like in his attitude and action. The Greek word was used to express unreserved love for another out of pure generosity of heart and with no thought of reward. For Paul, grace was rooted in the cross. It can only be understood and experienced in the context of judgment. When we see what we have done with the gift of life, ourselves, people, the world; when the anxiety of separation from God because of our willful rebellion finally gets hold of us; and when the knowledge that God loves us in spite of all that we have done or been amazes us—that's grace! It means forgiveness, acceptance, and a new beginning we never deserved. . . .

Peace is the result of grace. It literally means, "to bind together." In other words, the peace which comes from unmerited, unearned love can weave and bind our fragmented lives into wholeness. And the civil war of divergent drives, which makes us feel like rubber bands stretched in all directions, is ended. The Lord is in control. He has forgiven the past, he is in charge of now, and shows the way for each new day.

LLOYD OGILVIE

Quoted from *Let God Love You* (Waco, TX: Word Books, 1974), p. 17.

Jesus Christ, the same yesterday, and today, and for ever. **18**
Hebrews 13:8

IN OUR CHANGING WORLD, just about the only thing we can be sure of is that things will change! Clothing styles are constantly changing; skirts go from short to long; jeans are bell-bottom this season, and tight-leg the next. Even our vocabulary changes from year to year and generation to generation. Sometimes we older people have trouble understanding what our children are trying to say, and vice versa! And the fads in popular music change as often as the wind, it seems. In entertainment, politics, and sports, fame is fleeting. Yesterday's hero is today's forgotten man. What can we hold on to? This one fact: "Jesus Christ [is] the same yesterday, today, and forever." He is the only One in this whole world that we can count on—and we can depend on him without fear of his failure! With the psalmist David I shout, "I will praise the Lord all my life" (Ps. 146:2, NIV).

I have given you authority . . . over all the power of the enemy. . . . **19**
Yes, ask anything, using my name, and I will do it!
Luke 10:19, RSV; John 14:14, LB

YOU REMEMBER that in the Lord's Prayer, the Master taught us to say, "Deliver us from evil." A modern rendering of that would read, "Rescue us from the evil one (Satan)." Christ has given us "authority . . . over all the power of the enemy," and we are rescued from the evil one by using that authority *in Jesus' name*.

But not everyone can use the Master's name. Some men in Ephesus tried to use it, to cast out evil spirits by speaking His name as they had heard the disciples do. But the demons knew full well who had a right to use that name, and they caused the men in whom they dwelt to jump upon the offenders and tear them and leave them bleeding. They did not have the right to use that name. Obedience is the requirement for the Lord Jesus' name, and with obedience always goes "faith." And faith is this: knowing that Jesus *is* the Victor. That scarred Jesus, that crowned Jesus—it is to have no doubt about *Him!*

A missionary from Tunis told me of an Arab woman, a Mohammedan with all the fanaticism, ignorance, and superstition that marks that strange belief. She was won to Christ, and her family did everything in their power to force her to recant, but failed. So they secretly put poison in her food. After the woman had eaten it, she knew immediately what had happened. Greatly alarmed, she did not know what to do. Unconsciously at first she began to repeat the name of Jesus, the great name above every name; not aloud, but now with all the intensity of one who felt the sentence of death in her body, she kept repeating that marvelous name: "Jesus! Jesus! Jesus!" For several days that went on until at last she was completely restored. That was only a physical rescue, but to each true and obedient believer Christ has given "authority . . . over *all* the power of the enemy"—in His glorious name!

S. D. GORDON

20

Then Jesus came from Galilee to the Jordan to be baptised by John. But John tried to prevent him. "I need you to baptise me," he said. "Surely you do not come to me?" But Jesus replied, "It is right for us to meet all the Law's demands—let it be so now." Then John agreed to baptise him.

Matthew 3:13–16, PHILLIPS

FOR A LONG TIME I couldn't grasp the significance of this baptism. I was with John in his wonderment at Jesus' request to be baptized of *him*. John's baptism was defined as "the baptism of repentance for the remission of sins." Jesus was sinless. Why did he need that baptism? He had no sin to confess, and he could not repent. Then it dawned on me. On the cross Jesus did more than suffer as the Sinless for the sinful. He *identified* himself with us in our sinfulness so completely that he *submitted* to John's baptism. And he used the term "us." In doing so, he was perhaps saying to John, "It is right for *me* to submit to this ordinance, as the Savior, and for *you* as my Forerunner to administer it. Otherwise you cannot completely fulfill your mission." Jesus' attitude here reminds me of the Good Samaritan parable. It is said of the Good Samaritan that he came right up to where the wounded man lay. He didn't provide his help from a distance, as I am so prone to do. He came to "where he lay." That's what Jesus did in submitting to John's baptism and going on to submit to the cross as well.

21

He calls his own sheep by name and leads them out.

John 10:3, RSV

THREE STRIKING THOUGHTS emerge as we contemplate this verse: First, there is divine *possession*. Those of us who believe in Jesus Christ belong to the Good Shepherd. We are "his own sheep." He has set his mark upon us, and he distinguishes his own in a way that can never allow them to be confused with the children of the world. Second, there is divine *knowledge.* He knows their names. In verse 14 he says, "I am the good shepherd, and know my sheep, and am known of mine." He is intimately acquainted with them so that he can call each one by name. And, third, there is divine *guidance:* he "leads them out." He goes before them each day to lead them into fresh pastures, new paths of service, or untrodden fields of patient following. If the Shepherd knows his sheep, it is so that the sheep may know the Shepherd. This mutual knowledge implies sympathy, love, community of nature (1 John 4:7; Gal. 4:9; 1 Cor. 8:3; John 17:3, 25). Christ first took our nature that we might afterward receive his. He who has laid down his life *for* us now gives his life *to* us.

But whoever drinks of the water that I shall give him will never thirst; the water that I shall give him will become in him a spring of water welling up to eternal life.

John 4:14, RSV

22

NOT MANY OF US live with wells today. We just reach for a faucet and the water flows at our touch. But in my younger days I lived on a farm that was supplied by a constantly flowing well. Whether we used it or not, the water kept coming—cooling the milk cans, supplying all the pure drinking water we could possibly use, and more. No matter how much we used, there was always plenty—and so far as I know that well is still supplying the needs of the people who live there now. That, in miniature, is a picture of the endless supply Jesus is talking about here. There's no water bill at the end of the month. It doesn't slow down to a trickle during the heavy usage periods. This is the "well in the heart" which comes from the infilling of the Holy Spirit. Like that old well on our farm, our lives will overflow with the goodness of God if we are his.

The Word became flesh and lived for a while among us. We have seen his glory, the glory of the one and only Son, who came from the Father, full of grace and truth.

John 1:14, NIV

23

THERE IS A MAJESTY about these words in the King James Version: "And the Word was made flesh, and dwelt among us . . ." but the NIV gives this grand truth of our faith a flavor of immediacy and right-now-ness: ". . . and lived for a while among us." What does it all mean? People have pondered this question for centuries, ever since Jesus Christ first came to earth, but clear-cut answers have eluded them. As early as the second century Irenaeus said confidently, "The Word of God, Jesus Christ, on account of his great love for mankind, became what we are in order to make us what he is himself." And this is a valid answer. Hundreds of years later, Martin Luther said in *Table Talk*: "The mystery of the humanity of Christ, that He sunk Himself into our flesh, is beyond human understanding." That, too, is an authentic answer. Thank God that even though we cannot understand the Incarnation of Christ, we can *experience* it personally. Jesus Christ becomes real to us as we open our lives to his control. Another ancient theologian, Hilary of Poitiers (c. 315–368) summed it up: "He did not cease to be God by being born as man, or fail to be man by remaining God."

---

24 *Nevertheless death reigned from Adam to Moses, even over them that had not sinned after the similitude of Adam's transgression, who is the figure of him that was to come.*

Romans 5:14

THERE IS a messianic thread running straight through the Scriptures. The Old Testament looks forward to the coming of the Messiah, and the Gospels report that coming in the person and ministry of our Lord Jesus Christ. The rest of the New Testament writers look forward to his coming again, this One who has come. In a very real sense, Jesus belongs to every age; he is the One "who is and who was and who is to come" (Rev. 1:4, RSV). According to Paul, Adam was a "figure of him that was to come" or, as the New International Version has it, "a *pattern* of the one to come." It is glorious to know that this One "is come to seek and save that which was lost" (Luke 19:10). John reports Jesus' statement that "*I am come* that they might have life, and that they might have it more abundantly" (John 10:10). Thus divine salvation has come to men—and our Savior offers us not just life, but abundant life! Yet there is an even broader concept here—this One who *has* come *will* come again! We stand between his first and second advents—what a glorious perspective!—and we may well see his dramatic reappearing on the world's gigantic stage.

Who was delivered for our offenses, and was raised again for our justification.

25

Romans 4:25

BY THE RESURRECTION, God declares that he has accepted and is satisfied with the settlement Christ has made. I am thus declared righteous in God's sight. If we are ever troubled with doubts as to whether God has accepted the offering Christ made, we have only to look at the empty tomb and the risen Lord.

The crucifixion loses its meaning without the Resurrection. Without the Resurrection the death of Christ was only the heroic death of the Son of God. It shows the death to be of sufficient value to cover our sins, for it was the sacrifice of the Son of God. In it we have an all-sufficient ground for knowing the blackest sin is atoned for. My sin may be as high as the highest mountain, but the sacrifice that covers it, is as high as the highest heaven.

R. A. TORREY

And the Lord direct your hearts into the love of God, and into the patient waiting for Christ.

26

2 Thessalonians 3:5

THIS BOOK would not be complete without recognition of the Lord's soon return. I know that note has been sounded for centuries, and he hasn't come yet—but that doesn't shatter my confidence that he *is* coming. After all, on the time clock of God only a couple of days have passed since Jesus' first coming, for a day in God's sight is as a thousand years, and a thousand years as a day. In this verse Paul is calling for a lifestyle characterized by love and patience. Note that the love stems from God, but it is not the shallow and sometimes syrupy love the world worships and sings about. And our waiting is to be patient—a quality also foreign to our human nature. We'll wait if we have to, but don't ask us to be patient about it! I'm glad Paul included verse 16 in this chapter: "Now may the Lord of peace himself give you peace at all times in all ways. The Lord be with you all" (RSV). That is the secret of fulfilling his call on us. If the source of our peace were in ourselves, we'd blow it for sure—but as it is, the One for whom we wait is already here!

September

27

> *If, because of one man's trespass, death reigned through that one man, much more will those who receive the abundance of grace and the free gift of righteousness reign in life through the one man Jesus Christ.*
>
> Romans 5:17, RSV

DO YOU REIGN in life? If not, the reason may be that you do not distinguish between *praying* and *taking*. There is a profound difference between *entreating* for a thing and *appropriating* it. You may admit that God's abundant grace is near you through Jesus Christ, and yet you may not quite see the necessity of learning how to take it. Some people are always telegraphing to heaven for God to send a cargo of blessing to them; but they are not at the wharfside to unload the vessel when it comes in. How many of God's richest blessings for which you have been praying for years have come right close to you, but you do not know how to lay hold of and use them! Mark—"Those who *receive* the abundance of grace shall reign." The emphasis is not on grace, not on abundance, but on *receiving* it; and the whole grace of God may surround your life today, but if you have not learned to take it in it will do you no good.

F. B. MEYER

28

> *We look for the Saviour.*
>
> Philippians 3:20

ACCORDING TO THE RSV, "we await the Savior." "The form of the verb implies a waiting full of attention, perseverance, and desire" (H. C. G. Moule). We are looking for him out of heaven—waiting for him as the Savior in the full and complete sense. Now we have the salvation of our souls. But when he shall come he "shall change our lowly body to be like his glorious body" (Phil. 3:21, RSV). He shall save us then from the very presence of sin, and from temptation and sorrow and pain. The return of the Lord and Savior Jesus Christ is *the* hope of the waiting Church. The salvation for which we wait is emphatically that of the body (Rom. 8:23). "To the ancient philosopher the body was merely the prison of the spirit; to the Apostle, it is its counterpart, destined to share with it, in profound harmony, the coming heaven" (Moule on the Epistle to the Philippians). Let this be the attitude of the soul each day: "Looking for that blessed hope, and the glorious appearing of the great God and our Saviour Jesus Christ" (Titus 2:13).

EVAN H. HOPKINS

Behold, I come quickly. . . . The Lord direct your hearts into the love
of God, and into the patient waiting for Christ.

29

Revelation 22:7; 2 Thessalonians 3:5

THE LAST MESSAGE the risen Christ gave his people was the promise of
his soon return. Couple this with Paul's admonition to the Thessalonian
Christians and you get a good rule for life: Live both expectantly and
patiently, and you will be fulfilling the Lord's will until he returns.

What are some of the blessings awaiting the believer when Jesus
Christ comes back? First of all, the faithful ones can confidently expect
to be rewarded for their faithfulness. This is a matter of scriptural record,
for in foretelling his return in Matthew 16:27 (RSV), Jesus promised:
"For the Son of man is to come with his angels in the glory of his
Father, and then he will repay every man for what he has done."

There is also a clear-cut promise of reward to the obedient Christian.
"And being made perfect he became the source of eternal salvation to all
who obey him" (Heb. 5:9, RSV). Besides these promises of reward for
faithfulness and obedience, Jesus has also promised to deliver his
followers from the great tribulation awaiting the world at the end time.
Paul told the Thessalonian believers "to wait for [God's] Son from
heaven, whom he raised from the dead, Jesus, who delivers from the
wrath to come."

In the light of such promises, our response should be, "Even so,
come, Lord Jesus!"

But in addition to waiting expectantly, we are also admonished to wait
patiently, to "occupy 'til he comes." And while we are waiting, we are to
be yielded to the "love of God" operative in our lives. If the love of God
flows through us, we will find ourselves sharing that love with those
around us, for God is love, and that love is bigger than its container, the
Christian, so it must overflow. Those around us long for love, for our
world is full of hate, Satan's legacy since the Garden of Eden episode.
Let us as Christians share God's love as we await the return of his Son
from heaven.

Let us lift up our heart with our hands unto God in the heavens.

30

Lamentations 3:41

IN OUR DAY it is becoming increasingly common for worshipers to lift
their hands as an outward sign of their adoration and love for God.

September

Apparently it was the same way in the Old Testament ritual of worship. In Psalm 141:2 David says, "Let . . . the lifting up of my hands [be] as the evening sacrifice." In Psalm 143:6 he prayed, "I stretch forth my hands unto thee." But this outward sign of worship must be reflected in the heart to have any meaning with God—and that is why Jeremiah here in Lamentations says, "Let us lift up our *heart* with our hands." He is decrying empty worship, the mere formality often characteristic of our so-called devotion. David frequently spoke of lifting up his *soul* to God: "Unto thee, O Lord, do I lift up my soul" (Ps. 25:1). This act of lifting was no mere formality in his worship—it was real. In Psalm 143:8 he even claimed it as an evidence of his sincerity in prayer: "Cause me to know the way wherein I should walk; for I lift up my soul unto thee." Both of these aspects are necessary if our prayer is to rise above our heads: the outward sign of reverence (lifted hands) and the inward reality of spirit (lifted heart). Let the body as well as the spirit be involved in all our worship.

October

Living in the Spirit

Ye are dead, and your life is hid with Christ in God. 1

Colossians 3:3

MORE LITERALLY it is, "for you died" (NIV). The words do not describe a *condition of deadness*, as many have assumed, but they point to the fact that death, as a crisis, has been passed through. And if we recognize the principle that all the great *facts* of redemption find their accomplishment first of all in Christ, rather than in our individual experience, then we see that the death referred to here took place on the cross. "For you died" with Christ when he died. You were identified with him in his death. This is the meaning of your baptism: "Know ye not, that so many of us as were baptized into Jesus Christ were baptized into his death?" (Rom. 6:3). "Into *his* death," remember, not into *your* death. The fact with which faith is concerned is not something which finds its center in yourself but in Christ. "For you died." When? When you were baptized? No. When you experienced that wonderful blessing? No. But when *Christ* died, and you, in the eye of God, died with him. This is the foundation of all experimental and experiential knowledge. We must begin with the judicial *fact*, or we have no solid base to rest upon.

EVAN H. HOPKINS

Yet a little while, and the world seeth me no more; but ye see me: 2
because I live, ye shall live also.

John 14:19

CHRIST LIVES with every person who puts his trust in him. The resurrection means the presence of the living Christ. He said, "Lo, I am

167

October

with you always, even unto the end of the world" (Matt. 28:20, KJV). This is Christ's own guarantee: life has a new meaning. After the crucifixion, the disciples were in despair. They said, "We had hoped that he was the one to redeem Israel" (Luke 24: 21, RSV). They were full of anguish because they thought of Christ's death as such a tragedy. Life had lost its meaning for them. But when he rose from the grave, they saw the living Christ, and life took on purpose once more.

BILLY GRAHAM

Quoted from *How to Be Born Again* (Waco, TX: Word Books, 1977).

---

3   *By their fruits ye shall know them.*

Matthew 7:20

THERE ARE THREE THINGS in the Christian life that should be distinguished—fruit, gifts and works. A person may be busy in Christian work without abounding in fruit. Fruit is something higher and more spiritual than works. It is the outcome of the divine life in the soul. The fruit of the Spirit is absent from the life of the one who is habitually grieving the Holy Spirit, however active in work and zealous in doctrine he may be. We have to be "fruitful in every good work" (Col. 1:10). It is not by their *works* ye shall know them, but by their *fruits*.

Then, again, remember that fruit and gifts are not to be confused. A person may be gifted as a preacher or teacher of the Word who is nevertheless lacking in the fruit of the Spirit. Those "gifts" may draw crowds, and hundreds may even come to Christ through the Word preached, and yet if we judged the person's true spiritual condition by his "gifts," we should come to the wrong conclusion. "By their *fruits* ye shall know them." Let there be genuine humility, an ignoring of self, and you have then "fruit," which is distinct from "works" or "gifts."

EVAN H. HOPKINS

---

4   *The attitude you should have is the one that Christ Jesus had.*

Philippians 2:5, TEV

HERE IN PHILIPPIANS Paul has pleaded for unity and oneness in Christ. He uses disposition as a synonym for the Spirit living in us. The quality of humility, self-giving, and interest in the welfare of others is possible only as a result of the remolding of our disposition around the character of Christ.

The secret of discovering this is not to try to be more loving to please our Lord. Many of us were taught that we should make an effort to honor Christ by reproducing Christian characteristics to win his affirmation. These Paul clearly delineates as the fruit of Christ's Spirit in us. In Galatians 5 he listed the elements of Christian disposition: love, joy, peace, patience, kindness, goodness, faithfulness, gentleness, self-control. Without root there can be no fruit. And our Lord put it bluntly, "Abide in me, and I in you. As the branch cannot bear fruit by itself, unless it abides in the vine, neither can you, unless you abide in me . . . for apart from me you can do nothing" (John 15:4, 5, RSV).

Who in your life would want to find Christ because of your disposition?

LLOYD OGILVIE

Quoted from *Let God Love You* (Waco, TX: Word Books, 1974). p. 61.

There is no fear in love; but perfect love casteth out fear.
1 John 4:18

5

ONE OF THE most famous pronouncements concerning fear was made by the crippled but courageous President Franklin Delano Roosevelt. He said: "We have nothing to fear but fear itself" as he led his countrymen to battle against the Great Depression and later into an even greater battle, World War II. But despite his advice, and that of the Scriptures, fear seems to be our constant companion in this earthly life. We have all kinds of fears: the fear of failure; the fear of death; the fear of growing older; the fear of being rejected by those we love and our peers. Everyone has experienced some or all of these fears. They sometimes come so thickly that they almost overwhelm us. But John gives us the answer here. Think upon your heavenly Father and the message he has for you in his Word. You can't keep fear from entering your mind, but you can keep it from settling in. As Paul tells us in Romans 8:15, "For ye have not received the spirit of bondage again to fear; but ye have received the Spirit of adoption, whereby we cry, Abba, Father." His perfect love casts out our fear!

October

6

We who are strong ought to bear with the failings of the weak, and not to please ourselves; let each of us please his neighbor for his good, to edify him.

Romans 15:1–2, RSV

A BEAUTIFUL STORY is told of the Agassiz brothers. Their home was in Switzerland on the shore of a lake. One winter day the father was on the other side of the lake, and the boys wanted to join him. The lake was covered with thick ice. The mother watched as the boys set out. They got on well until they came to a wide crack in the ice. Then they stopped, and the mother became very anxious, fearing they might be drowned. The older boy jumped over easily, but the little one was afraid. Then, as she looked, she saw Louis, the older brother, get down on his face, his body stretched over the crack, making a bridge of himself, and then she saw his little brother creep over him. This story is a beautiful parable of love. We should be willing to make bridges of ourselves on which others may pass over the chasms and the streams that hinder them in their way. We have many opportunities to do this in helping our brothers over the hard places, out of temptation, through sickness, or in some other way of living. It is not pleasant to lie down on the ice, or in the wet, and let another use us as a bridge; but Christ did it. His cross was just a laying of His own blessed self over the awful chasm of death and despair, that we might pass over Him into joy and hope and heaven. He endured the cross, despising the shame, that He might save us. We cannot call ourselves Christians if we balk or falter or hesitate to endure suffering, loss, or shame, to help others. "He that saveth his life shall lose it."

J. R. MILLER

7

And I, when I am lifted up from the earth, will draw all men to myself.

John 12:32, RSV

PUT A PIECE OF IRON in the presence of an electrified body and that piece for a time becomes electrified. It is changed into a temporary magnet in the mere presence of a permanent magnet, and as long as you leave the two side by side they are both magnets alike. Remain side by side with him who loved us and gave himself for us, and you too will become a permanent magnet, a permanently attractive force; and like him you will draw all men unto you, like him you will be drawn unto all men. That is the inevitable effect of Love.

HENRY DRUMMOND

Walk in love, as Christ also hath loved us. . . .

Ephesians 5:2

8

"WALKING" is the analogy Paul frequently uses to emphasize the practical or everyday aspect of the Christian life. With our souls as well as our bodies, we need exercise to bring out our full potential. We cannot enjoy health unless we are putting into practice that which we have learned in terms of our faith. Unused limbs atrophy—and so does unused faith. Love is the power that has drawn us sinners to God, that has melted our hard hearts, that now puts us under obligation to live for him. Let's face it, love is the common sphere of the Christian's activity: "God is love; and he that dwelleth in love dwelleth in God, and God in him" (1 John 4:16). We Christians are called to be followers, imitators of God. Paul makes no distinction between our being the objects of the love of God and our being objects of Christ's love. Therefore we are to "walk in love." Earlier in Ephesians Paul wrote: "And be ye kind one to another, tender-hearted, forgiving one another, even as God for Christ's sake hath forgiven you" (4:32). If we imitate God in this respect, we will forgive one another. This love is not only for contemplation and rejoicing, it is "Where the rubber meets the road"—without love our claims to Christianity are empty. Let's put some muscle and meaning into our walk!

My deep feeling for you all comes from the heart of Christ Jesus himself.

Philippians 1:8, TEV

9

As I SIT in my study, I look out over the Lake Hollywood Reservoir surrounded by magnificent mountains. I am a few minutes away from downtown Hollywood and the Los Angeles area I serve. The water in the lake is portioned off each day for the needs of the city below. Often when I look out over the lake, I wonder how there can be enough water for the millions of people in the city. Early one morning I took a walk around the lake, and at the north end I was amazed to hear the rushing of water tumbling into the lake. I discovered that the rush of water came from the Colorado River and replenished the lake every day. What looks to me like a loch in a Scottish highland glen is really a widening in the passage of water from the Colorado River to faucets in the homes of Hollywood.

Loving is like that. I would like to be an endless resource of loving attitude and thought. I would like people to look at me as some do at Lake Hollywood and believe that I have an endless supply within myself.

Not so! The gushing, sparkling inflow of water is like the indefatigable inflow of Christ's love to me. I am a channel, not a reservoir.

LLOYD OGILVIE

Quoted from *Let God Love You* (Waco, TX: Word Books, 1974), p. 25.

10
[Paul said,] I have showed you all things, how that so laboring you ought to support the weak, and to remember the words of the Lord Jesus, how he said, It is more blessed to give than to receive.

Acts 20:35

THIS REMINDER to be charitable or generous is a note that rings throughout the New Testament. In 1 Corinthians 13:3 Paul says, "If I give all I possess to the poor and surrender my body to the flames, but have not love, I gain nothing" (NIV). Jesus often talked about the importance of a generous spirit and recommended it as a way of life. And, to quote Paul again, the apostle particularly recommended it to the youthful Timothy: "Don't let anyone look down on you because you are young, but set an example for the believers in speech, in life, in *love*, in faith and in purity" (1 Tim. 4:12, NIV) and again: "Flee the evil desires of youth, and pursue righteousness, faith, *love* and peace, along with those who call on the Lord out of a pure heart" (2 Tim. 2:22, NIV). We used to call giving for good causes "charity," but it's more aptly called "love in action." As Erich Fromm says, "Not he who has much is rich, but he who gives much." And the great French poet, novelist and dramatist, Victor Hugo, said, "As the purse is emptied, the heart is filled."

Beloved, let us love one another: for love is of God.
1 John 4:7

11

"GOD IS LOVE." What a world of meaning is wrapped up in these three short words! What should this mean to me as a Christian? Do I really care about other people? I have no problem loving those who love me, and those who are "my kind of people." But what about those who are different from me, or those who actively oppose me, who are my enemies? Do I love them? Would I be telling the truth if I answered yes? God's brand of love has no reservations. It is not dependent on the object, but comes unlimited from its Source—God himself.

If our troubled world's greatest need could be summed up in a word, *love* would be it. Everywhere we look we see the results of a lack of love—war, hatred, and anger. Have you ever lived, even for a short time, in an atmosphere of real, accepting love, where those around you put God first, others second, and themselves last? Then you know what John was talking about when he wrote, "Love is of God."

Then he poured water into a basin, and began to wash the disciples' feet, and to wipe them with the towel with which he was girded.
John 13:5, RSV

12

MY RELATIONSHIP TO GOD embraces every faculty; I am to love Him with *all* my heart, *all* my soul, *all* my mind, *all* my strength; every detail is instinct with devotion to Him; if it is not I am disjointed somewhere. Think what you do for someone you love! The most amazingly minute details are perfectly transfigured because your whole nature is embraced, not one faculty only. You don't love a person with your heart and leave the rest of your nature out, you love with your whole being, from the crown of the head to the sole of the foot. That is the attitude of the New Testament all through. In 1 Corinthians 15 the Apostle Paul has been speaking about the stupendous mystery of the resurrection, and suddenly, like a swinging lamp in a mine, he rushes it right straight down and says, "Now concerning the collection . . ." The New Testament is continually doing it—"Jesus knowing . . . that the Father had given all things into His hands . . . began to wash the disciples' feet." It takes God Incarnate to wash feet properly. It takes God Incarnate to do anything properly.

OSWALD CHAMBERS

October

13

Love does no wrong to a neighbor; therefore love is the fulfilling of the law.

Romans 13:10, RSV

YOU REMEMBER the profound remark which Paul makes. "Love is the fulfilling of the law." Did you ever think what he meant by that? In those days men were working their passage to heaven by keeping the Ten Commandments, and the hundred and ten other commandments which they had manufactured out of them. Christ said, I will show you a more simple way. If you do one thing, you will do these hundred and ten things, without ever thinking about them. If you love, you will unconsciously fulfill the whole law.

HENRY DRUMMOND

ON OCCASION, I've been tempted to think this an oversimplification of what Jesus meant when he set forth the law of love—but that happens only when I lose sight of what his brand of love really means!

14

I hope in the Lord Jesus to send Timothy to you soon, so that I may be cheered by news of you. I have no one like him, who will be genuinely anxious for your welfare.

Philippians 2:19–20, RSV

CARLYLE'S WIFE, Jane Welsh, was often a disturbance and a bore to him, and he treated her badly. But after her death, he wrote, "Oh, if I could see her once more, were it but for five minutes, to let her know that I always loved her, through all that. She never did know it, never."

Jesus told us that within us would flow rivers of living water. There's a dry and thirsty land, a desert parched for love in the people around us.

We wonder if Timothy was there with Paul when he wrote about him to the Philippians. Did he overhear Paul's dictation to his scribe? What an encouragement that would have been to him! Paul was not a capricious flatterer, motivated by insecure solicitousness. He was able to be direct and honest with his companions about things they needed to change, but he was also open and free to express his feelings of love.

LLOYD OGILVIE

Quoted from *Let God Love You* (Waco, TX: Word Books, 1974), p. 87

A merry heart doeth good like a medicine. **15**

Proverbs 17:22

EACH OF OUR LIVES has a direction which it seems to travel naturally. Some of us make others happy when we come in contact with them, and some spread gloom and despair by their attitude toward life. Philosophers of the past and early psychologists assumed that our attitude toward life was predetermined. Some were destined to be optimistic and happy, and others seemed doomed to melancholy by their "built-in" disposition. But it is clear from the Scriptures (this passage among others), that Christians are not to be doomspreaders. Rather it is our mission to spread happiness wherever we go by the very joy of our presence. The secret lies in the source of the happiness. It does not come from ourselves but from the indwelling presence of the Holy Spirit in our lives. As the New International Version has it, "A cheerful heart is good medicine." In his biography of Samuel Johnson, Oliver Edwards has his character say, "I have tried too in my time to be a philosopher; but, I don't know how, cheerfulness was always breaking in." What kind of "medicine" is my life?

The joy of the Lord is your strength. **16**

Nehemiah 8:10

WHAT IS THIS JOY? It is *divine*. There is a joy of youth, of circumstances, of prosperity. But the joy of the Lord rises above all these. Its source is heavenly, its nature divine. It is the joy of *the Lord*. And so we can understand why it is an *abiding joy*. It does not come and go, but continues: "That *my* joy might *remain* in you" (John 15:11). Thus the apostle could say, "Rejoice in the Lord *always*." "As sorrowful, yet *always* rejoicing." It is a *satisfying* joy. One of the characteristics of all earthly joy is its unsatisfying nature. But the Lord's joy not only calms the mind, it fills the heart. Then it is a joy of great *practical* value. It is the secret of power for service: "The joy of the Lord is your *strength*." For *testimony*. It is when the heart is full of joy that the mouth can speak. The life itself then has a witness apart from our words. For *suffering*. It is when there is joy within that we can endure patiently. For *temptation*. Not simply in the sense of trial, but of allurements. When the heart is satisfied with the Lord's joy it will not be drawn aside by the world's enticements.

EVAN H. HOPKINS

October

17

O God, my heart is fixed: I will sing and give praise. Awake up, my glory; awake, psaltery and harp.

Psalm 57:7–8

DAVID WAS IN A CAVE hiding from King Saul when he wrote this psalm. Yet instead of saying, "O God, my heart is frozen with fear," he declares, "O God, my heart is fixed"—calm, happy, resolute, firm, established. His soul is among lions, yet he cries as if to arouse himself to the spiritual joy that is beyond the reach of one's enemies, "Awake up, my glory; awake, psaltery and harp."

Many of us need at times to make this same call upon ourselves to awake. The harps are hanging silent on the walls. The figure of speech showing instruments of music sleeping is suggestive. They are capable of giving forth rich melodies, but not a note is heard from them. There are two thoughts suggested by this prayer. One is that life is meant to be glad, joyous. It is pictured as a harp. The other is the splendor of life— "Awake up, my glory."

It is to a life of joy and song we are called to awake. Life is a harp. There is a legend of an instrument that hung on a castle wall. Its strings were broken. It was covered with dust. No one understood it, and no fingers could bring music from it. One day a stranger saw the silent harp, took it into his hands, reverently brushed away the dust, tenderly reset the broken strings, and then he played upon it, and the glad music filled all the castle.

This is a parable of everyday life, which is a harp, made to give out music, but broken and silent until Christ gets possession of it. Then the song awakes. We are called to joy and joy-giving. "Awake up, my glory."

J. R. MILLER

18

These things have I spoken unto you, that my joy might remain in you, and that your joy might be full.

John 15:11

CHRIST IS THE SOURCE of joy to men in the sense in which he is the source of rest. His people share his life, and therefore share its consequences, and one of these is joy. His method of living is one that in the nature of things produces joy. When he spoke of his joy remaining with us he meant in part that the causes which produced it should continue to act. His followers, that is to say, by *repeating* his life

October

would experience its accompaniments. His joy, his kind of joy, would remain with them.

HENRY DRUMMOND

Rejoice in the Lord always: again I will say, Rejoice. **19**
Philippians 4:4, RSV

THE BIBLE insists upon joy as an element of Christian life. Christ spoke of his desire that the disciples should have his joy fulfilled in themselves. Paul exhorts Christians to rejoice always, and speaks of joy as one of the fruits of the Spirit.

Christian joy is not hilarity. One may be sorrowful, and yet have the joy of the Lord in the heart. It is an inner joy—a fountain in the heart, supplied from heaven. Every Christian should have this joy. It belongs to the ideal of the complete Christian character. It is evident, however, that there are many Christians who do not have it. Their spirits go up and down like the mercury in the tube of the thermometer, varying with the atmosphere. When things are pleasant they have joy. When circumstances are hard or painful they have no joy.

We ought to know how to get the joy of Christ. One secret is absolute devotion to the will of God. Another is serving others. Only as we learn to live the life of love—"Not to be ministered unto, but to minister"— can we find true, deep love. Every self-denial or sacrifice of love for another's sake adds to the Christian's joy. We reach the ideal life only as joy lives in our heart, and shines out in our life.

J. R. MILLER

And your heart shall rejoice, and your joy no man taketh from you. **20**
John 16:22

A LIFE SURRENDERED to the control of the Holy Spirit is a life of joy and peace and freedom. There is no anxiety in such a life, there is no fear in the presence of God.

The Spirit-filled life is always joyful and jubilant and nothing can disturb its joy. No matter how adverse the circumstances, its joy abides; for its joy is not in circumstances but in him, who is the same yesterday, today, and forever.

It is the joy of knowing our salvation is complete. Completed

177

salvation includes not merely the salvation of the soul; it includes the salvation of the body, that we shall possess when the wondrous promises about our being transformed into the perfect likeness of Jesus Christ, not only spiritually but physically, have their fulfillment; and unto that salvation God keeps us: "When he shall appear, we shall be like him; for we shall see him as he is" (1 John 3:2).

R. A. TORREY

21

A merry heart maketh a cheerful countenance. . . . he that is of a merry heart hath a continual feast.

Proverbs 15:13, 15

AN ANONYMOUS WRITER has expanded on this thought: "Cheerfulness removes the rust from the mind, lubricates our inward machinery, and enables us to do our work with fewer creaks and groans. If people were universally cheerful, probably there wouldn't be half the quarreling or a tenth part of the wickedness there is. Cheerfulness, too, promotes health and immortality. Cheerful people live longest here on earth, and afterward in our hearts." And out of her rich spiritual insight, blind Helen Keller wrote: "Keep your face to the sunshine and you cannot see the shadow." That says it all. If our eyes are fixed on the face of the sun, our Savior, and our faces are turned toward him, then we'll be able to follow this divine prescription for a happy face and a victorious life.

22

But let all who take refuge in thee rejoice, let them ever sing for joy; and do thou defend them, that those who love thy name may exult in thee.

Psalm 5:11, RSV

WHERE DOES JOY come from? I knew a Sunday school student whose conception of joy was that it was a thing made in lumps and kept somewhere in heaven, and that when people prayed for it pieces were somehow let down and fitted into their souls. I am not sure that views as gross and material are not often held by people who ought to be wiser. In reality, joy is as much a matter of cause and effect as pain. No one can get joy by merely asking for it. It is one of the ripest fruits of the Christian life, and, like all fruits, must be grown.

HENRY DRUMMOND

You are always in my heart! And so it is only right for me to feel as I **23**
do about you. For you have all shared with me in this privilege that God has given me, both now that I am in prison and also while I was free to defend the gospel and establish it firmly.

Philippians 1:7, TEV

ONE MORNING when I was studying this verse I was overcome with the realization of how delighted Paul was in the expression of his feelings for the Philippians. He knew all the problems and differences they were having, but his letter was written in the context of affirmation that they were "his people" regardless of what happened. It's one thing to talk about grace, something else to incarnate it. There is no evidence that he would hold back his feelings of joy over them until they measured up.

"You are always in my heart!" Paul wanted the Philippians to know the depth of his feelings. I am sure that the reason they were so open to Paul was because they felt the enjoyment he had in them. Real communication begins with delight in the person to whom we want to relate significantly.

LLOYD OGILVIE

Quoted from *Let God Love You* (Waco, TX: Word Books, 1974), p. 22.

Great peace have those who love thy law; nothing can make them **24**
stumble.

Psalm 119:165, RSV

I SOMETIMES THINK all the wisdom of the ages is distilled in Psalm 119—and this verse has to be one of the most pungent and compelling statements in the entire Book. Peace seems to be the great prize for which our modern world is striving. Presidents and generals have sought it diligently—and indeed concentrated on it sometimes to the exclusion of other highly important goals. Ever since the Fall in the Garden of Eden peace has been the goal of armies and kings, but always it seems to

October

elude our grasp. Could it be that men have forgotten the last part of this verse, "those who love thy law"? Can we have peace aside from allegiance to the Prince of peace? Only in the society where God's law is supreme and operative is true peace possible.

25

He went up unto them into the ship; and the wind ceased.

Mark 6:51

THERE IS A TREMENDOUS spiritual truth lying within "waves" of this remarkable story of Jesus' power over the elements. J. R. Miller notes: "When Jesus comes to us our trouble ceases. At his bidding the wildest storm instantly becomes a calm. The trouble itself may not go away from us, but it is no longer a trouble when he is with us. The wind may not cease to blow without and beat upon our lives, but he makes peace within. It is far better to have so much grace that our hearts shall be quiet and quiet in the fiercest storm, than to have the storm itself quieted, while our hearts remain as restless as ever. Peace within is far better than mere calm without." With Christ in the boat of our life, we don't have to worry about the storms surrounding us.

26

. . . let us run with patience the race that is set before us.

Hebrews 12:1

RACES APPEAR to be the rage today—and physical fitness is one of our modern gods, it seems. Far be it from me to disparage this movement, for since our bodies are the temples of the Holy Spirit (1 Cor. 3:16), we need to treat them as such, seeking to keep them in the best physical condition possible. Paul here is likening life itself to a race, and he asks us to run it with patience. As one of the fruits of the Spirit, patience is an important ingredient in the Christian life (see Gal. 5:22–23). It seems to be tied in so closely with all the other fruits that what we have here is not just one fruit, but part of the total cluster that characterizes the Christian. Patience is just one facet of the sparkling diamond that is the Christlike character. Running and patience don't seem to go together— for running is thought of as active and patience is considered passive. But true patience takes work, as James 1:3 points out: "Knowing this, that the trying of your faith worketh patience." As I run my race, I'm to relax in the knowledge that my God works in me "both to will and to do of his good pleasure" (Phil. 2:13).

. . . be thou faithful until death, and I will give thee a crown of life. He that hath an ear, let him hear what the Spirit saith unto the churches; he that overcometh shall not be hurt of the second death.
Revelation 2:10–11

27

J. R. MILLER is one of my favorite devotional writers. Even though he died in 1912, his spiritual insight is applicable in any century. On the subject of faithfulness he says: "Men do not fly up mountains; they go up slowly, step by step. True Christian life is always mountain climbing— heaven is above us and ever keeps above us. It never gets easy to go heavenward. It is a slow and painful process to grow better. No one leaps to sainthood at a bound. No one gets the victory once and for all over his faults and sins. It is a struggle of years and every day must have its victories if we are ever to be final and complete overcomers. Yet while we cannot expect to reach the radiant mountaintop at one bound, we certainly ought to be climbing it step by step. We ought not to sit on the same little terrace, part way up the mountain, day by day. Higher and higher should be our unresting aim." That's a good motto for a young person today to live by!

Set a watch, O Lord, before my mouth; keep the door of my lips.
Psalm 141:3

28

HERE IS ONE of the most practical prayers in all of Scripture. Someone has said that the Lord must have intended for us to listen twice as much as we speak, for he gave us two ears—but only one mouth! Of course, some may argue, but he gave us two lips with which to form our words. But let me remind you that he still gave us only one tongue—the main organ involved in speaking. This prayer of David's echoes in my own heart. Too often I'm inclined to watch what I do, but not what I say. But my words can often hurt others more than my actions. In fact, words can sometimes wound beyond healing and break beyond mending. My

October

Christianity should affect how I use my lips. How fittingly David prays, "Set a guard over my mouth, O Lord, keep watch over the door of my lips!" (RSV).

29

A word fitly spoken is like apples of gold in pictures of silver.

Proverbs 25:11

HAVE YOU EVER BEEN troubled with "foot-in-mouth" disease? I'm afraid it happens to me on occasion, although I'd like to think that the older I get the less often it happens! Despite my age, however, I still sometimes speak before my mind is in gear . . . and what comes out I have to regret at leisure. Wise old King Solomon has a word of advice for me and my fellow-sufferers. The NIV renders it: "A word aptly spoken is like apples of gold in settings of silver." Isn't that a beautiful picture of what our words *should* be? Did you ever realize that our tactfulness and diplomacy glorify the Lord? Oh, the Lord can use the bumbler and the bumpkin—but how much better for all concerned if my words smooth and soothe rather than bruise and batter. As I begin my day or end it, I make this my prayer—that my words may be "fitly spoken."

30

A gossip goes around spreading rumors, while a trustworthy man tries to quiet them.

Proverbs 11:13, LB

JAMES, the brother of our Lord, had a great deal to say about that flimsy little organ, the tongue. His New Testament Epistle is a masterful analysis of the trouble the tongue can cause and the importance of exercising a little restraint, a little "won't" power in our tongue control. Solomon, too, realized the damage the tongue could do, as he points out here in Proverbs 11. And Jean Paul Richter, the German author, has said in more recent years, "A man never discloses his own character so clearly as when he describes another's." I rather like what Solomon says just before our verse for the day: "A man who lacks judgment derides his neighbor, but a man of understanding holds his tongue" (Prov. 11:12, NIV). If you can't say something good about your neighbor (across the room, the street, or the world) it's best to hold your tongue. Good advice from any source!

In the multitude of words there wanteth not sin: but he that refraineth his lips is wise.

31

Proverbs 10:19

PROVERBS IS A delightfully practical book—and humorous at times. I particularly like the *Living Bible*'s translation of this verse: "Don't talk so much you keep putting your foot in your mouth. Be sensible and turn off the flow!" God surely has a sense of humor! But on the serious side, the tongue can create some real problems for all believers, young and old alike. In the New Testament James especially decried the damage the tongue could do and called for Christian self-control in that area of the life. Though soft to the touch, the uncontrolled tongue can become a two-edged sword of destruction. On the other hand, the Christ-controlled tongue can bring blessing and healing. The danger to which the wise writer of Proverbs, Solomon, refers to here is in how often a hasty word, a sharp and cutting comment, escapes in the "multitude" of our words. The gift of God to his children is a calm and well regulated mind, a loving and considerate heart, and lips guarded against words that might hurt and hinder others. As James said, this is true wisdom "without wrangling."

November

Living Thankfully

1

Who is able to stand before envy?

Proverbs 27:4

WHENEVER YOU ATTEMPT a good work you will find other men doing the same kind of work, and probably doing it better. Envy them not. Envy is a feeling of ill-will to those who are in the same line as ourselves, a spirit of covetousness and detraction. How little Christian work even is a protection against un-Christian feeling! That most despicable of all the unworthy moods which cloud a Christian's soul assuredly waits for us on the threshold of every work, unless we are fortified with this grace of magnanimity. Only one thing truly need the Christian envy—the large, rich, generous soul which "envieth not."

HENRY DRUMMOND

2

Therefore, as God's chosen people, holy and dearly loved, clothe yourselves with compassion, kindness, humility, gentleness and patience. Bear with each other and forgive whatever grievances you may have against one another. Forgive as the Lord forgave you.

Colossians 3:12–13, NIV

SOMETIMES I THINK "forgiveness" should have been listed among the fruits of the Spirit Paul mentions in Galatians. Indeed, forgiveness would not be possible aside from these fruits. These verses convict me of a shortfall in my own life. I'm afraid I'm hardest on those who are closest to me. There's a line in that old song, "Home on the Range": ". . . where seldom is heard a discouraging word." Can this be said about my home? Do I encourage my loved ones or discourage them by my words and actions? How often do I praise them for the little things in life, the everyday things that I take for granted? Am I quicker to complain than to compliment? J. R. Miller once said, "Silence, in the presence of needs that words will fill, is sinful." Is this the sin "no one talks about"? I want to live the way Paul encourages the Colossians to live—with a forgiving spirit.

If we confess our sins, he is faithful and just to forgive us our sins, and to cleanse us from all unrighteousness. **3**

1 John 1:9

GOD HAS CALLED every one of us to a victorious life, and the secret of this victorious life is looking to Christ for victory. Through looking to Christ crucified, we obtain pardon and enjoy peace. Through looking to Christ risen, we obtain present victory over the power of sin. If you have lost sight of the risen Christ, confess your sin and know it to be forgiven, and the vision of Christ will be restored.

R. A. TORREY

I am with thee to save thee and to deliver thee, saith the Lord. **4**

Jeremiah 15:20

THE RICHES of this twofold promise are unfathomable. A saved soul needs a daily salvation and a continuing deliverance. He needs not only daily deliverance out of the hand of the wicked, he needs to be saved from evil thoughts and desires, and kept in a state of deliverance from self-seeking and self-confidence. This salvation is found in the Lord's ongoing promise of his presence: "I am with thee." But there is a proviso connected with this promise. In verse 19 the Lord says: "If thou return, then will I bring thee again, and thou shalt stand before me: and if thou take forth the precious from the vile, thou shalt be as my mouth. . . ." I like the way the NIV clarifies the meaning of this verse: "If you repent, I will restore you that you may serve me; if you utter worthy, not worthless, words, you will be my spokesman." What the Lord declares he will do for the prophet, every true witness may take as a divine assurance for himself. But a repentant, realistic spirit is the condition for that promise.

November

5

And Samuel spake . . . If ye do return unto the Lord with all your hearts, then put away the strange gods . . . and prepare your hearts unto the Lord, and serve him only: and he will deliver you out of the hand of the Philistines.

1 Samuel 7:3

I'M CONSTANTLY thrilled as I see the Old Testament mirrored in the New. Jesus was saying much the same thing as Samuel when he said, "No man can serve two masters: for either he will hate the one, and love the other. . . . Ye cannot serve God and mammon" (Matt. 6:24; Luke 16:13). All through its history Israel was guilty of this senseless dichotomy, even in Jesus' day. Samuel offers the only antidote:

First, *return* unto the Lord. Change the direction of your life and attitude. Become a person with a one-track mind, fastened on the Lord. Second, *put away* the strange gods. If your returning and your repentance are genuine, they will have this sure effect: your actions will be in harmony with your words. Third, *prepare* your hearts unto the Lord. The attitudes of our hearts are open to God. It is the condition of our hearts "unto the Lord," or in relationship to him, that is the great point of Samuel's formula for a fruitful life as a Christian.

6

He that putteth his trust in me shall possess the land, and shall inherit my holy mountain.

Isaiah 57:13

I THINK THAT WITH all we know of the divine heart of Jesus, he would far rather see a soul trust him too much, if that is possible, than trust him too little, which we know is possible enough. When a man who has sinned, and who, like Simon Peter, has not a shadow or a ghost of an excuse to offer for his sin, has so known Christ that he never thinks of him as one to be appeased, never doubts for an instant that if he is forgivable he is forgiven, and so lets his hatred of his old sin break out in an utterance of his love for the Holy One, and lets his sorrow for his treason only show itself in his desire for loyal work, then that poor sinner's sin is dead and gone.

Is not Christ the mountain into which the believer goes, and in which he finds the divine idea of himself? As a mountain seems to be the meeting place of earth and sky, the place where the lowering skies meet the rising planet earth, the place where the sunshine and the cloud keep closest company with the granite and the grass—so Christ is the meeting place of divinity and humanity; he is at once the condescension of divinity and the exaltation of humanity; any one wanting to know God's idea of man—anyone wanting to know God's idea of him—must go up into Christ, and he will find it there.

PHILLIPS BROOKS

And be ye kind one to another, tender-hearted, forgiving one another,
even as God for Christ's sake hath forgiven you.

Ephesians 4:32

7

KINDNESS IS ONE of the fruits of the Spirit least talked about and perhaps least practiced in Christian circles. Here Paul couples it with forgiveness, which is a striking combination. Frederick William Robertson, an Anglican minister of the nineteenth century, said: "We win by tenderness; we conquer by forgiveness." And our Lord placed forgiveness at the very heart of his model prayer (the Lord's Prayer). A forgiving spirit is just as basic to victorious Christian living as is a thankful attitude. Alexander Pope in *An Essay on Criticism* wrote: "To err is human, to forgive divine." I've mouthed that saying as a platitude for decades, but only recently have I realized the truth that lies behind these seven short words. In this book about Christian living, I must emphasize at least once the vital importance of a forgiving spirit in the living of our lives. May God help me to live my life this way!

Your sins are forgiven you for his name's sake.

1 John 2:12

8

WHAT A STUPENDOUS PROMISE! Throughout the New Testament we learn that the one who receives Christ as Lord and Savior also receives, immediately, the gift of forgiveness. The Bible says, "As far as the east is from the west, so far hath he removed our transgressions from us" (Ps. 103:12).

"Forgive me." "I'm sorry." "I didn't mean it." How often we use those words, and they echo back with a hollow sound. But God's forgiveness is not just a casual statement; it is the complete blotting out of all the dirt

November

and degradation of our past, present and future. The only reason our sins can be forgiven is because Jesus Christ paid their full penalty on the cross.

BILLY GRAHAM

Quoted from *How to Be Born Again* (Waco, TX: Word Books, 1977).

9   *Take heed to yourselves: If thy brother trespass against thee, rebuke him; and if he repent, forgive him. And if he trespass against thee seven times . . . thou shalt forgive him.*

Luke 17:3–4

OH, THE FREEDOM with which the gates of the divine forgiveness are thrown open! The Bible trembles and burns and overruns with offers. They crowd on one another. Not waiting to be asked, not giving it reluctantly, but following to tempt them with it, in his open hands the eager Savior brings his free forgiveness. The great wonder of the Incarnation was the great miracle of that free pardon—as if sin, with all its enormity, had yet this accidental glory, almost transfiguring it, that it gave a new license of utterance to the unutterable love. The Forgiver stands upon the heights of human tragedy and summons man to be forgiven.

When God has fulfilled in us his promises, we have a new reason for loyalty to him. He is not only our Creator but our Benefactor, the God of grace to us. So Jacob felt as he came back with many blessings to the place where God had given him encouraging promises, and where he had vowed to make the Lord his God (Gen. 32). So he puts away the "strange gods." In the same spirit should we, through God's goodness leading us to repentance, put everything away that dishonors him. May the Holy Spirit help us to do so!

PHILLIPS BROOKS

10   *When ye stand praying, forgive, if ye have aught against any; that your Father also which is in heaven may forgive you your trespasses.*

Mark 11:25

FORGIVENESS lies at the heart of our Christian faith. If we cannot learn to forgive others who have hurt or hindered us, how can we expect forgiveness from our heavenly Father? Forgiveness is not so much an action as it is an attitude. Once we as Christians grasp how much we have been forgiven, we will experience what it means to really forgive those who have injured us in spirit or in body.

Jesus is our pattern or model in this matter of forgiveness. On the cross he prayed, "Father, forgive them; for they know not what they do" (Luke 23:34), asking his heavenly Father to forgive the very men who were killing him! When Peter asked, "Lord, how oft shall my brother sin against me, and I forgive him?" he was so cocky he answered his own question: "till seven times?" (Matt. 18:21). Jesus replied, "I say not unto thee, Until seven times: but, Until seventy times seven" (v. 22). I don't think we're meant to take that literally, for if by some stretch of human endurance and forbearance one were to forgive 490 times, but change his attitude on the 491st opportunity to forgive, it would show that one's spirit from the start was wrong—judgmental instead of truly forgiving.

One of the primary guidelines for the young Christian (and any Christian, for that matter) is the importance of a forgiving spirit. In Psalm 86:5 David prayed, "For thou, Lord, art good, and ready to forgive; and plenteous in mercy unto all them that call upon thee." Really, the Christian creed calls for us to go beyond forgiveness and live in the fruit-bearing spirit of Paul when he wrote, "Be ye kind one to another, tender-hearted, forgiving one another, even as God for Christ's sake hath forgiven you" (Eph. 4:32).

Freely ye have received, freely give. . . . Give, and it shall be given unto you; good measure, pressed down, and shaken together, and running over.

11

Matthew 10:8, Luke 6:38

THE ART OF GIVING is a gift! While it's not one of the nine fruits of the Spirit listed in Galatians 5:22, it is an attitude that underlies many of those gifts, for example, love. Richard Braunstein says, "It is possible to give without loving, but it is impossible to love without giving." John Raleigh Mott, one of the founders of the early ecumenical movement, summed it up:

The world asks, How much does he give?
Christ asks, Why does he give?

Gracious and generous giving is praised throughout the Bible, and stinginess is condemned. I don't know whom we think we're fooling! Jesus knows our very hearts, and he knows our attitude toward our possessions. Do we possess them—or are they so important to us that *they* possess *us?* Affluence can be a blessing or a curse, depending upon how we handle it. "Freely ye have received, freely give. . . ."

12 *"We have here only five loaves of bread and two fish," they answered.*
Matthew 14:17, NIV

THERE IS A STRIKING principle of divine mathematics being expressed here. God doesn't give out his gifts to be clutched in a miserly way to one's breast. Instead, he delights to give his gifts to those who will share them with others. This is one of the most important spiritual lessons we can learn. Jesus goes on to tell his disciples to "Bring them here to me" (v. 18, NIV). This is his command to us. We are merely to be channels through which he can work—and a clogged channel is pretty useless. There's another truth expressed here: those gifts of ours that are turned back to him are then multiplied many times over by the divine hand—spiritual math again at work. Surrender your loaves and fish to him and watch what miracles he will do with them!

13 *He that giveth, let him do it with simplicity; . . . Distributing to the necessity of saints; given to hospitality.*
Romans 12:8, 13

I LIKE the way the NIV handles this, for it broadens our responsibility for hospitality: "if it [a man's gift] is contributing to the needs of others, let him give generously. . . . Share with God's people who are in need. Practice hospitality." Billy Graham has said, "God has given us two hands—one to receive with and the other to give with. We are not cisterns made for hoarding; we are channels made for sharing." What a world this would be if it were filled with Christians who lived by the "channel" principle. Not only should we be generous to our fellow Christians, we should also follow the admonition of the writer to the Hebrews: "Do not forget to entertain strangers, for by so doing some people have entertained angels without knowing it" (13:2, NIV). Another apostle has said, "Use hospitality one to another without grudging. As every man hath received the gift, even so minister the same one to another, as good stewards of the manifold grace of God" (1 Pet. 4:9–10). Melvin Jones in *Lion Magazine* put it in very practical terms: "What you give humanity you get back. Bread cast upon the waters is much more wholesome and nourishing than pie in the sky."

. . . remember the words of the Lord Jesus, how he said, It is more blessed to give than to receive.

14

Acts 20:35

THE MOST OBVIOUS lesson in Christ's teaching is that there is no happiness in having and getting anything, but only in giving. And half the world is on the wrong scent in pursuit of happiness. They think it consists in having and getting, and in being served by others. It consists in giving, and in serving others. He that would be great among you, let him remember that there is but one way—it is more blessed, it is more happy, to give than to receive.

HENRY DRUMMOND

And they, continuing daily with one accord in the temple, and breaking bread from house to house, did eat their meat with gladness and singleness of heart, praising God, and having favour with all the people.

15

Acts 2:46–47

THE EARLY CHRISTIANS gave themselves continually to praise and thanksgiving; these were among the most noticeable and notable characteristics of their lives. The same thing is true of the holy men and women of the Old Testament. I cannot think of one good man mentioned at all prominently in the Bible of whom it is not definitely recorded that he thanked God for some act of his goodness.

In approaching God to ask for new blessings, we should not neglect to return thanks for blessings already granted. This attitude of praise is the key to power in prayer. As Paul exhorts us: "Be careful for nothing; but

November

in every thing by prayer and supplication with thanksgiving let your requests be made known unto God" (Phil. 4:6).

R. A. TORREY

16 *O praise the Lord, all ye nations: praise him, all ye people. For his merciful kindness is great toward us: and the truth of the Lord endureth forever. Praise ye the Lord.*

Psalm 117

A TREMENDOUS SPIRITUAL TRUTH resides in this shortest of the Psalms. Some anonymous writer has summed it up for us: "We who are the objects of his mercy should be the trumpets of his praise." It's a note sounded in another Psalm as well: "For the Lord is good; his mercy is everlasting; and his truth endureth to all generations" (100:5). And in the New Testament Paul echoes: "Praise the Lord . . . and laud him, all ye people" (Rom. 15:11). What are the writers saying? I think each in his way is calling God's people to a life of thankfulness. Gratitude to God for all his goodness should be as natural to us as breathing. In the best-known psalm of all David says, "Surely goodness and mercy shall follow me all the days of my life" (23:6). Although gratitude cannot permeate my every waking moment, my life does go better when I give God thanks.

17 *Who satisfieth thy mouth with good things.*

Psalm 103:5

THE LIVING BIBLE'S translation of this verse reads: "He fills my life with good things!" The Christian young person can say that with assurance. Does this mean everything's going my way, everything's coming up roses? If it did, and the word got out, I suppose the world would be beating a path to God's door! You and I both know that's not happening. No, a quick look at some of the other verses in this Psalm reveals that the Christian has his problems too. If you don't believe it, check with Job. His life wasn't always filled with "good things." But it *was* filled with the ability to cope with whatever came and still say, "The Lord gave, and the Lord hath taken away; blessed be the name of the Lord" (Job 1:21). We deserved the bad, but God gave us the ultimate good—and along the way he gives us grace to say, "He fills my life with good things."

192

In every thing give thanks: for this is the will of God in Christ Jesus concerning you. **18**

1 Thessalonians 5:18

I'VE SAID THAT the spirit of thanksgiving might well be the key to living the Christian life victoriously and successfully. Paul apparently believed this, for he frequently sounds this note in his writings: "We give thanks to God and the Father of our Lord Jesus Christ, praying always for you" (Col. 1:3); "I thank Christ Jesus our Lord, who hath enabled me, for that he counted me faithful, putting me into the ministry" (1 Tim. 1:12). Praising prayer should be a natural part of our lives. When it is, remarkable things happen. Joni Eareckson, the quadriplegic woman who conquered her paralysis of body by experiencing the freeing of her spirit, says: "I believed that if God took something away from me, He would always replace it with something better. My experience had taught me this as I relied on the sovereignty of God. 'Delight thyself in God,' the psalmist said, 'trust in His way.' As I did so, it became easier to express true gratitude for what He brought into my life—good as well as suffering. The suffering and pain of the past few years had been the ingredients that had helped me mature emotionally, mentally, and spiritually." * This is giving thanks "in everything."

*Quoted from Joni Eareckson and Joe Musser, *Joni* (Grand Rapids: Zondervan, 1976), p. 205.

It is a good thing to give thanks unto the Lord, and to sing praises unto thy name, O Most High. **19**

Psalm 92:1

IN THE ALMOST FORTY YEARS of my walk with the Lord, one of the greatest lessons I have learned involves the importance of a thankful spirit. At the risk of oversimplifying the Christian life, I might say that this attitude of thankfulness underlies everything we do as Christians if we are living above instead of "under the circumstances." In the Psalms, certainly, thankfulness is a note frequently sounded. It was this spirit that inspired Paul to write, "For I have learned, in whatsoever state I am, therewith to be content" (Phil. 4:11). And he told Timothy "And having food and raiment let us be therewith content" (1 Tim. 6:8). And the author of the Epistle to the Hebrews echoed Paul's sentiments: "Be content with such things as ye have: for he hath said, I will never leave thee, nor forsake thee" (Heb. 13:5). These passages aren't talking about a spirit of passive acceptance—they're demanding the best that we can give in terms of our attitude toward everything that comes into our lives. "It's a good thing to give thanks unto the Lord!"

20

O give thanks unto the Lord; for he is good: because his mercy endureth forever.

Psalm 118:1

I'M AFRAID most of us are guilty of failing to give thanks "in all things." By that I mean we are prone to thank God for the positive things that happen to us, but not for the negative mercies. Let me explain what I mean: Some years ago my family and I were involved in a rather serious automobile accident, but only the car was a casualty. The Lord saved us all from serious injury, even though he allowed the automobile to go to the graveyard. Since that time I've often thanked him for many aspects of the accident: no serious injuries to anyone in our family; no other people or cars involved; the closeness of friends who took us in even though we were far from home. I could go on and on. That was a close call—but what about the routine daily care each of us as a child of God enjoys? How blessed we are in the things he does not allow to happen to us! Indeed, his mercy *does* endure forever.

21

Honor the Lord with thy substance, and with the firstfruits of all thine increase.

Proverbs 3:9

THERE IS A POWERFUL spiritual principle being expressed here. It's probably more understandable in the *Living Bible* rendition: "Honor the Lord by giving the first part of all your income, and he will fill your barns with wheat and barley and overflow your wine vats with the finest wines" (vv. 9–10). It is not only our souls the Lord would have us put into his hand, but also our substance, our possessions. This is a lesson we cannot learn at too young an age. It is marvelous to me that God would use those things which are of the earth, earthy, in his plan and purpose for his world—but he does! As we honor him with our "substance," our money, gifts, talents, our entire selves, he blesses our endeavors. Our thank-offerings of self delight him and honor his name. By our giving, he knows that we ascribe all our prosperity to his mercy and goodness. When we confess by our actions as well as our words that we believe he who is the God of our spiritual gifts is also the Giver of all our temporal blessings, we "honor the Lord."

I will sing unto the Lord, because he hath dealt bountifully with me.
Psalm 13:6

22

SINGING AND A SPIRIT of thankfulness seem to go together. Maybe that's why the Psalms, which were written to be sung, so often speak of giving thanks and being thankful. This verse certainly gives us in brief scope the reason we should be thankful. Our Lord has indeed "dealt bountifully" with us. If you're feeling down (and I guess all of us do at times), try this experiment: Think of someone in your family or circle of friends who is "worse off" than you. I've done this many times, and do you know, I've never failed to find someone in poorer straits than I. And many times these same people are an inspiration to others in the way they handle difficulties. Of course, I'm speaking here of Christians. There are courageous and even victorious non-Christians, but they aren't "singing unto the Lord." Try this approach next time you're tempted to carp and complain. You'll discover that God has indeed "dealt bountifully" with you!

Only fear the Lord, and serve him in truth with all your heart: for **consider** *how great things he hath done for you.*
1 Samuel 12:24

23

AS A FATHER I have tried to share an "attitude of gratitude" toward God with my children. It has become a priority with me. God is so good to us—but too often we live our lives quite unaware of this great fact, quite complacent in crediting our own efforts with the blessings we enjoy. Samuel's words to the ancient people of Israel deserve new emphasis in our affluent age. "Consider" or think upon God's past mercies toward you and his current blessings on a daily basis. Such action will deepen our faith in his future blessings—and our sense of personal unworthiness as well. Remembering what he has already done for us and "meditating" on his goodness will dispel our doubts and turn the clouds of discouragement into sunshine before us. The divine logic of "He that spared not his own Son, but delivered him up for us all, how shall he not with him also freely give us all things?" (Rom. 8:32) bears out Samuel's words in a New Testament setting. Paul believed in this principle as well as Samuel did! No, we cannot wholly grasp the breadth of his goodness, but "considering" it in a meditative spirit will certainly deepen our thankfulness and put us in a spirit of prayer. "Bless the Lord, O my soul, and *forget not* all his benefits" (Ps. 103:2).

---

24 *For the Lord God is a sun and shield: the Lord will give grace and glory: No good thing will he withhold from them that walk uprightly.*
Psalm 84:11

THE FIRST PART of this striking verse speaks of the majesty and power of God. To our finite minds, describing God as a sun is to place him at the pinnacle of the solar system, for the sun is that star around which our solar system revolves. From it we receive the light, heat, and energy we need to function. Without it, we would be literally dead! In a sense, this "sun" description for God is a picture of him as Creator and Sustainer of his universe and all of us in it. Still, that same all-powerful Being is our "shield," a figurative expression for his protection as well as his nature, as Truth personified. Faith in God itself is described as a shield in Ephesians 6:16. This transcendent Being, God, cares about me! That is the marvel. In fact, our verse says that "no good thing will he withhold from them that walk uprightly." Because of his great love for us, he gave the greatest gift of all—his Son! And with his strength, we *can* walk uprightly; in fact, "He . . . preserveth the way of his saints" (Prov. 2:8)!

---

25 *Jesus answered and said unto him, Verily, verily, I say unto thee, Except a man be born again, he cannot see the kingdom of God.*
John 3:3

EXCEPT A MINERAL be born "from above"—from the kingdom just *above* it—it cannot enter the kingdom just above it. And except a man be born from above, by the same law he cannot enter the Kingdom just above him. There being no passage from one kingdom to another, whether from inorganic to organic, or from organic to spiritual, the intervention of Life is a scientific necessity if a stone or a plant or an animal or a man is to pass from a lower to a higher sphere. The plant stretches down to the dead world beneath it, touches its minerals and gases with the mystery of life, and brings them up ennobled and transformed to the living sphere. The breath of God, blowing where it listeth, touches with its mystery of Life the dead souls of men, bears them across the bridgeless gulf between the natural and the supernatural, between the spiritually inorganic and the spiritually organic, endows them with its own high qualities, and develops within them those new and sweet faculties by which those who are born again are said *to see the kingdom of God.*

HENRY DRUMMOND

Being asked by the Pharisees when the kingdom of God was coming, he answered them, "The kingdom of God is not coming with signs to be observed; nor will they say, 'Lo, here it is!' or 'There!' for behold, the kingdom of God is in the midst of you."

26

Luke 17:20–21, RSV

THE CHRISTIAN LIFE is stamped all through with impossibility, human nature cannot come anywhere near what Jesus Christ demands, and any rational being facing His demands honestly, says, "It can't be done, apart from a miracle." Exactly. In our modern conception of Christianity there is no miracle; the emphasis is put not on the regenerating power of the Cross, but on individual consecrations, individual fasting and prayer, individual devotion. It is simply individualism veneered over with religious phraseology. There is no need for the Cross of Christ for all that kind of thing. The only entrance into the Kingdom is the Cross; then when we are born again by means of the Cross and are in the Kingdom of God, we have to live out its laws. It is not that we take the precepts of the Sermon on the Mount and try to live them out literally, but that as we abide in Christ we live out its precepts unconsciously. Being in the Kingdom, we are fit now to live out its laws, and we obey Jesus Christ's commands because of our love for Him.

OSWALD CHAMBERS

November

27

Not that I have already obtained all this, or have already been made perfect, but I press on to take hold of that for which Christ Jesus took hold of me.

Philippians 3:12, NIV

OFTEN IN THIS BOOK we have talked about surrender to the will and way of God as the path to victory in the Christian life. Surrender or submission is just one side of the coin, however. The other side involves physical effort and energy. As the writer to the Hebrews said, "let us run with perseverance the race marked out for us" (12:1, NIV). We need to give our human best to God to do with as he sees fit. Both David, who vowed he would not offer God "that which doth cost me nothing" (2 Sam. 24:24), and Paul, who spoke the words of our text, are examples of God-centered men who sought for excellence in their spiritual lives— and we should do the same. Back in the nineteenth century Robert Browning wrote:

Ah, but a man's reach should exceed his grasp,
Or what's a heaven for?

May my deep desire as a Christian be to reach higher rather than to be satisfied with the spiritual status quo.

28

For I the Lord thy God will hold thy right hand, saying unto thee, Fear not; I will help thee.

Isaiah 41:13

DR. BILL BRIGHT of Campus Crusade for Christ is fond of pointing out that "God has a plan for your life." And he has! Indeed, as G. Campbell Morgan says, "God is not making an experiment with you. We are not pawns upon a chessboard, moving which, God may win or lose. Every movement is arranged. I did not know what was to come to pass today, but God was in this day before I came into it. Doing what? Choosing the place for me, making arrangements, controlling everything." In the secure knowledge of God's involvement in my little life, should I consider any event insignificant or meaningless? From my perspective after walking with the Lord for more than thirty years, I don't believe anything in the life of the Christian is "happenstance" or coincidence. The chessboard of my life is known completely to him. "He knows the end from the beginning." It is my responsibility to fit in with his plan by seeking his will and putting him first in my life.

Hear, O heavens, and give ear, O earth: for the Lord hath spoken; I **29**
have nourished and brought up children, and they have rebelled
against me.

Isaiah 1:2

ALL OF US had to start out as children. Undoubtedly some reading these pages were the kind of children described by God in this verse. Many are outwardly rebellious—and almost all of us know what it means to experience inner rebellion. In spite of our rebellion, however, God loves us, and he does not cease to love us because of our rebellious actions. G. Campbell Morgan has a unique perspective on this whole matter: "The Fatherhood of God was a fact before the coming of Jesus. He illuminated it for men, so that since His coming they have understood it as never before. Though men had wandered and lost their sense of relationship, God was ever their Father, and His presence their home." Isn't it a comfort to know that our Father God is faithful? Our actions do not alienate us from him, even though they can temporarily separate us. It is Isaiah who says, "Comfort ye, comfort ye my people, saith your God" (40:1). What a blessing to know that the same God against whom we have rebelled forgives us because of what Jesus Christ accomplished on the cross.

You are to rejoice before the Lord your God in everything you put your **30**
hand to.

Deuteronomy 12:18, NIV

THOMAS CARLYLE once wrote, "A well-written life is almost as rare as a well-spent one." If one were to follow the advice of Moses here, he would go a long way toward living a "well-spent" life. Moses was talking about work, and he was saying that we are to do "everything as unto the Lord." Since work makes up so much of our living, and takes up so much of our lives, our attitude toward it will pretty well determine the "flavor" of our living. As you launch a career—or prepare yourself for one—examine your attitude. Is it one of rejoicing? If so, yours will be a life "well-spent."

December

The Understanding Life

1

O Lord, how manifold are thy works! in wisdom hast thou made them all: the earth is full of thy riches.

Psalm 104:24

THE OLD SAYING IS, "Go from nature up to nature's God," but it is hard working uphill. The best thing is to go from nature's God down to nature; and, if you once get to nature's God, and believe Him, and love Him, it is surprising how easy it is to hear music in the waves, and songs in the wild whisperings of the winds; to see God everywhere, in the stones, in the rocks, in the rippling brooks, and hear Him everywhere in the lowing of cattle, in the rolling of thunders, and in the fury of tempests. Get Christ first, put Him in the right place, and you will find Him to be the wisdom of God in your own experience.

CHARLES H. SPURGEON

2

Know therefore that the Lord thy God, he is God, the faithful God, which keepeth covenant and mercy with them that love him and keep his commandments to a thousand generations.

Deuteronomy 7:9

THE CONSTRUCTED WORLD of man is not the created world of God. The sin of man has polluted the material earth, and it will have to go through a cremation, out of which will emerge "new heavens and a new earth, wherein dwelleth righteousness." That which God created can never finally be bad. God demands of His children the practical belief that all that stands for Creation is upheld by His righteousness. The One who made the world and who upholds all things by the word of His power, is the One who keeps His saints.

OSWALD CHAMBERS

For whatever is born of God overcomes the world; and this is the victory that overcomes the world, our faith.

1 John 5:4, RSV

IF EVIL WERE STRONGER than God, he would never have sent his Son to show us how to overcome it. God in his wisdom knew that evil could be defeated. God, in the person of his Son, faced the cruel facts of evil and pain and death unflinchingly for us. The crucifixion was the seeming triumph of evil, and God allowed it. The resurrection, however, was God's secret weapon and with it he triumphed by demonstrating his power to replace evil, suffering, and death with the creative force of love and life. The resurrection tells more about God and his power to overcome evil than any other event in history.

But. . . . if God has infinite power and infinite love, why does he allow the terrible things that daily menace our loved ones and our own happiness and security? Why are there hurricanes, earthquakes, fires, famine, disease, accidents? No human being can explain the whole mystery of human suffering. The greatest minds in history have struggled with the problem of pain. God's explanation is Jesus. He is like the shaft of light which a lighthouse throws on a black, turbulent sea. As we come into the beam of this light, through faith and prayer, we begin to understand. God sent Jesus, not to take the insecurity, danger and challenge from life, but to teach us to live and pray so that we might joyfully cry with St. John: "Who is it that overcomes the world but he who believes that Jesus is the Son of God?" (1 John 5:5, RSV).

HELEN SMITH SHOEMAKER

4

The Lord is King for ever and ever.

Psalm 10:16

THOSE OF US who have never lived in or under a monarchy may not fully grasp what this verse means. What is "kingship"? A king is one who holds by life tenure, and usually by hereditary right, the chief authority over a country and people. Looking at this verse, G. Campbell Morgan says, "The history of human sin is the history of man's attempt to deny the Divine Kingship, and to resist its claims. In spite of all this terrible history of rebellion and failure, God has not resigned His throne, He has not abandoned His sceptre, He has not yielded the reins of government. . . . His right to reign does not depend upon the vote of a crowd."

December

These firm words describe our divine King, the One whom we worship and serve—not because we have to, but because it is our privilege and honor to do so!

5

Trust in the Lord with all thine heart; and lean not unto thine own understanding. In all thy ways acknowledge him, and he shall direct thy paths.

Proverbs 3:5–6

WHAT A MARVELOUS motto for a glorious life! The formula set forth here is simple and straightforward—trust and find direction. Our problem is that we want to test God rather than trust him. We want to experiment with him rather than rely on him. We're like the boy who tests the doubtful ice instead of skating confidently where God is leading. What is our faith worth if we don't trust *completely?* It is perfectly natural to trust in our own understanding, to rely on our own natural strengths, gifts, or talents (and indeed some modern prophets tell us to do so!). But it is the walk of faith to *trust* his teaching and direction. Give him first place and let him have precedence. This is the secret of safe guidance and peaceful progression. Simple dependence *upon* him, committing our all *to* him, obeying him implicitly—this is how to acknowledge him "in all thy ways." As St. Augustine said centuries ago, "Beware of despairing about yourself: you are commanded to put your trust in God, and not in yourself."

6

Behold, I set before you the way of life, and the way of death.

Jeremiah 21:8

THESE ARE THE WORDS of the Lord himself in answer to the prayer of King Zedekiah. And they come down to us today with just as much impact. Here are two vastly contrasting ways—and yet our decisions in life today will determine the way that we take. Each one of us, personally, comes to the crucial crossroad when we choose our direction. Jesus said, "I am come that ye might have life." And Satan said to God, "Skin for skin, yea, all that a man hath will he give for his life" (Job 2:4). Paul said, "For if ye live after the flesh, ye shall die"

(Rom. 8:13). In Job 34:15 Elihu says, "man would return to dust" (RSV). So we are moving in one direction or the other—eternal life or eternal death. How can I describe life? Jesus said, "I am the Way, the Truth and the Life"—so life must be inextricably interwoven with him who is Life. I see created life all around me—in the flowers, in everything that has breath and movement. But all of these will die. Only the essence of life remains, the One who created and sustains it. If I am not connected by faith to him, I cannot live. I am bound to die. Life is indefinable but death is the cessation of it. In Christ I have defeated death and I am on "the way of life."

The wicked is driven away in his wickedness: but the righteous hath hope in his death.

7

Proverbs 14:32

HOW DO YOU get ready to die? It is a common error to think that eternal life begins when one dies. Eternal life is not out yonder somewhere. Eternal life is fellowship with God. It begins now. Every person must live in two worlds. Eternal life, the heavenly life, begins when one commits his life to Jesus Christ. That life is never interrupted thereafter. Death can't interrupt it. Death then becomes simply the way ordained by God for our passage from one stage of life to another. We do not stop loving, or growing just because we die. Why do some people come close to death and panic? Because they haven't prepared. . . . Jesus demonstrated the way to die. On the cross, he said to his Father, "Father, into thy hands I commend my spirit" (Luke 23:46). What an example of trust. What a way to die. Then he said to his disciples: "Let not your heart be troubled: ye believe in God, believe also in me" (John 14:1). Our best approach to death is a commitment of life to Jesus, so that life for us becomes a growing, maturing fellowship with him.

T. CECIL MYERS

Quoted from *You Can Be More Than You Are* (Waco, TX: Word Books, 1976), pp. 39–40.

Happy is the man that findeth wisdom, and the man that getteth understanding.

8

Proverbs 3:13

IN PROVERBS 8 Wisdom is no mere abstract quality, but a Person—Jesus Christ himself. He says in verse 4: "Unto you, O men, I call; and my voice is to the sons of man." Verses 34 and 35 promise: "Blessed is the man that heareth me, watching daily at my gates, waiting at the posts of my doors. For whoso findeth me findeth life, and shall obtain favor of the Lord." Wisdom is thus embodied in the Divine Person. To find wisdom is not something attained by human effort. It is to receive him "who of God is made unto us wisdom" (1 Cor. 1:30), and "in whom are hid all the treasures of wisdom and knowledge" (Col. 2:3). To find Christ is to find life—it's as simple as that. "Happy is the man that *findeth* wisdom." Every such person is *found* by him who is Wisdom. As we find righteousness complete and perfect, when we find Christ, so we find in him wisdom also. It is the gift of the Holy Spirit to unveil to the heart and mind of the believer all those treasures of wisdom stored up in Christ.

EVAN H. HOPKINS

9

Happy is the man who finds wisdom, and the man who gets understanding, for the gain from it is better than gain from silver and its profit better than gold.

Proverbs 3:13–14, RSV

I WONDER HOW MANY of us would pray as Solomon did, "Give thy servant therefore an understanding mind to govern thy people, that I may discern between good and evil; for who is able to govern this thy great people?" (1 Kings 3:9, RSV). We read: "It pleased the Lord that Solomon had asked this. And God said to him, 'Because you have asked this, and have not asked for yourself long life or riches or the life of your enemies, but have asked for yourself understanding to discern what is right, behold, I now do according to your word. Behold, I give you a wise and discerning mind, so that none like you has been before you and none like you shall arise after you'" (1 Kings 3:10–13, RSV). How priceless wisdom and understanding are! What better equipment could we have to face the pressures and problems of modern life? Lord, help me to make Solomon's prayer the prayer of my own heart!

10

But where shall wisdom be found? And where is the place of understanding?

Job 28:12, RSV

I'M WITH JOB! If I had my life to start over again, I think wisdom and understanding would be high on my list of priorities—not for what I could gain thereby but, like King Solomon, for what I could give. Job answered his own question when he records, "And he [the Lord] said to man, 'Behold, the fear of the Lord, that is wisdom; and to depart from evil is understanding'" (28:28). Way back in the fourth century A.D. St. Augustine wrote, "Understanding is the reward of faith. Therefore seek not to understand that you may believe, but believe that you may understand." May spiritual understanding be my supreme goal as a Christian—and may I find it in my God!

For the Lord giveth wisdom: out of his mouth cometh knowledge and understanding.

11

Proverbs 2:6

KNOWLEDGE AND UNDERSTANDING together make up what we call wisdom—and what greater gift could a young person have than this? Daily decisions demand our best, and we deeply desire the insight to handle the problems and challenges that come our way. The writer of Proverbs tells us where to look for this insight. Wisdom—the instinctive combination of knowledge and understanding—is more than a gift from God: "But of him are ye in Christ Jesus, who of God is made unto us wisdom" (1 Cor. 1:30). Wisdom is not so much a gift we are to seek apart from Christ, but that which we actually find *in* him! He is our Wisdom as truly as he is our Righteousness and Strength. Just as in our weakness his strength can find its greatest manifestation, so in our ignorance his wisdom can find its greatest perfection. Our need measures our capacity. He is ready and willing to fill our emptiness with his blessing and grace. The Lord doesn't just *give* wisdom, he *is* wisdom!

For the Lord giveth wisdom: out of his mouth cometh knowledge and understanding. He layeth up sound wisdom for the righteous: he is a buckler to them that walk uprightly.

12

Proverbs 2:6–7

WISDOM is our greatest need today. We need it for our responsibilities and relationships. It is the missing quality in most leaders, the lacking ingredient in society, the reason for the impotence and ineptness of most Christians.

We worship at the shrine of fact, place our oblations on the altar of

December

knowledge, and bow down before our capacity to solve the mysteries of life. We live as paupers of the mind because we lack the power of wisdom.

True wisdom cannot be earned or acquired by human effort. Nor is it reserved for old age, or the result of experience alone. We can have lived long and squeezed the fruit of life dry and not have wisdom. Wisdom is a gift. It is imparted by God, imputed in communion with him, and infused by his Holy Spirit. It is beyond acquired skills. Deeper than insight. More profound than learning.

Do you have the gift of wisdom? You can! The first step to greatness, effectiveness, and inner power for living is wisdom. You can receive the gift today. Right now. An understanding heart filled with wisdom can be yours.

LLOYD OGILVIE

Quoted from *When God First Thought of You* (Waco, TX: Word Books, 1978), pp. 75–76.

---

13   *The entrance of thy words giveth light; it giveth understanding to the simple.*

Psalm 119:130

PSALM 119 seems to come from the heart of a young person (see v. 9). What a prayer for the "best in life" it is—a plea for wisdom or understanding. Young King Solomon was a prime example of the wisdom asked for in this prayer psalm. His spiritual perception early in his reign was phenomenal, almost legendary. He was, indeed, the wisest man of his generation, if not of all time. But somewhere along the way Solomon got off the track. He was no longer where God could bless him—and the latter end of his life was a tragedy and a travesty. His reliance upon God was replaced by reliance upon self. The secret of spiritual insight lies in the "entrance of thy words," the very words of God. As the Word lives in our lives, it expands our understanding so that we live beyond our native intelligence (whether great or small) in the "light" which Divine Wisdom sheds.

---

14   *The fear of the Lord is the beginning of knowledge; but fools despise wisdom and instruction.*

Proverbs 1:7

THE WISDOM of the ancients—where is it? It is wholly gone. A schoolboy today knows more than Sir Isaac Newton knew. His knowledge has vanished away. You buy the old editions of the great encyclopedias for a few pennies. Their knowledge has faded away. And all the boasted science and philosophy of this day will soon be old.

HENRY DRUMMOND

DRUMMOND died in 1897. What would he have said of earthly wisdom if he had lived in our day? I have a feeling he would not have changed his assessment at all. Even now with the explosion and proliferation of knowledge, man's wisdom becomes obsolete overnight. Only the precepts and principles of the Scriptures live on century after century.

Teach me to do thy will; for thou art my God: thy Spirit is good.
Psalm 143:10

15

THERE ARE SO MANY possibilities in life, in attainment and achievement, and so many opportunities of doing good, that it is a glorious thing to live. Surely, then, we ought to make the most of our life, not failing to become what Christ would have us to be, or to do the sweet things he would have us do as we pass along the way.

Yet life's lessons must always be learned slowly. Paul was well on in life when he said, "I have learned, in whatsoever state I am, therein to be content." The words suggest that the lesson was not easily learned; that it required time and struggle. It is only fair to infer that Paul could not have written thus in his earliest epistles. There is comfort in this for us common mortals, who in younger or middle life grow discouraged because we have not Paul's contentment. If only we are really learning the lesson, there is hope that some day we shall be able to say we have learned it.

J. R. MILLER

Take my yoke upon you, and learn of me; for I am meek and lowly in heart: and ye shall find rest unto your souls.
Matthew 11:29

16

WE HAVE TO LEARN to live, if ever we live worthily. No one becomes a fine pianist without learning. No one can take a piece of canvas, with palette, paints, and brushes, and at once make a great picture.

Life itself is not easier than music or painting. We must learn to live;

December

and the lessons are hard, requiring long years of patience and practice. But we ought to learn the lesson, whatever the cost may be.

Life is a sacred trust. We are accountable for it to God who gave it to us. We are required to make the most of our powers, training them to their best capacity; by self-discipline getting the perfect mastery of our being, then doing the things which we were made to do. Yet many people never seriously try to learn to live. This is unworthy of a being endowed with immortality and sent forth on a divine errand. We should live in a way which will not shame us when we come to the end.

J. R. MILLER

17

Does not long life bring understanding? To God belong wisdom and power; counsel and understanding are his.

Job 12:12–13, NIV

SOMEONE HAS SAID, "There is no substitute for experience." There's a strong element of truth in that statement from the spiritual point of view. One never "arrives" spiritually—there is always some new discovery waiting behind the next experience with God. I think John Wesley must have had that truth in mind when he wrote: "When I was young I was sure of everything; in a few years, having been mistaken a thousand times, I was not half so sure of most things as I was before; at present, I am hardly sure of anything but what God has revealed to me." In our verse for today, Job had been "through the mill," too—and he had learned his lessons well. He retained a teachable spirit rather than concluding that because of his vast experience with affliction, he had all the answers. I pray that I'll react the same way as I go through life.

18

If any of you lacks wisdom, let him ask God, who gives to all men generously and without reproaching, and it will be given him.

James 1:5, RSV

GOD IS MORE READY to give wisdom than we are to ask. James also speaks of the meekness of wisdom (3:13). There's the condition of humility again! The word *meekness* implies the willingness to be led. The Greek word for meek, *praus*, is used for an animal which has been domesticated and trained to obey the command and the touch of the reins of its master. The Greeks also used the word *meek* for the opposite of *hupsēlokardia*, which means lofty-heartedness or arrogant resistance to be taught. Without a realization of our ignorance there can be no learning. Quintilian, the great Roman orator, said of his students, "They would no doubt be excellent students if they were not already convinced of their own knowledge." Meekness is the humility of knowing we need forgiveness, the cross, and the gift of wisdom from the indwelling Lord of our hearts. And the Lord's promise is sure and irrevocable: "Blessed are the meek, for they shall inherit the earth."

We have come full circle back to Solomon's prayer for an understanding heart. A hearing heart. A receptive heart. A Spirit-filled heart. A heart of wisdom. Is that what you'd ask of God if he gave you one wish?

John would want us to know that wisdom is not ours just for the asking. It's ours for the using. Wisdom has already been given. The issue is our anointing. If we have accepted the anointing of the Lord, he abides in us. Our prayer then is, "Lord, thank you for abiding in me. I know I belong to you and that all my days are in your hands. Help me to appropriate the wisdom you have given me. Use my intellect and intuition to know and do your will."

LLOYD OGILVIE

Quoted from *When God First Thought of You* (Waco, TX: Word Books, 1978), pp. 82–83.

Now when John had heard in the prison the works of Christ, he sent **19**
two of his disciples, and said unto him, Art thou he that should come,
or do we look for another?

Matthew 11:2–3

I CAN IDENTIFY with John here. When I was a young Christian, to doubt was tantamount to heresy (at least in my theological circle). In my generation questioning one's faith and religious heritage was frowned upon—indeed, one could be "banished from the kingdom" if he dared to honestly express his intellectual struggles with "the faith once delivered to the saints." I'm glad that there is a new openness today toward honest inquiry. In his *Maxims and Moral Sentences*, Stanislas I (King of Poland) said: "To believe with certainty we must begin with doubting." And Henry Drummond wrote in *How to Learn How:* "Christ never failed to distinguish between doubt and unbelief. Doubt is *can't believe*; unbelief is *won't believe*. Doubt is honesty; unbelief is obstinacy. Doubt is looking for light; unbelief is content with darkness."

20

And Isaac went out to meditate in the field at the eventide: and he lifted up his eyes, and saw, and, behold, the camels were coming.

Genesis 23:63

ISAAC WAS A YOUNG MAN at the time of this experience—on the threshold of his marriage to Rebecca. And we don't normally combine youth and meditation. Young people tend to *move* rather than *meditate!* But there is nothing more needed in this busy age than quiet times alone with God. Prayer is not to be our only concern at the throne of grace. We are not to draw near to God merely to make our requests known to him. We come to hear his voice and to discover his will. As we meditate on his Word we are preparing for future action. As we submit our hearts and minds to his Word we become possessed by it and conformed to the image of his Son. Jeremiah says, "Thy words were found, and I did eat them" (15:16). Only by quiet and prayerful meditation can this assimilation of spiritual food take place. Then, says the prophet, ". . . thy word was unto me the joy and rejoicing of mine heart." We may not be able to follow Isaac's example and go into the fields to do our meditating, but we must find a quiet place somewhere, or we risk going bananas in our whirling world.

21

The Lord upholdeth all that fall, and raiseth up all those that be bowed down.

Psalm 145:14

GOD NEVER GETS TIRED helping us learn our lessons. No matter how often we miss, he is ready to give us another chance. When we fail to have our lesson learned, he does not give us up, putting us out of his school, but tells us to take the lesson over again and try to get it better. Only think how often we have to try before we do things as he wants us to do them, how often we fall in trying to walk before we learn to walk. If our great Teacher were not patient with us we should never become like Christ; but he never wearies of our slowness. He is pleased with our efforts, however faulty they are, and has for us always an encouraging word.

J. R. MILLER

Thy gentleness hath made me great.

2 Samuel 22:36

22

WHAT CONSTITUTES true greatness? Are not the godlike ones the great? Is long life greatness? But who can live so long as he who through faith in Christ has begun to live eternally? Is privilege greatness? Who is as privileged as he whose sins are washed away? Is character greatness? Whose character is comparable with that of him to whom has been imputed the righteousness of Christ? Are riches greatness? Who is so rich as an heir of glory? Is fame greatness? Who are more famous than those whose names are written in the Book of Life? Is power greatness? Can there be a greater exercise of power than that which overcomes the world? Is human family greatness? Whose kin takes precedence over the sons and daughters of the Almighty?

JAMES M. GRAY

He that judgeth me is the Lord.

1 Corinthians 4:4

23

THERE IS A STORY of a young composer whose music was being performed. The audience was enthusiastic, applauding wildly as the composition was played. But the young man seemed utterly indifferent to all this applause. He kept his eye fixed intently on one man in the audience, watching every expression that played upon his features. It was his teacher. He cared more for the slightest mark of favor on his face than for all the applause of the great company. So in all our life we should watch the face of Christ, caring only that he should be pleased. It matters far more what he thinks of our performance than what all the world besides thinks. If we live to win his approval, we shall not be afraid to have all our deeds laid bare at the last before the judgment throne.

J. R. MILLER

December

24

Thou art weighed in the balances, and art found wanting.

Daniel 5:27

SUCH WAS GOD'S MESSAGE to Belshazzar through his servant Daniel. The words should be read in connection with verse 23: "The God in whose hand thy breath is, and whose are all thy ways, hast thou not glorified." Here is the standard by which men's hearts and lives are to be judged. Every life will be found wanting which has not for its end the glory of God. It is not a question of whether we have committed few or many sins, small or great transgressions. A life may be moral, according to the highest earthly standard, and yet be sadly lacking when weighed in the balances of eternity. God has called us not only out of darkness into light, but out of a course of self-seeking into a life which has for its end "the praise of the glory of his grace" (Eph. 1:6). Self is the center of every life that has never come under the renewing power of God's grace. It may be strictly moral, and even religious, but it will be essentially self-centered until the great change has taken place.

EVAN H. HOPKINS

25

The unspiritual man does not receive the gifts of the Spirit of God, for they are folly to him, and he is not able to understand them because they are spiritually discerned.

1 Corinthians 2:14, RSV

OURS IS AN AGE when knowledge is mushrooming and science seems to be riding high, taking great strides forward in a "computerized" world. But in the midst of this proliferation of scientific advance there is more famine, poverty, and human degradation than ever before, simply because there are more people in the world than ever before. Our scientific genius does not seem able to cope with this fact. G. Campbell Morgan once said, "Intellect divorced from Deity deals only with dust. All scientific investigation has been almost exclusively occupied with the investigation and tabulation of material things." Paul's words to the Corinthians really cut to the heart of the world's problem today—true knowledge cannot exist apart from the Spirit of God. And God has largely been relegated to a "back seat" in our "enlightened" age. What a joy it is, from time to time, to meet knowledgeable scientists who acknowledge their dependence upon God! Would that their tribe might increase!

26

For consider your call, brethren; not many of you were wise according to worldly standards, not many were powerful, not many were of noble birth; but God chose what is foolish in the world to shame the wise, God chose what is weak in the world to shame the strong, God chose what is low and despised in the world, even things that are not, to bring to nothing things that are, so that no human being might boast in the presence of God.

1 Corinthians 1:26–29, RSV

HOW GRATEFUL we should be that our faith does not depend upon our intellect! If it did, most of us would fail to pass the test because we could not understand all the ramifications of faith. G. Campbell Morgan wrote: "The keenest intellect and most cultured mind are unable to understand the mystery of redemption, and therefore cannot explain it to others. Whoever can say light has broken upon the cross, and the eternal morning has dawned, is able to do so through the direct illumination of the Holy Spirit; and apart from that, there can be no witness and no service." It is this same illuminating power of the Holy Spirit that enables us to grow in grace, so we should not boast, but be thankful for the understanding he gives us.

27

Jesus then said to the Jews who had believed in him, "If you continue in my word, you are truly my disciples, and you will know the truth, and the truth will make you free."

John 8:31–32, RSV

IT SEEMS that so many young people today are feeling disintegrated in their lives. They appear to be searching for something, a unifying adventure which will bring into a single focus all of their abilities and energies. I guess I am projecting my own experience on them, because that is what I was looking for all my life: an adventure with a meaning and purpose beyond my grasp—an hypothesis with which to integrate all truths. I guess if I were a professor, I would go and tell them what a relief it is to have found such a unifying adventure in the Christian life . . . because it certainly is.

Lord, help me to realize fully the paradoxical freedom that is found through trying to commit all of life to You. Sometimes I am amazed that this commitment has issued in creativity and a freedom to look in

December

all areas for truth, when I had thought it would mean a narrower, restricted intellectual life. . . .

KEITH MILLER

Quoted from *Habitation of Dragons* (Waco, TX: Word Books, 1970).

28

Yes, if you cry out for insight and raise your voice for understanding, if you seek it like silver and search for it as for hidden treasures; then you will understand the fear of the Lord and find the knowledge of God. For the Lord gives wisdom.

Proverbs 2:3–6, RSV

THIS IS a very important part, the intellect, one of the most useful servants of truth; and I need not tell you as students that the intellect will have a great deal to do with your reception of truth. I was told that it was said . . . last year that a man must crucify his intellect [to be a Christian]. I venture to contradict the gentleman who made the statement. I am quite sure no such statement could ever have been made in your hearing—that we were to crucify our intellects. We can make no progress without the full use of all the intellectual powers that God has endowed us with.

HENRY DRUMMOND

THE INTELLECT of the wise is like glass; it admits the light of heaven and reflects it.

AUGUSTUS WILLIAM AND JULIUS CHARLES HARE

29

If ye then be risen with Christ, seek those things which are above. . . .

Colossians 3:1

WHAT ARE YOU SEEKING? Where do you and I place our priorities? Are we actively involved in a search for "things" at the expense of our spiritual growth and health? Paul's label, "those things which are above," does not necessarily designate things that are other-worldly. The "things above" are those attitudes which grow out of our desire to express the love and compassion of Christ in our daily relationships. To be "risen with Christ" does not mean to be "out of this world." It means to see the world with Christ's eyes and to feel with his heart. "Where your treasure is, there will your heart be also" (Matt. 6:21), Jesus said. Both Paul and Jesus call for an active and involved discipleship, a "follow-ship" that can be characterized in the words, "Set your affection on things above, not on things on the earth" (Col. 3:2). That's what it means to be "risen with Christ." That's the way to have "your life . . . hid with Christ in God" (v. 3). That's what it means to be *in* the world but not *of* it. What's your spiritual address?

Do not labor for the food which perishes, but for the food which endures to eternal life. **30**

John 6:27, RSV

WE NEED TO BE continually reminded of the unsatisfying nature of the things of this world, and exhorted to seek the real things in life. We live in a material age, when the quest of men is for money, for power, for things of the earth. Bunyan gives a picture of a man with a muck-rake, working hard, scraping up the rubbish under his feet, not seeing the crown that hangs in the air above his head. It is a picture of the great majority of the people in this world. They are wearing out their life in gathering rubbish out of the dust, not thinking of the heavenly treasures, the divine and imperishable gifts, which they might have with half the toil and care.

> Bubbles we buy with a whole soul's tasking;
> 'Tis heaven alone that is given away,
> 'Tis only God may be had for the asking.

We ought not to spend our life in picking up things which we cannot carry beyond the grave. If we are wise we will seek rather to gather treasures and riches which we can take with us into eternity. Whatever we build into our character, we shall possess forever. Money which we spend in doing good, in Christ's name, we lay up as safe and secure treasure in heaven. All true service for Christ stores up rewards for us in the future. What we keep we lose; what we give in love we keep.

J. R. MILLER

December

31

I know that whatever God does endures for ever; nothing can be added to it, nor anything taken from it; God has made it so, in order that men should fear before him.

Ecclesiastes 3:14, RSV

CAN WE SAY of anything that man does that it "endures for ever"? Entire civilizations have risen and fallen at the whim of man. Vast cities have grown up as a result of man's efforts only to slide into oblivion through war or pestilence, or the irresistible erosion of eons of time. The old-time hymnwriter wrote, "Only what's done for Christ will last." His was simply another way of saying that when God is the Author the book lasts—whereas the books of man rise in an arc of sudden popularity only to fall into oblivion a year or a generation later. God's handiwork is not like that—and my salvation is his handiwork!

Quoted Author Index

Author Index

Medina, Harold 13
Mercier, Cardinal 56
Meyer, F. B. 26, 29, 118, 119, 126, 164
Miller, J. R. 35, 41–42, 48, 54, 58, 62–63, 69, 80, 83–84, 85, 86–87, 89, 90, 91, 95–96, 100–101, 105, 114, 123–24, 135, 170, 176, 177, 180, 181, 185, 207–208, 210–11, 215
Miller, Keith 55, 213–214
Morgan, G. Campbell 39–40, 70, 86, 113, 128, 131, 153, 198, 199, 201, 212, 213
Mott, John Raleigh 189
Moule, H. C. G. 66–67, 164
Myers, T. Cecil 13–14, 81–82, 132, 135–36, 203
Ogilvie, Lloyd 18–19, 31, 36, 43, 46–47, 89–90, 108–109, 112, 158, 168–69, 171–72, 174, 179, 205–206, 208–209
Phillips, E. Lee 129
Pope, Alexander 187
Quintilian 209
Ramakrishna 110
Richter, Jean Paul 182
Riney, Earl 153
Roberts, John 56
Robertson, Frederick William 187

Roosevelt, Franklin Delano 169
Seneca 45
Sheen, Bishop Fulton 56
Shoemaker, Helen Smith 64–65, 130–31, 141, 201
Shoemaker, Sam 14–15, 17–18, 27, 33–34, 133–34, 145–46
Simpson, A. B. 38, 95
Smith, Hannah Whitall 22
Southcott, Ernest 141
Spurgeon, Charles H. 30–31, 31–32, 67–68, 110, 200
Stanislas I 209
Tennyson, Alfred Lord 31
Thoreau, Henry David 88
Tolstoy, Leo 56
Torrey, R. A. 22–23, 28, 38–39, 64, 96, 115–16, 117–18, 120, 125, 133, 138–39, 140, 143–44, 147, 151–52, 163, 177–78, 185, 191–92
Wallace, Lew 68
Webb-Peploe, Hammer William 63
Webster, Daniel 139
Wells, H. G. 154
Wesley, John 208
William, Augustus 214
Wilson, O. G. 56
Woodberry, George Edward 44

Subject Index

abiding in Christ 23–24
Abraham's faith 73–74
affliction and suffering 51
agitation 44
anxiety 49–50
approval of God 211
attitude of gratitude 195–96

bearing one's cross 103
being "religious" 150
belief 16–17
believing 68
Bible 136, 137–38, 139–40
body of Christ 142–43
brevity of life 90, 91, 105–106

character growth 15–16
cheerfulness 178
choice 202–203
Christ
    as guide 121
    eternal 159
    in our lives 19–20, 33–34, 39–40
    incarnation 161–62
    our example of faith 73
    our light 40–41
    our wisdom 205
    presence 36
    source of joy 176–77
Christian conduct 107–108
Christian growth 10
Christian life 89–90, 96, 99, 106–107, 197
    relational 84
Christian walk 110

Christian work 86, 106
Christians 38
Christlikeness 14–15, 20, 22, 35, 38, 91
circumstances 53–54
    and character 52
confidence in God 11–12
consecration 17
controlling speech 182
Creator 200
Cross 167

Daniel 72–73
death 202–203
dedication 103–104
deliverance 60–61
denying Christ 94
dependence on God 10, 56–57
discipleship 102–103
distorted dogma 150, 157
divine guidance 125
doubt 209–10

envy 184
eternal life 157, 203
evil 59–60

faith 65–66, 67–68
    and God's protection 196
    and guidance 202
    in the midst of suffering 78
    of the four 113
    strength through 24
    through the centuries 64–65